Praise for *Never Ride a Rollercoaster Upside Down*

"Meeting, knowing, and working for Jeff Smulyan gave me the confidence to leave Indianapolis and seek fame and fortune in our sister city of Hollywood. I will never be able to repay Jeff for his faith, kindness, and motivation. Please read the book and phone me.*"

*Anyone attempting to phone Mr. Letterman will be subject to prosecution.

—David Letterman, comedian and former TV host

"Jeff is a natural storyteller and makes me laugh out loud every time he shares the highs and lows of his life as an entrepreneur in sports and media. Full of insight, humor, and an honest voice, *Never Ride a Rollercoaster Upside Down* is cleverly paced and a delight for the reader."

—Andrew Luck, former quarterback for the Indianapolis Colts

"Jeff Smulyan is the kindest, funniest, and smartest person I've ever known . . . except for everyone else I've ever known. Read *Never Ride a Rollercoaster Upside Down* and you'll find out why."

—Jerry Reinsdorf, owner of the Chicago Bulls
and the Chicago White Sox

"Jeff Smulyan brought fun to baseball. He also brought us together as the only father and son to ever play in the major leagues together. If you read this book, you won't play in the major leagues with your father or your son, but you will have fun reading it and you will learn some great life lessons."

—Ken Griffey Sr. and Ken Griffey Jr., former MLB players

"Jeff and I have been best friends for decades and his book, *Never Ride a Rollercoaster Upside Down*, chronicles the experiences of a classic entrepreneur. Told in a humorous, engaging style, Jeff provides the lessons that anyone who has ever thought about starting a business needs to know. Some of his experiences are death-defying, some are bizarre, but all of them have led to a life filled with joy and accomplishment. I'm not in favor of cloning, but if I did, I'd suggest Jeff Smulyan be cloned."

—Evan Bayh, former Governor of Indiana
and former United States Senator

NEVER RIDE A ROLLER COASTER UPSIDE DOWN

NEVER RIDE A ROLLER COASTER UPSIDE DOWN

The Ups, Downs, and Reinvention of an Entrepreneur

Jeff Smulyan

Matt Holt Books
An Imprint of BenBella Books, Inc.
Dallas, TX

Matt Holt is an imprint of BenBella Books, Inc.
10440 N. Central Expressway
Suite 800
Dallas, TX 75231
benbellabooks.com
Send feedback to feedback@benbellabooks.com

BenBella and *Matt Holt* are federally registered trademarks.

Printed in the United States of America
10 9 8 7 6 5 4 3 2 1

Library of Congress Control Number: 2022013473
ISBN 9781637742228 (hardcover)
ISBN 9781637742235 (electronic)

Editing by Phyllis Strong
Copyediting by Scott Calamar
Proofreading by Jenny Rosen and Leah Baxter
Indexing by WordCo Indexing Services, Inc.
Text design and composition by PerfecType, Nashville, TN
Cover design by Brigid Pearson
Cover image © Shutterstock / Scarlette2020_
Printed by Lake Book Manufacturing

Special discounts for bulk sales are available. Please contact bulkorders@benbellabooks.com.

To my family, you make everything worthwhile: especially my wife, Heather, and my children, Cari and Brad, and his wife Leslie and my grandchildren, Liam and Quinn. And of course, my daughter Sammie, who convinced me to write this book. I love you all very much; know that this book is for you. Finally, to my Emmis family, who have meant so much to me for so many years: I love all of you, too.

Contents

Foreword

If you were ever under the impression that being an entrepreneur is an easy one-way bet to endless reward, Jeff Smulyan's long career in broadcasting, radio and whatever else he found along the way will quickly disabuse you of that notion. Smulyan makes it no secret; being an entrepreneur is hard, particularly if the chosen area of focus is an industry of endless challenge that requires constant reinvention all while the fickle capital markets constantly threaten to shut you down.

This book is as much textbook as memoir, offering countless lessons on the way to build a career in business. You want to learn what it feels like to start a radio station, build a TV station business, run a radio empire, start the first all-sports radio station and own a Major League Baseball team? Smulyan has the answer, and he teaches in the most effective way: by sharing his many mistakes along the way. The journey of Jeff's life in business proves that nice guys don't always finish last, but they sure don't always finish first.

I've known Jeff for long enough to remember when his company, Emmis, was significant enough to merit regular mention on CNBC. Those days are long gone, but there was so much I had forgotten or never known about the radio business and how Smulyan always managed to fight on despite the obstacles to success. His retelling of both the halcyon days of radio and the near-death experience brought on by a suddenly stingy capital market was particularly insightful for someone who has covered markets for decades. As his story unspools you'll meet a wonderful cast of characters along with some well-known names from broadcasting (who do you think gave David Letterman his start?). But it's the intricacies of dealing with the daily challenges of trying to build a company that will stay with you. That and the fact that Smulyan is funny. Or at least his many stories are funny. His humor draws you in so that you find yourself rooting for him to succeed—or at least not fail too badly.

Should he have sold Emmis when he had the chance years ago? Probably. Should he have tried to hang on to the Seattle Mariners with losses mounting and a city turned against him? Possibly. And did he really need to sell WFAN, one of the most successful and groundbreaking stations of all time? I will leave that for the reader to decide.

One thing not in question is Smulyan's love for radio. It lives on. As does something else he shares with those who have faced setbacks in business but ultimately persevere. He is relentless. And I mean that in the best possible way.

—David Faber

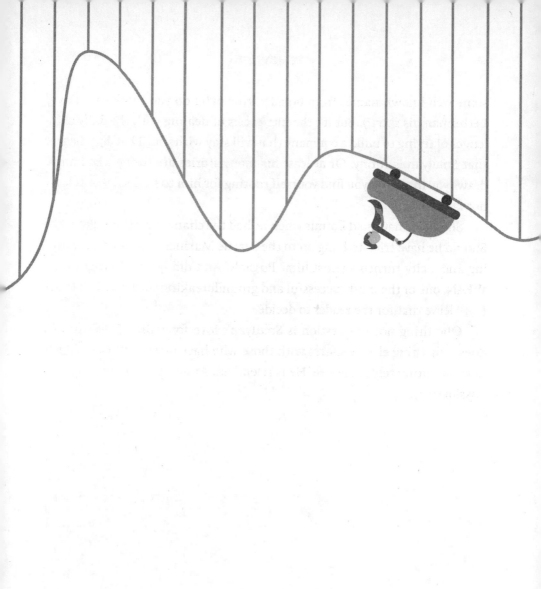

Top: My parents, Sam and Natalie, with me. *Bottom:* A family photo from a recent holiday card: Heather, Sammie, Me, Jude (a.k.a. Junior), and Savannah (a.k.a. Fozzie).

Prologue

I originally wanted to call this book *What Have We Learned*, after the first question I invariably ask when I start a meeting with my managers. The phrase summarizes my desire to learn what others are thinking, and it's the interaction that best explains how members of my team deal with each other. However, as I started recounting the stories of my life and career, I realized that my life is best described as a long, strange rollercoaster ride. Given the sometimes tumultuous turns I have taken, the title *Never Ride a Rollercoaster Upside Down* is far more appropriate.

I'm a fanatical believer in lifelong learning. In fact, one of my favorite movie scenes is from *Three Days of the Condor*, a classic spy film from the 1970s. Robert Redford is a researcher for the CIA, and he returns from lunch to find his entire section has been murdered. Later he realizes that he was the target of the attack. Incredulously, he asks: "Why would they target me? I'm just a reader." I've thought about that line thousands of times, because at heart, that is what I am—just a reader—and I've found much of my success has come from absorbing information.

My three children put it best: "Dad is a lesson guy." I am aware that over the years, Cari, Brad, and now Sam have been driven to distraction by my constantly asking, "What have we learned from this?" However, as a proud father, I can tell you that all three have taken many of those lessons to heart, and Cari and Brad have become very kind, compassionate, and inquisitive adults, and Sam is on her way. I'm certain all three of them will leave this world a better place than they found it.

Moreover, my managers will quickly add that "Jeff is also a 'story guy.'" Some of the stories are funny, some provide valuable insights, some are straight-out bizarre, and many are just remembrances of an old guy who has been amused by the many strange events of his life. Rest assured, all of them are true. I've tried to curate the stories in this book so they will give you a behind-the-scenes view, not only of my company, but of the world of media and sports and the fascinating characters you find around every corner. The lessons that arise from these stories are the same ones I have learned (or at least tried to) over a fifty-year career.

And since I am an entrepreneur, this book will provide the unvarnished truth about what that really means. This isn't a book about inventing a revolutionary product that changes the world or a story about scaling the mountaintops of commerce and emerging unscathed. Instead, it's about what happens in some fascinating businesses when things go spectacularly right and just as often when they go painfully wrong. Anyone who wants to be an entrepreneur needs to understand that to succeed, you absolutely have to know how to handle failure, and this book will provide lots of examples of both.

Never Ride a Rollercoaster Upside Down is not exclusively about business because a life is (or should be!) so much more. To that end, this book will provide a number of lessons that are critical to understanding how to navigate the rollercoaster ride that will be your life. Some of these may be ones you've heard of before, while others may be surprising. Regardless, all should be relevant to anyone who wants to captain their own ship.

This book also provides insights into the economics of media and sports, to show you another intriguing look behind the scenes of these industries that have such a foothold in our lives. Through a host of interesting stories— told in plain terms we can all understand—you will peel back the curtain on how media and sports really work. Some of those insights will probably surprise you, and some should amuse you as well.

Writing this book has been one of the most cathartic, enjoyable experiences I've ever had. I hope you will have fun reading it and come away with an understanding that will help you in all of your endeavors.

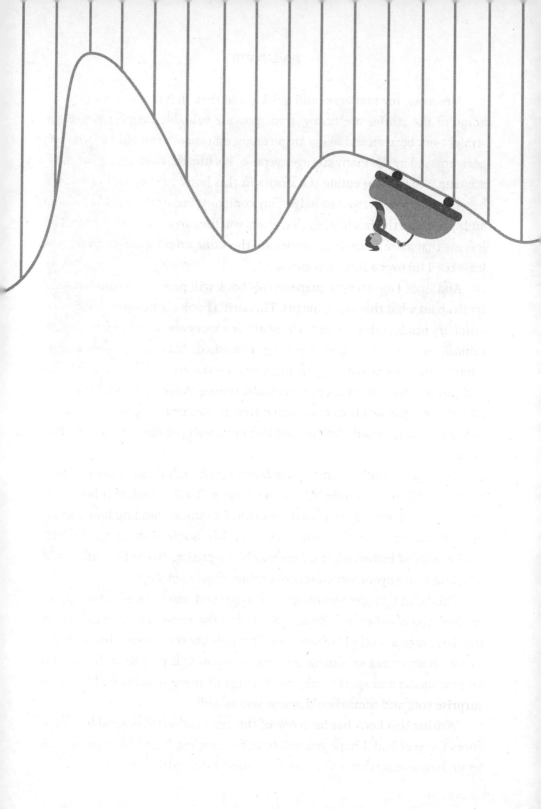

Top: Years ago, my sister, brother, and I decided to do the "speak no evil, hear no evil, see no evil" monkey pose. Here are me, my sister Dale, and my brother Jim doing the pose. *Bottom:* For fun, years later, my children reprised the famous monkey photo: Here are Brad, hear no evil; Sammie, speak no evil; and Cari, see no evil. (*Photo credit: Lori B. Adams*)

Do What You Love

Over the past fifty years, I have had an immensely rewarding, albeit sometimes bizarre, career in media, sports, entertainment, and even a slice of government. Most people know me because I invented radio's all-sports format with the launch of WFAN, New York. Others have heard of me because of my controversial tenure as owner of the Seattle Mariners baseball team. For years, I've told friends that I had to be an entrepreneur because I'm not capable of being hired in a free society.

My entrepreneurial roots run deep. I come from a family that was part of the first wave of Jewish immigrants in the 1880s and 1890s, most escaping from the pogroms in Russia and Ukraine. My father's father came through Ellis Island and ultimately moved west to Indiana, where he worked for himself. Doing what? I'll give you a tip that will serve you well at cocktail parties. When you meet someone who is Jewish from the Midwest, ask if their family was in scrap or dry goods. They will be amazed at your perceptive skills. It's a trick question: Every Jew in the Midwest was in scrap or dry goods. My father's father was a peddler, selling his wares in several small towns in

Indiana, until he settled in Indianapolis where he started a poultry business that operated successfully for many years.

My mother's father, who had also landed in Indiana, was a classic entrepreneur. In 1912, he started one of the first, if not *the* first, automobile finance companies in the United States. The business was wildly successful all through the next three decades, and he prospered even as the country was ravaged by the Depression. After my dad returned from active duty during World War II, both his father and his father-in-law wanted him to join their respective businesses. My mother lobbied hard, and my dad agreed to join her father's company, Indiana Finance. While it had enjoyed a terrific niche market before World War II, Indiana Finance gradually declined as banks realized that automobiles were valuable collateral. By 1960, when my grandfather died, the business was still profitable, but on a much smaller scale. My dad and my uncle, seeing little future in Indiana Finance, branched out into Howard Johnson's motels and a sizable apartment complex.

For the past eleven years, I've had the pleasure of driving my younger daughter, Sammie, to school every morning. We talk about everything, and my lessons bubble up naturally from the stories of my life. One time we were discussing how to have a successful career, and I surprised her by telling her she had to be prepared to fail. I know when you're starting out, you think success is going to be a straight line to the top, but setbacks are inevitable. Life is really a rollercoaster ride of ups, downs, dips, and wild turns. The key to staying on the rollercoaster is to enjoy the ride—and for that, you need to find something you love doing. Sammie gave me a skeptical look; she had heard that her great-grandparents weren't in love with their successful businesses. I countered that they loved the family life their work afforded, but that's not the same as loving your career. To press my point, I brought up the adage: "If you do what you love, you'll never work a day in your life." Sammie liked that, but she wondered how I knew so early what my lifelong passion was going to be. And that led to telling her how I began my career.

As a young child, I grew up with a passion for radio. It's hard to describe how different radio was in the 1950s and 1960s, compared to the medium we know today. With the advent of television, broad-based programming declined, and radio became a niche medium. Radio stations could no longer rely on national programs like *The Jack Benny Show* or *Fibber McGee and*

Molly to survive—those series had made the transition to television. As a result, radio was pronounced dead in the early fifties, but it reinvented itself by narrowing its programming into various formats: country music, adult hits, easy listening, rhythm and blues, and—the most successful format— Top 40. Between the rise of transistors and the explosion of the baby boom, it seemed that every pre-teen and teenager carried around a transistor radio, the first pocket-sized receiver available. With transistors, inefficient vacuum tubes could be reduced to a series of tiny wires, and thus everyone could listen to their favorite stations wherever they went. Transistor radios became ubiquitous, and with them, the stations that defined the lives of nearly every young American. In the late fifties, Top 40 radio began to skyrocket, fueled by iconic artists like Elvis Presley. I'm sure there were kids who were immune to Top 40 radio, but I never met any of them. Listening to the latest hits, either on stations in Indianapolis or from Chicago or Detroit, provided the entertainment for my generation. In addition, as a baseball fan, I could hear my favorite team, the San Francisco Giants, merely by listening to the games on radio stations from other National League cities. Through clear-channel stations (strong signals that carried across the United States), I could listen to my beloved Giants when they played in Chicago, Cincinnati, Pittsburgh, Philadelphia, St. Louis, and New York. This was long before the wall-to-wall coverage on cable TV (actually long before cable TV!), and radio was the only way to consume most sports in the late fifties and early sixties. Radio was our escape, listening to the hits in our rooms at night and even listening to late-night ball games with our transistor radios under our pillows, hidden from parental curfews. It's amazing how many friends in my industry had the same experiences, turning down the radio so our parents thought we were doing our homework and pretending we were asleep while being mesmerized by the late innings of a baseball game, transmitted from the comfort of our pillows.

Nearly every city had at least one Top 40 station. In Indianapolis, that was WIFE. Don Burden, a classic entrepreneur from Omaha, bought a failing station at 1310 on the AM band and launched a radio revolution in the city. With ubiquitous billboards, contests, bumper stickers, and a slick presentation, he took the city by storm. It was impossible to find a teenager who didn't listen to WIFE, night and day; in addition, the nonstop contests and promotion pulled a sizable number of adults into the fold. Within six months, WIFE turned its ratings around, taking an unprecedented 35 percent of all listeners and sending long-time market leader WIBC spiraling downward. The two stations developed an intense rivalry that led to Burden, many years later, losing the licenses for all his stations (Indianapolis, Omaha, and Portland) for violating Federal Communications Commission (FCC) rules prohibiting free airtime to US senators. Many believed that Burden's downfall was hastened because WIBC was owned by the politically connected Richard Fairbanks—a descendant of US vice president Charles Warren Fairbanks—who delighted in using his influence to put pressure on Burden. And Burden didn't make matters simple for himself either, with his legendary hubris making him an easy target for the FCC. My favorite Burden story is about one night, when he was quite inebriated, he called into the request line at WIFE and demanded that disc jockey Scott Wheeler, then on the air, play the 1912 hit "My Melancholy Baby." Scott naively responded, "Sir, we don't play 'Melancholy Baby,' it's not on our playlist." To which Burden replied, "You stupid SOB, I'm Don Burden—I own this station and it's on the playlist now." Wisely, Scott dug up "My Melancholy Baby" and interrupted a few Beatles songs to play it.

There were other Top 40 stations all over America and in every city; teenagers were addicted to their favorites. When I started college in 1965 in Los Angeles, KHJ had just made its debut and completely took the city by storm. With its tight playlist, catchy jingles, vivid imaging, and brilliant disc jockeys, KHJ sped to the top of Los Angeles's ratings and stayed there for many years. KHJ's two stars were Robert W. Morgan who did mornings, and "The Real Don Steele" who did afternoons. Morgan's impact was so great that Morgan in the Morgen (*Morgen* is German for morning), spawned imitators from coast to coast. In radio, if something works spectacularly well in one city, it is guaranteed to be copied everywhere very quickly. In Indianapolis, we had *Roger* W. Morgan, Detroit had *Chuck* Morgan, and on and on. None had Robert W's wit, but at least they could copy the name. Like just about everyone in Los Angeles, I was hooked on KHJ and found Morgan to be as talented as anyone I had ever heard on the air. In those days, it was impossible to roll down your windows at a stoplight and not hear KHJ coming from multiple cars. The movie *Once Upon a Time in Hollywood* used KHJ as a soundtrack to inform the audience that the film was set in the lead-up to the 1969 Manson murders. Because the Top 40 format required the personalities to fit their humor into segments of less than a minute, Morgan's quick wit was perfect for the station. Ironically, years later, I hired an aging Robert W. Morgan for our first station in Los Angeles. While the keen wit was still there, too many years of too much alcohol had turned his natural acerbity into an anger that generated a hostile workplace. I spent many hours on the phone with his agent resolving the challenges Robert W. presented to his fellow employees.

Near the end of the KHJ era, NBC was trying to save its weekend show *Monitor*. *Monitor* had been a relic of earlier days in radio, a broadly based entertainment program that had trouble staying relevant in a now more segmented industry. To update the show, NBC decided to hire the two most talented disc jockeys in America, Morgan and Don Imus, and put them together to see if they could save it. The effort ultimately failed, but Morgan and Imus became best friends. The story I'm about to relate may be apocryphal, but it has to be the most retold story in the history of American radio. Supposedly, Imus and Morgan had been out carousing in Hollywood all night long and at 5 AM, they were both standing at an intersection in a drunken stupor when a little old lady drove up and asked for directions to Sunset and Vine. One of the two supposedly unzipped his pants, pulled out his penis, and pointed to one of the veins and said "This is Sunset, go down three blocks," and then, pointing to the other vein, added, "This is Vine. That will get you there." For a variety of reasons, there are no more stories like that in American radio today!

Everything about the radio business mesmerized me. Unlike television, in which you were largely a captive of your network, and beholden to program whatever is sent down the line, radio was a complete blank slate. You picked the format and the talent, devised the marketing, and summoned all of your creativity to build a business. For someone with entrepreneurial genes, a radio station was the perfect place to launch a career, and at an early age, I knew it was what I wanted to do. When I finished my senior year of college, before starting law school, I decided to look for a summer job in radio, and one of my fraternity brothers had a distant cousin at KABC: George Green, then the station's sales manager. George agreed to speak with me as a courtesy, but he told me up front, before the meeting, that he didn't have any jobs. After we talked for about thirty minutes, he commented "How do you know all this stuff about the industry?" I told him I read *Broadcasting Magazine* every week, cover to cover, and that I also studied the industry in my spare time; radio was my hobby. He hired me on the spot, launching my radio career.

I had always intended to pursue a graduate degree; my first inclination was to get a master's in telecommunications, and I targeted Stanford's program. However, after seeking advice from several people, including my dad, the consensus was: If you want to be an entrepreneur, get a law degree. When you get out of school, you'll have the instant credibility a master's degree won't give you. So, I chose law school at USC. Looking back, I'm fascinated that not one person suggested an MBA. Today the advice would be 100 percent to get an MBA or a joint JD/MBA degree, but back then, most people thought little of a graduate degree in business. It's amazing how much the world has changed. At USC, I earned my degree, writing my law review article on the FCC's clear-channel doctrine, and was ready to tackle the world. I've been a member of the Indiana State Bar Association for nearly fifty years but have been on inactive status for most of that time. I've joked that if I actually decided to practice law, I would be disbarred within the week. My attorneys constantly tease me that I don't even have the patience to listen to most of their legal analyses, let alone do the analysis myself.

After law school, I joined forces with a few friends and, for nearly a year, we chased radio deals, always coming up empty. Then my dad called with an offer: He and my mom wanted me to come home to Indiana, and he had a cousin with a small radio station in Indianapolis that happened to be failing. My dad said he would invest in the station if I would agree to come home—that way I could run the station for a while until I found other, more promising radio deals and could start my own company. Not wanting to leave California, I resisted his entreaties for a number of months, but I finally realized this was the right way to start and headed home. For the first few months after my return, I wondered what in the world possessed me to come home to Indiana. As time went on, however, I began to fall in love with all the exciting developments that were taking place in Indianapolis. The city of my youth, which had given rise to the John Birch Society and other reactionary elements, was a thing of the past, replaced by a tolerant, imaginative community that was willing to try different approaches to compete in a global marketplace of ideas and talent. For many, many years, as my company's holdings grew, friends always asked why I stayed in Indiana, when we owned stations in New York, Los Angeles, and other seemingly more desirable locales. I explained that Indianapolis was a growing, dynamic city, and it was fun to be a part of a community that embraced change so completely.

When I came back, I decided to switch the station, WNIR, from a country format to WNTS, which stood for news, talk, and sports. Perhaps the best way to describe running WNTS was Warren Buffett's adage about the impossible project. To paraphrase, Buffet said, "Show me an impossible project and give me good people working on it, and three years later, you'll find a project that is still impossible and worn-out good people." I'm not sure how good my team and I were, but trying to make a daytime-only station work at 1590 on the AM radio dial, where signal reception is much worse than on the other end of the dial (e.g., 540), did turn out to be an impossible project. I've seen a few businesses like this in my career, and I've developed my own adage: "If you need to kick a seventy-yard field goal into the wind to win the game, you probably shouldn't be on the field!" WNTS was facing insurmountable odds, but it was a remarkably fun, if challenging, station to run. I'll always look back on WNTS as one of the great lessons of my life. Throughout this book you'll hear my old saying, "you do your best work in the most difficult situations," and that's what we did at WNTS.

We marketed WNTS as the scrappy underdog, going up against the city's behemoth, WIBC, which in the post-WIFE era had reasserted itself as Indianapolis's undisputed leader. While our rival was primarily an adult music station, it had a large news department and was the one station everyone went to for information. We had a news block from six to ten every morning and sports in the afternoon, from three until whenever we had to sign off, which depended on what time sunset was, sometimes as early as 5:15 PM. There's nothing like saying goodbye to your listeners in the middle of evening drive time. These days, WNTS is known for its original midday host, David Letterman. Dave was working as a weekend weatherman for the local ABC TV station as well as hosting a farm show; my brother, then in college at Indiana University, insisted "you have to hire Letterman." I knew of him; we are exactly the same age (five days apart), and he had gone to neigh-boring Broad Ripple High School. I had seen him on TV and his weather reports were legendary. Once, he announced that "A significant snowstorm is approaching from the west, but don't worry about that, because ICBMs are approaching from Russia." Another time he stated that it was forty-nine degrees in Kokomo and forty-nine degrees in Muncie, and they would play off that tie at a later date. And once, he announced that hail the size of giant canned hams was approaching later that night. His reports were brilliant and incredibly offbeat—not something you would normally see in staid, conservative Indiana.

I hired Dave immediately and every day was an adventure. When he took the job, he told me, "In a year, I'm going to go to Hollywood to see if I can make it as a writer." It's hard to describe how funny he was or how lit-tle difference it made in our ratings. The experience taught me everything about reaching the audience available to you. Dave resonated with my age group. We found him brilliant every day. My friend, David Klapper, who would eventually found the athletic retailer Finish Line, was working at his dad's liquor store when Letterman debuted on WNTS. Klapper knew Let-terman because they were a year apart at Broad Ripple High School. Klapper became part of a cadre of twenty-five-year-olds (or thereabouts) who were addicted to Letterman. They listened every day and marveled at his bril-liance. Unfortunately, 95 percent of the people who listen to AM talk radio are conservative sixty-five-year-olds. To say that our listeners didn't get Dave was an understatement. Once, upon returning from lunch, I got an angry phone call from an aging listener: "Sir, Dave Letterman is a communist!" When I asked why he thought that, the listener replied, "I told him the com-munists were all over Carmel (a suburb of Indianapolis) and we needed to do something about it, and do you know what he said?" Of course, I didn't, but I braced myself as he continued, breathlessly: "Letterman said to give Carmel to the communists; the schools are overcrowded, parking is a mess, and the streets are always torn up! Let's let them keep Carmel and hold the line at Nora [a nearby suburb]." I managed—barely—to hold back explosive laughter, but I mollified the shocked listener by assuring him I would discuss the whole thing with Dave, immediately.

Dave had one elderly gentleman who would call regularly and spout largely insane, nonsensical things, and since AM stations at 1590 don't get a wide variety of callers, this guy was able to hog a great deal of airtime. After a few times, Dave decided that the only way to make the calls tolerable was to play sound effects in the background. Sometimes, bombs would go off during the calls, sometimes mooing cows, but every time it was different and every time it was hilarious. Once, Dave announced that the city of Indianapolis had sold the monument in the middle of Monument Circle to Guam, in exchange for a 150-foot asparagus stalk. He noted, with his typical deadpan delivery, that the stalk would add greenery to the middle of downtown. Listeners actually called to express their disgust that the city would sell their beloved monument. Another time, Dave announced that the Indianapolis Motor Speedway had decided to accommodate all of the fans who wanted to watch the 500-Mile Race on the main straightaway, and had decided to hold the race on Interstate 70 from Indianapolis to Kansas City, almost exactly five hundred miles. People called in to ask how the tickets would be sold. The more nonsensical Dave's bits were, the more confused our listeners became. After a year, Dave moved to California as he had promised, leaving behind a number of younger listeners who revered him (including everyone on our staff), and the great majority of our audience who were merely dazed and confused. To help Dave get started in Los Angeles, we paid him a small stipend to report from California. One of my favorite Letterman bits was that, to save the Tournament of Roses Parade from being cancelled because of the skyrocketing cost of roses, the parade had made all of its floats from pork and pork by-products. He noted that any savings were eliminated by medical costs necessitated by parade goers who had been sickened by the stench of rotting pork. On the other hand, Dave noted that the all-pork Minnie Mouse looked absolutely lovely!

Despite Letterman's hilarious commentary, it was clear from the beginning that making WNTS a success was going to be nearly impossible. A daytime signal on the worst position on the dial clearly left our station with both hands tied behind its back. WIBC and the other full-time stations had all of the resources and practically all of the listeners. I once joked that Fred Heckman, WIBC's longtime news director, had immense credibility in the market and that if we put Walter Cronkite on WNTS, most Hoosiers would still think that Fred Heckman was a superior, more credible commentator.

Although I was nearly manic in putting the station together, hiring an air staff, working on the programming elements, and writing sales presentations, something happened during my first few months that taught me some valuable lessons about myself and, ultimately, prepared me for the rest of my career. Probably sensing the impossibility of making WNTS successful, I went into a complete funk. It's the only time in my life I could have been characterized as clinically depressed, and in retrospect, I'm sure that I was. After all, this was my first chance to manage something, to build success out of a project I had conceived, and I'm certain when I came to grips with the odds of success, I began to realize that it was destined to fail. I've seen fear of failure in myself and other people throughout the years, and it is absolutely paralyzing. I've since developed the ability to be my calmest when things are at their very worst, and it's an attribute that has served me very well during the absolute toughest times of my life, when faced with the death of loved ones or a significant setback in life or in business.

It's hard to describe how it happened, but shortly after the start of WNTS, I drifted into an almost zombielike state. I was unable to sleep, eat, or manage coherent conversations. I know that the rest of the staff didn't know what to make of me. It was early in a new venture, and the general manager had disappeared into the ozone. Like an artery or vein that forms to get blood flowing when a main artery is blocked, they just managed to avoid me, knowing that any interaction was likely to be useless. About the only appetite I had was spent eating several of the donuts that one of our salesmen brought in every morning. Once, talking about the futility of dealing with me, Dave Letterman noted to our production director, "Let's see, our general manager has donut frosting all around his mouth and he is babbling incoherently, not exactly the leadership we need around here." Dave, as usual, was correct, and my "syndrome" lasted for several months. I couldn't shake the terrifying feeling that the station was doomed to fail, and my career would be going down the drain before it had even started. Obviously, being missing in action was making a difficult situation worse, but nothing seemed to help me. In retrospect, I should have run over to Eli Lilly and gotten an early prototype of Prozac, or at least sought professional help, but I had never encountered anything like it and wasn't capable of taking action to help myself.

The paralysis seemed to last for an eternity, but it was probably less than three months. One night, while having dinner with my sister, Dale, and her husband, Zeke, they prescribed the medicine I really needed. Dale observed, "Look, you're driving yourself crazy here. I have one question: Do you understand your business as well as anyone?" I meekly answered, "Yes." Zeke added, "Of course you know this stuff and if it's fixable, you'll find a way to fix it. If it's not, so be it. You have to have the confidence to do your job and the rest will take care of itself." Something about this conversation snapped me out of it. It's almost like the infamous Al Franken/Stuart Smiley bit on *Saturday Night Live*: "I'm good enough and I'm smart enough and doggone it, people like me!" Whatever it was about those words that cured me, they changed my thinking forever. I realized that I knew the business, and I knew how to work with people; after that, my fear of failure disappeared—although I know, at times in my career, it probably would have helped if it had come back. I developed a mindset that I was going to tackle the challenges others wouldn't and, beyond that, I kindled a desire to accomplish what no one else could. It was a complete 180-degree reversal, and as I have said, it sometimes has led me to attempt things that no one else would even think of trying, but it has made my life vastly more interesting than it would have been if I had played it safe. In this book, you'll see some of the challenges that I took on, and in more than a few cases, you'll probably wince at the risks I took.

Rick Cummings, now president of Emmis programming, and I have discussed his first few months working at WNTS and encountering me in my trancelike state: "I would characterize you as beleaguered. You were working sixteen-hour days with a bad radio station, no sales, poor equipment, and the pressure pretty much rendered you useless. Until you snapped out of it, I never really knew you at all." Another great experience from my WNTS days was first meeting Rick. A recent Butler grad who had been laid off from his production job at WFMS and was seeking gainful employment in Indianapolis, Rick found a comparable position at WNTS. As I emerged from my trance, I began to recognize what a remarkable talent, and human being, he was. Diminutive because of a rare bone disease, Rick is as adept at understanding the industry and its people as anyone I have ever met.

Throughout this book you will see myriad references to him, but in the early days, he moved from production director to program director to Letterman's replacement on his talk show when Dave moved on to California after a year. Probably the most fun I had working at WNTS was when I would fill in as a host on talk shows, and Rick and I ended up doing a regular sports talk show on Saturday afternoons that we still laugh about. Early on in our relationship I told him: "When I start my company, I want you to program it." That's exactly what happened, and nearly forty-five years later, we're still together. To succeed in life, you have to be lucky, and meeting Rick was one of the greatest strokes of luck I would ever experience. I'm convinced that in the history of American radio, there has never been anyone who understood listeners and programming as well as Rick, and you will see a number of examples of his remarkable talent throughout this book. One more thing: We have been working together for nearly five decades and have disagreed thousands of times. Yet I don't remember us ever getting angry at each other. Our exchanges have always been filled with incredibly humorous moments. Rick can make me laugh constantly, and I do the same for him. Although once, after a nonstop session when he exploded with laughter, I asked: "Rick, am I that funny, or do you just laugh because I'm your boss?" Without missing a beat, he said, "Jeff, trust me, you're funny, but I laugh extra hard because you're my boss!" It's been that way for all of these years, and there's no doubt, having someone you respect and trust completely makes all of the difference in any endeavor.

After my rocky start at WNTS, our day-to-day settled down, but my original fears were ultimately realized. The station had some ratings growth and the losses narrowed, but it was clear that it was never going to be a competitive player in the market. By the late summer of 1975, less than two years after it was launched, we decided to shift direction. By then, Dave Letterman had gone to California, and six months later, Rick Cummings had a terrific offer to do the overnight shift at WTIC, Hartford. While the time slot was awful, WTIC was one of America's most dominant stations, and it was a great chance for Rick to get into radio's big leagues. Despite losing two key members of the team, we caught a break when NBC decided it needed to put some form of programming on all of its FM radio stations. Bob Mounty led the effort to develop the NBC News and Information Service ("NIS"). It was basically an upbeat version of the all-news stations that CBS and Westinghouse had developed in the major markets. NBC provided as much as sixty minutes an hour of news and features, and stations, if they wanted, could use several windows to provide local information. NIS syndicated the format to other non-NBC stations, such as WNTS. Those stations that wanted no overhead at all could simply take the NBC feed twenty-four hours a day, seven days a week, without the expense of any local news employees. For WNTS, it was a very elegant solution. We could eliminate most of our expenses, and merely employ a few newsreaders for local inserts. The service was provided on a barter basis, meaning NBC gave us the content without charge but kept a number of advertising minutes per hour to sell, thus using the affiliates' inventory to defray the costs of NIS.

It was clearly a win-win situation, and we decided to jettison the local news, talk, and sports format for a chance to provide a much lower cost alternative that would give the station a chance at profitability. Critics noted that if NBC really had any faith in the format, they would have placed it on their big AM stations around the country, but instead they merely inserted NIS on their own FM facilities that had anemic ratings at the time. In the mid-seventies, the rise of FM radio was still on the horizon, and NBC wasn't about to risk the value of their primary AM stations with an untried format. During our first year with NIS, our ratings dropped, but our costs dropped even more, and the station was perpetually on the verge of profitability. However, in the fall of 1977, NBC abruptly pulled the plug on NIS. The network wasn't getting significant ratings on NBC's own FM stations, and it was saddled with a number of weak affiliates around the country (like us) who weren't able to generate ratings either, thus leaving NBC's sales force with largely unattractive inventory.

Once our programming provider had vacated the space, we had to figure out what to do with the station. It was very clear we weren't going to go back to the expense of providing news/talk and sports, so it was my job to figure out our next move. After talking to a good friend, Dick Shaheen, a media broker from Chicago, I realized that there was only one answer for WNTS: religious radio. Without a full-time signal and with limited power, lesser AM stations became a haven for religious, "time-brokered" formats. I researched the format and we quickly made the decision to switch WNTS to religion. Religious radio today is more diverse than it was in the latter part of the 1970s. There are Christian music stations, talk stations, as well as the time-brokered stations that predominated in 1977 when we made the switch. But back then, it was a totally different experience from running a regular commercial station. My job was primarily to call national religious programs and convince them to buy time on WNTS. Most time was sold in fifteen-minute and thirty-minute blocks. Calling it "religious" radio is a bit of a misnomer. Almost every religious station in America broadcasts some form of evangelical Christianity. Within the evangelical community are various forms of Baptist, Pentecostal, and other faiths, but invariably, this evangelicalism was intertwined with a brand of fundamental conservatism that was beginning to engage more aggressively in partisan politics. Many were led by charismatic preachers such as Jimmy Swaggart, Jerry Falwell, and Pat Robertson, to name a few. All of them booked time on stations around the country. These ministries understood that the success of their shows depended on the scale of contributions they received in each market. I learned early on that if your station didn't pull in the requisite amount of financial support in a reasonable amount of time, the ministry would cancel the program. It was a reasonably sophisticated financial model and WNTS, with its 5,000-watt signal in a very conservative Midwestern market, was able to generate good returns for its clients. WNTS might not have had enough signal strength to compete with the biggest broadcasters in our market, but compared to lesser suburban stations also selling religious time, we were a very significant competitor.

While it sounds a bit crazy to look at it all these years later, I actually developed a great rapport with a number of the ministers who became our best customers. As a moderately liberal Jewish Democrat, I was on the opposite end of the spectrum from almost all of my clients; I learned at a very early age that to succeed in business, you have to be able to relate to just about anyone. My time selling religious programming taught me that rapport was possible with anyone, no matter how different, and the ministers and program brokers were actually very enjoyable to work with. Fortunately, WNTS reached profitability fairly quickly as a religious station, and that was a relief. However, there's no question I was bored doing a form of radio that wasn't like anything I had ever envisioned. With lots of time on my hands, I ramped up my efforts to start my own company and continued talking with a few investors about bidding on stations. I also decided to write a novel, which was called *The Emmis Region*. It was about sports, espionage, and politics, and it allowed me to escape from religious radio during down times. I never finished the book, but it was a fun diversion. It also provided me with the name of my company, Emmis, which is the Hebrew word for truth.

The religious radio business was the perfect antidote for the signal strength problems of WNTS. The station became nicely profitable and we had the opportunity to buy another. Bob Gibson, the Hall of Fame pitcher, had bought two stations, an AM and an FM, in his hometown of Omaha. His original idea, programming two stations for Omaha's Black population, had been a great gesture for his hometown, but the economics didn't work. By the late 1970s, it was becoming clear that he had to sell. The FM station had more potential; Mike Lynch and Mike Oatman of Great Empire Broadcasting decided to buy it and convert the urban format into country music, which was their specialty. The AM, another daytime-only station, was available, and we decided to buy it and switch the format to religion. During the sale process, I got to know Gibson quite well and found him to be a likable, very intelligent man. I even attended his second wedding. His image as a tough-as-nails competitor who would take the head off of any opposing batter softened considerably when I got to know him.

Shortly after the Omaha purchase, I accelerated my attempt to start a company. My proposition was simple. Although FM at the time was a decidedly lesser band for radio, it was going to become dominant because, with its superior fidelity, FM was going to make listening to music much more enjoyable. With FM also able to broadcast in stereo, I was convinced it was only a matter of time before most music stations transitioned from the AM band. While the observation seems obvious today, it was a bit revolutionary in the late seventies. Most companies ignored their FM stations and focused on their cash cows, their AMs. I assembled a group of investors, led by Michael Gradison, and we located an FM station in Milwaukee that we thought it made sense to buy. However, the deal fell through. I then turned my sights to Indianapolis. My theory was that while there were a number of FM stations in the market, there were also two full-signal FMs in adjacent counties. Both had 50,000-watt signals, and with tower improvements could reach the entire Indianapolis market easily. My first choice, WSMJ in Greenfield, was on the market, and I approached the sellers but was quickly outbid by Cecil Heftel, who offered $1 million for the station and gobbled it up. By this time, I needed new investors, because Gradison had joined a group that was trying to win the license of WIFE-FM, which the FCC had taken away from Don Burden for his influence-buying scheme with several senators. Because the FCC essentially picks the winner and gives the preferred group a free license, the opportunity for Gradison's investment partners was too tempting. Why partner with me and have to buy something when you have a chance at a free license? Michael still wanted to pursue an opportunity with me but was outvoted by his partners. Ironically, seven bidders came forward for that WIFE-FM license, and by the time Gradison's group lost four years later, my company was up and running with two very successful stations.

At that point, my accountant Bruce Jacobson put me together with Mickey Maurer and Bob Schloss—childhood friends—who were contemporaries of my sister, Dale. Bob's family was very prominent, the original owners of the Morris Plan, a financial institution that was an early lender to America's cable industry. When a number of the loans went bad, Bob's father turned the cable systems over to Mickey and Bob to find a way to make them profitable. The two of them were also early, successful investors in the racquetball craze, and by the time Bruce put me together with them, they had developed a reputation as very adept financial minds. Mickey, while in many ways the polar opposite of me, was clearly the financial wizard of the two and quickly grasped my plan. I had one other serious suitor, partners Buddy Yosha, one of the state's most successful trial lawyers, and Art Belford, who owned one of Indiana's most successful trucking companies. I knew those guys much better and was inclined to choose them, but Mickey and Bob made me an offer Buddy and Art couldn't match, and along with my understanding that Maurer and Schloss were more adept investors, I went with them.

By the time I partnered with Mickey and Bob, I had reached a tentative deal with John Hartnett and his partners at WSVL-FM, Shelbyville. Years earlier, John had put together a civic group to buy the town's AM station and later added an FM to the operation. WSVL-FM was unique, because it was the only other 50,000-watt station in a county adjacent to Indianapolis.

While it was merely a throwaway in Hartnett's operation, it would have significant value if it could be upgraded. In 1979, when we reached an agreement, WSVL-FM was putting on programming that wasn't deemed worthy for airing on the more dominant AM frequency. While WSVL-AM was broadcasting Shelbyville basketball games, the FM was carrying the games of smaller schools elsewhere in the county. If the AM broadcast Little League games, the FM carried minor Little League games.

When I approached John and his partners, they were excited by the hefty million-dollar price tag that WSMJ had commanded. With their operation strictly centered in Shelbyville, they had no interest in making all the changes necessary to compete in neighboring Indianapolis. Early on, John revealed that if we could get him a million dollars for WSVL-FM, he thought we could do a deal. Knowing that funding an all-cash offer would be difficult, I countered by raising the price to $1.2 million, with a down payment of $250,000 and the rest in a seven-year note. In March of 1979, we reached an agreement. The deal was contingent on our ability to build a new tower closer to Indianapolis, capable of transmitting a much stronger signal, and we had two years to construct it. Mickey and Bob agreed to put in $85,000 apiece, and I committed the final $80,000, only $40,000 of which I actually had, but I was certain I could raise the rest. We also agreed to find bank financing for working capital, which was made easier by Mickey and Bob's financial wherewithal.

In later years, I've joked that moving a tower is somewhat like invading Normandy, only with more violence waiting for you as you approach the cliffs. Admittedly, that's a bad analogy, but it's hard to describe how challenging the process was. I should also mention that when we made the deal for WSVL-FM, I had parted ways with my dad, and it was acrimonious. We patched up our relationship shortly after I started Emmis, and we became closer and closer through the rest of his life, but at that moment I was on my own. Starting a new company while also spending two years building that new tower and launching the revamped WSVL-FM took a major toll on my finances and my home life.

Those two years taught me that if you love something and want it badly enough, you will endure almost anything. To me, the experience was the ultimate lesson in persistence and grit, although most rational people might describe it as an insane lesson in futility. Here's how it went: Once we had our agreement to buy WSVL-FM, we determined that the best place to put the tower was closest to the metropolitan area, but still within the contours of Shelbyville coverage as required by FCC rules. Our spot was in southern Marion County, home to Indianapolis. It was clear that we would be able to reach all of the metropolitan area easily from this site, and we filed for a site change with the FCC. There was only one problem. Our consulting engineer missed the intermediate frequency rule. Rather than explain the nuances, suffice it to say that to comply with the regulation, our tower, with a planned frequency of 97.1, had to be 14.5 miles from the 107.9 frequency. Unfortunately, since 107.9 was the frequency of WIFE-FM, we had to be 14.5 miles from all seven applicants jockeying to acquire it (the FCC had not picked one yet). To make matters worse, most of the applicants were on the original WIFE-FM tower site, which was less than ten miles from our location. We decided that we had to approach the applicants and induce each of them to move to one of the tower sites on the north side of Indianapolis. Since the city was rapidly growing north (with the exploding suburbs of Carmel, Fishers, and Zionsville), we thought that the switch would provide better coverage in the highest growth areas and, with the proper inducement, would make sense to each of the bidders.

We started with Bob Kiley. Jack Marsella, our sales manager at WNTS, had been Kiley's sales manager at WIFE and they were lifelong friends. Because of their relationship, we thought that it was good to start with Bob. I always thought Joseph Stalin had a better chance of winning the license than Kiley; he had been the manager of WIFE during all of owner Don Burden's misdeeds, and common sense dictated that Kiley may have been aware of some of the issues. I couldn't imagine that, after taking Burden's licenses away, the FCC would reward someone who had been present during all of Burden's transgressions, and my instinct ultimately proved correct. But now we were at the initial stages, and our meeting with Kiley was an eye-opener, to say the least. He was indignant that we would do anything to interfere with "his license." His attitude was that it was just a matter of time before he won, and he was not going to do anything to alter his perfect bid. I quickly learned that talking with the bidders for a free FCC license is the best way to understand delusional thinking. Marvin Frank—Mike

Gradison's partner—was another bidder who exhibited the same attitude. In his view, the other bidders were merely cannon fodder; he was predestined to win and didn't want anyone wasting his time by suggesting that he make a slight modification to his perfect application that the FCC was certainly going to grant. Ultimately, Frank was as mistaken as Kiley about his chances for winning the license.

It was clear our approach to reaching an agreement with all seven bidders was futile. So we went back to Shelby County, where we found a tower site that was 14.5 miles away from all of the WIFE-FM applicants. It was in the town of Fairland, in the northern part of the county. While it wasn't ideal, we were certain the signal would be good enough to make us competitive in Indianapolis. We had to make sure that our frequency did not interfere with any air traffic, so we consulted with the Federal Aviation Administration (FAA) and picked a site that was acceptable. All we needed next was to win zoning approval. Zoning a tower is never easy, because there are always people in any neighborhood who believe that a broadcast signal causes cancer, the plague, or today, I'm certain, the dissemination of COVID-19. I can remember one hearing when we brought pictures of the Channel 13 tower, which was nearly across the street from shopping center magnate Mel Simon's home, certainly the most expensive residence in Indianapolis. That picture probably convinced a few people at the hearing that if Mel Simon lived across from a much larger tower, our tower probably wouldn't destroy property values or life expectancy in rural Shelby County.

We had a vastly greater challenge dealing with the Indiana State Aeronautics Commission ("ISAC"), a tiny department within the state of Indiana. It had very few employees, and its statutory obligation was to follow the rules of the FAA. In other words, they didn't have much to do, just listen to what the feds told them. Our case, however, caused a major fracas within the commission. The small staff concluded that our tower site was a great hazard to aviation safety, and they were determined to fight us to the death. The battle went on for over a year, and it was clear that they were going to kill our tower or die trying. I'm not a paranoid person, but all these years later, I'm absolutely sure somebody on that staff was on the take. Turning us down made no logical sense, yet every time we tried to discuss ISAC's statutory obligation to rely on the FAA's findings, their people countered, in no uncertain terms, that they didn't care what their own statute or the FAA said, they were going to block our tower. And this insane impasse was hardly an isolated incident; back in those days, broadcasting was like the Wild West and people pulled all sorts of stunts to prevent competitors from building their operations. A few years later, we encountered one of the craziest cases, when two big broadcasting companies devised a plan to prevent six competitors from moving their towers to the tallest building in Minneapolis.

All that time, as nothing was moving forward, I was finding the whole process incredibly painful. Having left my dad's stations (WNTS and KCRO), I wasn't making a living. Instead, I was spending all my time pushing to get the tower approved and WSVL-FM started. Although my wife Janine was working, I was depleting our meager savings, and on top of that, my relationship with my dad was strained. Then, in October of 1980, Janine and I adopted our daughter, Cari; with three mouths to feed and little income, the pressure to quit was significant. My mother-in-law pointed out that it was time to give up my ridiculous goal of starting a radio company and to find a way to take care of my family. I told her that I was not going to stop—I was going to get my station on the air, and time would prove that I could do it. While others might have abandoned the project, I had such a passion for this business that I was fundamentally incapable of quitting.

Finally, in early 1981, after eighteen months of trying to resolve the issue, and rapidly approaching our two-year deadline to complete the purchase, we filed suit in Marion County Superior Court to enjoin the state from blocking us. Ron Elberger, who has been my lawyer for most of the last fifty years, is a brilliant litigator, and I had confidence that if our case was winnable, he would prevail. Picking judges in superior court is a random affair, and while I was hopeful that we might have landed in a court of a sympathetic Democratic judge who might have known me or my family, we appeared to get the worse possible draw. Judge Richard Milam was not only a Republican, he was also a pilot. Since ISAC was claiming that the FAA decision was risking the lives of all pilots in the area, we were worried that Milam would agree and my career might disintegrate before my very eyes. Instead, Milam analyzed the case very quickly and clearly. Because he was a pilot, he was completely aware that ISAC's reasons had nothing to do with safety, and he even alluded to his concerns (and the source of my paranoia) when he told ISAC that he had no idea what was motivating them, but it certainly wasn't aviation safety. He quickly ruled in our favor. Elberger knew one of the reporters at the NBC affiliate, Channel 6, and they even reported about Milam's stern warning in a summary of the case.

After the ruling, I told the construction company to go ahead full speed and build the tower. Every day I checked on its progress, watching my dream become a reality. Truth be told, I was also terrified ISAC would get an injunction from an appellate court to stop our construction. It turned out we were able to complete the 679-foot tower before ISAC appealed the ruling. When they did, the case took several years to reach a resolution, and the State then granted us a formal permit. By that time, however, I had my company up and running, and I was in the midst of some of the most vibrant days of my life, doing what I loved.

Top: The original logo of KSHE's mascot, Sweetmeat the Pig, from a Blodwyn Pig album. *Bottom:* Sammie, the Sweetmeat Mascot, me, and St. Louis market manager John Beck.

2

The Golden Years

I was now ready to start my company, Emmis. Everyone liked the name, and it gave me a core value—truth—to uphold as I ran my venture. Moreover, I had found the perfect location for a small startup: Another radio station had recently vacated its building, a modular structure on Indianapolis's east side. I quickly reached an agreement with the site's market manager to lease the building. My first hire was local engineer Bob Hawkins, who would oversee the build-out of our WSVL tower and help get all the radio hardware up and running. After him, I reached out to Rick Cummings to head up programming. Rick had been fired from WTIC for referencing the Fannie Fox incident. Fox was a stripper who was discovered in the Washington Tidal Basin in the middle of the night with Wilbur Mills, the powerful head of the House Ways and Means Committee. At the time it was considered one of the greatest political scandals in American history, and ultimately ended Mills's career. On Rick's overnight talk show, a caller asked him about it, and he replied, "Oh Fannie, she Fox like a mink." Through a stroke of very bad luck, Rick's program director was listening at three in the morning. (I submit that any programmer listening at three in the morning should be fired on the spot.) Rick's boss thought the joke was in incredibly bad taste, and Rick was summarily dismissed. Rick then went to WSMB in New Orleans, a decidedly less prestigious station than WTIC.

It's hard to grasp how different the times were. Once, during that era, I reprimanded David Letterman for questioning why you can't say "pulling your pud" on the air. While this led to a hilarious discussion of what a pud was, I was certain the FCC would take the most common definition (a penis) and as a result would take our license away. Meanwhile, David argued that a pud could just as easily be a wad of chewing gum! But in that environment, I prevailed.

Anyway, through the years I had stayed in touch with Rick, and when I was ready to hire him at the beginning of 1981 to program our new station (which we had rechristened WENS), he decided to take a chance with us. Over the years, I've joked that if he had stayed at WTIC, he would have immediately spurned my offer. "Absolutely," he noted, "no chance I would leave Hartford to come to work for you," but I always thought he was kidding.

In the spring of 1981, with our tower under construction, Rick and I started to put together a small staff. One of our earliest additions was Steve Crane. He and I had grown up together and had been best friends since grade school. After Hanover College and a stint in the navy, Steve went to law school at Northwestern. Ironically, in the fall of 1974, while attending my first ever National Association of Broadcasters (NAB) convention, I ended up having dinner with Steve and his wife, Phoebe, at the Hyatt Regency where the convention was being held. Because they had to get home early to relieve their son Matthew's babysitter, I decided to go upstairs and have one drink alone, something I absolutely never did. As I went into the restaurant/bar, I met the hostess, Janine Ginger. It was a quiet night and we started talking and . . . well, to make a long story short, we began a long-distance relationship and were married a year later.

Steve had begun the practice of law at Hopkins & Sutter, a prestigious Chicago firm, and then followed mentor Don Reuben to the firm he founded, Reuben & Proctor. By 1981, Steve was miserable practicing law, so when I was getting ready to launch Emmis, he inquired about joining in some capacity. I told him, "Steve, the only job I can offer you is a sales job—it's going to pay nothing." He didn't care: "I'm willing to take a chance that you know what you're doing and this will work out." (Now, forty years later, he's aware I had no clue at the time!) With a new career waiting, Steve came back home to Indianapolis. When he arrived, a few weeks before we were ready to go on the air, I joked to him, "If I had known you had that ugly little yellow Datsun, I never would have let you come here!" Even today I remember that car; it was awful, but it served as reliable transportation for our lunches for several years.

Steve made even more of a commitment to Emmis, agreeing to invest just as we were ready to launch the station. We agreed he would pay $100,000 for 7 percent of the business (a calculation based on the appreciation of our station, now that it was ready to go on the air). Mickey and Bob and I all agreed to dilute our holdings, as we had done when we allowed my father and brother-in-law, Zeke, to invest a few years earlier. Even though my family was at odds at the time, they kept their small holdings for many, many years. As a result of the dilution, I was left with around 20 percent of free stock, and my $80,000 investment got me another 20 percent ownership in the company. Mickey and Bob retained 51 percent. When my partners and I had started Emmis, we had agreed they would control the first station, then continue to control the second station until it was profitable, after which I and the other investors would buy 2 percent ownership from them and have 51 percent of that second station. After the first two stations, Mickey and Bob's ownership would be reduced to 40 percent.

By the time we were ready to launch the station, I had a windfall that enabled me to add a bit of cash to improve my economic situation. While attending the NAB convention in Las Vegas, Janine and I were selected in a coffee shop line to be contestants on the game show *Las Vegas Gambit*. We ended up winning over $20,000, much of it in cash. The host, Wink Martindale, kidded me when I mentioned we were launching "The New WENS" in Indianapolis. Years later, Wink and I reconnected when Emmis owned Power 106 in Los Angeles; he claimed that he remembered us on the show. And it seems like every year, someone tells me they saw the segment on YouTube.

Through the years, people have asked me if I had any fears about putting all I had into that first station. The $80,000 came from my savings, my game show winnings, and everything I could borrow. Either I was incredibly naïve, or I had cast away my fear of failure after my WNTS experience, but I never worried about my prospects. Such is the confidence that can fuel an entrepreneur's rise or guarantee his demise. Nevertheless, I had no doubt we would make the station work—even after we discovered that the signal strength from our new tower was merely adequate, especially since we needed to reach the fastest growing parts of the market on the opposite side of the city.

In contrast, picking a format was easy. The FM band had nothing between Top 40 and "beautiful music." There was an urban station, a country music station, and an album-oriented rock (AOR) station. WNAP, the Top 40 station, could not play much mellow music, because it was careful never to duplicate the playlist of its sister station, WIBC, the dominant AM station that featured middle-of-the-road (MOR) music. WIBC owned the market in those days with ratings over 10 percent, a dominant news department, and legendary morning man Gary Todd, who after twenty years had reached iconic status. The WIBC/WNAP combination was clearly the city's powerhouse, and I knew that its owner, Fairbanks Broadcasting, was the one group that could block our entry with its incredible market power and generations of political clout.

All of us worked nonstop to launch the station. Rick was incredibly intuitive about programming, and although Steve knew nothing about radio, he was a remarkably quick study and an ideal sounding board. We also brought in a consultant, Bob Henaberry, who had developed a specialty in FM adult contemporary stations. One critical lesson in business: You have to assess your strengths and weaknesses, tearing each apart carefully, and that requires everyone's input. Once you pinpoint weaknesses in your plan, you can deal with them *before* you introduce that grand plan to the marketplace. As we said countless times, if we have a flaw, let's find it and try to fix it, because if we take it into the marketplace, our competitors will discover it, and when they do, it will cost us lots of money.

Of course, our strengths at WENS (which stood for We're Ninety-Seven) were simple. We had the music fidelity of the FM band and didn't have the clutter of any commercials on the air when we launched. The entire premise of Emmis, risky at the time, was that music sounded superior on the FM band and that, as a result, people would migrate to it to hear the same songs that they were listening to on AM.

What were our weaknesses? Money. We had none and our competitors had plenty, especially the WIBC/WNAP juggernaut. Money would pay for talented personalities, fund massive contests, and buy lots of billboard advertising and TV commercials. Our job, in a classic marketing sense, was to turn our competitors' strengths into weaknesses. With all the fervor of entrepreneurs putting everything on the line, we were merciless. Rick and I wrote a satirical take on the silly talk of our competitors and with the animators at Perennial Pictures created a TV commercial that highlighted its inanity. The commercial opened with the announcer intoning, "Doesn't it seem like most radio stations talk at you?" Our first goal was to reposition WIBC, our competitor playing similar music, and our target was their legendary host, Gary Todd. By then, Todd was so ingrained in the community that his show became a regular forum for his interactions with the power brokers of Indianapolis, which made him ripe for caricature. Our first line had an animation of Todd saying, "Tomorrow, I'm playing golf with the governor." We then went on to satirize other personalities and ended that segment with WNAP's buzzard mascot in a cast and crutches limping across the screen and falling down. The commercial then went on to note, "We're different, we're the new WENS, with music from Neil Diamond, Barbra Streisand, the Eagles, the Beatles. We don't talk at you." And then the spot ended with our tagline: "We let our music do the talking." Obviously, we had no idea if it would work, but clearly there was a hole in the market that you could drive a truck through, and if the message resonated, we were certain people would find us.

On July 3, we were preparing to launch the station. By six o'clock, Steve and I were about to leave and let Rick and Bob Hawkins complete their work. Bob was going to finish wiring the station's control boards, and Rick was going to get the format ready. Just as we were leaving, we realized we had no labels on our carts. In those days, all music was played on cartridges resembling eight-track tapes. The music had been loaded on the carts, but they hadn't been labeled. Steve and I thus spent the next six hours typing the labels of the six hundred songs we needed in order to go on the air. It was one of the first examples of what I call the legendary Emmis disorganization. When we finished, I asked Rick for a quick assessment of our preparations. "No chance we're going on the air tomorrow. Hawkins hasn't figured out the wiring. I'm not sure when he will but it ain't going to be anytime soon." With that I made it home at 1 AM and set my alarm for five thirty. On waking up, I called Rick and he said, "I'll be damned, Hawkins figured it out about three thirty and we're ready to go." So, at six in the morning, my dream venture was going to launch. We'd picked out our first song: "This Is It," by Kenny Loggins, which signified the perfect start for our venture. Naturally, at six, Tim McKee, our first disc jockey, reached down and played "Don't Let Me Be Lonely Tonight" by James Taylor. More Emmis disorganization, and not exactly the dramatic start we wanted, but we were up and running. A few hours later, Steve came by and we drove to every stereo shop in the northern half of Indianapolis to check the signal. In those days, every stereo had lights, usually red, to demonstrate the strength of the signal reaching the receiver. Our mission was to determine how well people in the fastest growing part of our market could hear our station. Our signal didn't light up as many lights as our competitors with closer towers, but it was clearly strong enough to be heard.

There have been a few times in my life when everything goes perfectly, and the launch of WENS was one of those times. Within the first couple of weeks, people were reporting they were hearing the station everywhere. One of my proudest moments was waiting in line to enter a movie, and overhearing the four people in front of me talking about the "I'm playing golf with the governor" TV commercial and how brilliant it was and how they loved the new station. In a few weeks, the 97.1 signal had gone from Little League games in Shelbyville to a formidable competitor in Indianapolis. Of course, there were growing pains, but the station was clearly skyrocketing. In its first Arbitron ratings book, the industry's measure for performance, WENS went from a zero share of the market to a 7 percent share, placing it firmly in the market's top tier. We quickly proclaimed it America's fastest-growing station and we were on our way. There's really no way to describe what happens when your dreams come true. For me, WENS was a quick validation that our vision for the media company of the future could be successful. Emmis was always a collaborative culture, built on respect for the worth of each individual, with a healthy dose of fun always baked into the enterprise. When I started it, I wanted a company that would foster a lifelong bond with its people, more along the lines of Japanese culture than the starker, more laissez-faire approach of American capitalism. Given the realities of modern capitalism, it was probably naïve, but the people-first approach of Emmis has always served us well.

For the most part, Mickey and Bob were thrilled with our prospects, although one meeting with Bob foretold problems. Bob was a likable guy, but I would describe him as someone "to the manor born." The phrase refers to someone who believes he has a higher status than everyone else, which leads him to expect others to do things he doesn't require of himself. I've encountered people like that my entire life and it is frustrating. Once, my friend Ginny Morris, whose family had started the prominent Hubbard Broadcasting Company nearly a century ago, asked me if she wasn't "to the manor born," too. Amused, I replied: "Ginny, not only are you to the manor born, but so was your father and his father, but you don't act like it. You don't treat everyone as if they're beneath you. That's a big difference." In fairness to Bob, he wasn't always that way, but the tendency surfaced every once in a while. One day at a meeting, I mentioned that I was bringing in a consulting engineer to measure our power in all directions, with the hope that he could tweak our signal to strengthen it in the direction of Indianapolis. Bob immediately interrupted, "You need to do this yourself, Jeff. Your problem is you delegate too much." I was incredulous: "Bob, I picked every record on the station, hired every employee, wrote the sales materials, made sales calls, and wrote the TV spot. I've delegated almost nothing, but I can't learn how to measure signals and understand antenna engineering." Bob reluctantly agreed to let me bring in a consultant, while Mickey sat amused in the corner.

The funny thing is, if Bob watched me today, his observation would be accurate, and I would be proud to admit it. If an enterprise is to grow, you have to delegate as much as possible and let your people do their jobs. The major failing of new managers is their inability to delegate, and when they do, their inability to let go of the projects they have delegated. My job as a leader is to attract great employees and give them the tools to accomplish their goals.

Back then, Bob's interference barely registered. We had hit a home run with the station, and from there things moved so quickly that we just went from success to success without thinking about the long term.

It was exhilarating and fun. After WENS's first Arbitron rating book, the station continued its climb, all the way to a ten share in the late spring of 1982. By then, we were actively looking for our second station: first, at one in Pittsburgh that never materialized, then at WLOL in Minneapolis, which we bought in the fall of 1982. The WLOL purchase highlighted a few fundamental tenets of our business approach. The first was that we could employ leverage to grow the company. When it works in your favor, leverage is a remarkable wealth creator. When it goes against you, you can watch your life's efforts go down the drain very quickly. I've seen both. If forced to choose, pick the former, not the latter! The purchase of WENS was $1.25 million, with a $250,000 up-front payment and a seller note for $1 million. When we bought the station, it had no ratings or revenues—what in radio would be called a "stick" because you have a license to broadcast at a certain frequency, but nothing else. The term "stick" refers only to the tower you had (although in the case of WENS, we didn't even start out with the stick!). We were betting we could generate enough cash flow to service our debt on the note. If we could produce $200,000 of cash flow, our leverage ratio would be five to one, or $1 million divided by the $200,000. This is a key factor in almost every business. If you want to earn outsized returns, you have to have debt; yet if you can't pay the interest, you will quickly lose your business. In its first year, WENS generated over $500,000 of cash flow—a spectacular return—with rating increases that indicated the number would go up. Since our note with the Shelbyville sellers carried an interest rate of 6 percent, we would have to pay them $60,000 per year. We had a choice: use the excess to pay down more debt, or fund new acquisitions. We usually decided on the latter. Our purchase of WLOL was for $6 million with an up-front payment of $3 million and a $3 million note from the sellers. That amount represented about fifteen times the station's cash flow. The station was not a true stick, since it was already generating profits, but we were willing to pay more than the traditional multiple of ten times cash flow because we liked WLOL's growth trajectory and we loved the Minneapolis market.

While we planned on keeping WLOL a traditional adult contemporary station, its general manager, Doyle Rose, was tinkering with the format not knowing that owners Bob Liggett and Larry Bentson were in deep discussions to sell the station. They never realized that Doyle made the switch to a straight Top 40 station as our sale talks progressed. We were aware of the changes and were encouraged that the station was moving in a better direction, ratings wise. When the sale was announced, WLOL's last rating book was a four share of Minneapolis radio. Whenever a purchase occurs, the FCC must approve the transfer, and in those days it usually took at least four months. When the sale was announced, we sent Steve Crane to Minneapolis to oversee the station during the transition period. Steve was to be the new general manager when the sale was approved.

While we were waiting, Steve had a number of meetings with Doyle and his team, and he called to say, "Look, this guy (Doyle) is great. There's no way I'd be better at running this station than he would be." It was a remarkable bit of honest self-reflection by Steve, and in the corporate world, that's almost unheard of. I'd like to say it's the type of culture we have at Emmis, but it's really the type of people we have. Steve's assessment of Doyle was absolutely correct: he was one of the best radio executives I've ever known. We not only took Steve's advice, but Doyle also became an integral part of Emmis's growth for more than twenty years, until he ultimately retired.

Also, during the transition period, my friend Stuart Layne, who headed CBS's rep firm in Chicago that handled our account, called us when he got an early look at the WLOL ratings. Breathlessly, he intoned, "You just went from a four share to a ten share at WLOL, you're at the top of the market!" Without missing a beat, I replied, "We're screwed." He responded, "I know." Doyle's bold, and largely surreptitious, switch to Top 40 had been a spectacular success. Why would this be bad news, with all of the potential windfall soon to come? Because Bob and Larry were suddenly selling a much more valuable station, and they were highly likely either to cancel the deal or seek to renegotiate. They were both honorable men, but there was no way they would ignore the change in the station's value. After a lot of posturing on both sides, we agreed that instead of a $3 million note for half of the purchase, we would pay them all cash, which because of a below-market interest rate on the note, gave them more value for the station. Because of our excess cash flow on WENS and the promise of more profitability at WLOL, we were able to increase our borrowings from our banks and close the all-cash purchase.

While we had absolutely nothing to do with the growth of WLOL, it led to my line that "It wasn't really Emmis management that made the difference in our success, it was merely the *threat* of Emmis management." It's a line I've used many times when something we purchased improved while we were waiting for government approval. Steve Crane latched on to that explanation when he gave me perhaps my greatest compliment: "Jeff, your absolute greatest strength is self-deprecation." To which I replied, "Steve, there's a lot here to self-deprecate!" However, Steve was absolutely right—if you can laugh at yourself, make fun of yourself, and never, ever take yourself too seriously, you can create an atmosphere where others will do the same. It's been a hallmark of Emmis that we can constantly laugh at ourselves, needle each other, and never take ourselves too seriously. In a later chapter, I'll describe the Eleven Commandments of Emmis, but the unofficial Twelfth Commandment is "Always take the cheap shot." It sounds ridiculous, but it's remarkable how much this playful spirit can lighten any serious discussion and how it creates an open atmosphere that brings out the best in everyone. Probably the greatest cheap shot in Emmis history came from Rick to me during my long period of bachelorhood: "Jeff, your problem is you always think with your dick. Unfortunately, you never think big thoughts!"

After the purchase of WLOL, we were clearly on a roll. Rick worked with Doyle to tweak WLOL, and it became known as one of America's most successful FM Top 40 stations. Clearly, in the two years since we had launched WENS, our original vision that music would transition to the greater fidelity of FM was being validated on a daily basis. It was impossible, even for the biggest AM music stations, to match the sound quality of FM, and powerhouses like WIBC (Indianapolis) were beginning a slow, inexorable decline. Its sister station, WNAP, hoping to protect WIBC, tried to match WENS, sometimes song for song; that merely created a perception that it was a badly programmed imitator, and the station never found its bearing. Years later, after we had purchased both WIBC and WNAP, I joked that "In 1981, we killed WNAP. The only problem is, now that we own it, it's still dead and we can't revive it."

With our cash flows growing geometrically, we were ready to buy more stations. I had studied the Los Angeles market and was enamored with its growth. With only twenty viable (full-signal) FMs, Los Angeles was, to me, the perfect radio market. Knowing the city from seven years at USC, I understood that people were captive in their cars, spending long hours on the myriad freeways with little to do but listen to their favorite radio stations. Having a great climate didn't hurt either, with people outside on beaches or jogging around neighborhoods with the ubiquitous Sony Walkman attached to their ears. It was the stereo descendant of the transistor radio, and listening to FM on it was a remarkable experience. By 1983, Los Angeles radio revenue was growing at a much faster rate than New York's and soon would pass it as the country's—and indeed the world's—largest radio market. From the early days of Emmis, we realized that the fixed costs in radio didn't differ much between the largest and the smallest markets, so we came up with the adage: "You're still going to pay the same light bill in Kokomo as you are in New York, but you can make a lot more money in New York than Kokomo." While success had certainly brought some hubris to our thinking, the math was essentially correct. If we were good at what we did, we could create outsized returns in the biggest markets. We also intuitively figured that some of the largest media companies—like networks ABC, NBC, and CBS—sometimes had bigger fish to fry than paying attention to their radio divisions, and that neglect fueled our fervor to take a shot at America's largest broadcasters.

My next target, Century Broadcasting, had been founded by two friends from Chicago, Howard Grafman and George Collias. In the days when it was impossible to buy big AM stations, they had cobbled together the funds to buy a few FMs with miniscule ratings. Ultimately, Century achieved success with their beautiful music station in Chicago, their pioneering album rock station in St. Louis, and their rock station in San Francisco. Their fourth was a perpetual laggard in Los Angeles. Howard and George wanted to sell their St. Louis and San Francisco stations. I had my heart set on KMGG Los Angeles, or Magic 106 as it was known. At one point we proposed buying three of the four stations, but I didn't want to purchase the San Francisco station. We believed it was going to face a difficult challenge maintaining its profitable market position, based on our study of the city. After a while, we settled on a $20 million deal, allocating $11 million for the never-profitable KMGG and $9 million for KSHE (St. Louis). Like WENS, the Los Angeles station was a true stick purchase: we were paying $11 million for a chance to compete in this market. Most observers thought the deal bordered on insanity, but we were confident we could make KMGG a viable competitor. My original analysis was that if we could just make it a player in the middle of the bottom quartile of LA FM stations, we would generate $2.5 million of cash flow, giving us a station with under five times leverage.

The night before closing the purchase, our attorney, David Wills, called to say we had a problem: "The sellers can't produce title to a part of the land where the transmitter is located." We were buying the transmitter site on Flint Peak, which also housed the transmitters of four other broadcasters in Los Angeles—we were about to become their landlords. Since Flint Peak was a forty-acre site, the question was: Where was the title defective? George Collias, who was not a man seriously concerned about the niceties of title transfer, suggested that we just complete the purchase and worry about the issue later. Our lawyers (and the rest of us) thought that was very unwise. We agreed to postpone the closing until the matter could be resolved. Soon thereafter, we found out that the parcel in dispute was the transmitter building, which housed all of the equipment for our and the other stations. We learned that an engineer, upset with something that Century had done to him, had for many years thrown the annual tax bills for the site into the wastebasket. After a while, with the company ignoring repeated requests by Los Angeles County to pay the property taxes, the city exercised its right to foreclose on the property. No one in the Century corporate offices ever knew about the problem. This would be a great case study, not only in proper management/employee relationships, but in corporate oversight as well, but Century was not exactly a buttoned-down enterprise. After we discovered the foreclosure, it took us a few weeks to convince Los Angeles County that it really didn't want to be in the radio business, and Century agreed to pay all of the taxes and fines to reclaim its site. A month later, our deal closed, and Emmis doubled in size while also entering America's best radio market.

We now owned KSHE (St. Louis), one of the very first FM album rock stations and an absolute institution in the city. Even today, nearly forty years later, I believe you can walk just about anywhere in the world with a KSHE T-shirt, adorned with its pig mascot, Sweetmeat, and you would be asked, "Are you from St. Louis?" I've had it happen countless times. Of course, my friend Dick Leventhal said that the only thing he ever saw me wear on weekends were T-shirts from one of our stations. "If you hadn't gone into radio," Dick laughed, "you'd have nothing to wear on Saturdays!" One of my proudest possessions is a massive photograph of the Berlin Wall, just before it fell in 1989, with "KSHE 95, St. Louis" scrawled in giant letters near the top.

KSHE was one of the most fun, exciting projects I've ever been involved with. We hired John Beck, the sales manager of CBS-FM in Detroit, to run the station. My first sales trip had been to Detroit when we started WENS. Steve and I went there on an overnight trip to court the automobile industry. Having limited funds, Steve and I shared a room, and in the morning we looked at each other and said, "We absolutely have to make this company successful enough to get separate rooms!" It wasn't exactly the same inspiring mission as Bill Gates's goal at Microsoft to put a computer in every home in the world, but it was a corporate mission for us, nonetheless. With our growth, we hired not only John from CBS, but also Stuart Layne, from CBS's office in Chicago. Both were bright, likable, young men who had been promoted to management quickly by CBS, and both were excited to leave its more staid culture for the vibrancy of the rapidly growing Emmis. Since Doyle's responsibilities were expanding, we shuttled Stuart between Minneapolis and St. Louis to give Doyle help as he focused on Los Angeles, and to help John tackle the marketing of KSHE.

The good news for KSHE was that everybody knew and loved it; however, not that many people actually listened to it, and even fewer bought advertising time. There's an old joke about an advertiser who refuses to buy time on a station with an undesirable audience. After a lengthy discussion with the beleaguered sales person, the advertiser finally blurts out: "Look, I'm not buying time on your station; your listeners are my shoplifters!" That was the KSHE image: grungy, unshaven, unemployed rock listeners who were the dregs of society. Known affectionately as Yard Apes, the KSHE audience was perceived as people who stayed in their basements and listened to rock and roll all day and night and who were never effectively integrated into polite society. Former owner Howard Grafman's brother, Shelly, had been installed at the station years earlier as its manager, and he fit the mold perfectly. While Shelly has never gotten his due as being one of the inventors of rock radio, he ran KSHE like his own fiefdom, playing whatever records he liked while being ensconced in his dark office and creating a station that was far more a cult than a viable business. Because of its image, KSHE was profitable, but we felt it could be markedly improved. Early on, while waiting for FCC approval, Stuart called me with a horror story about the sales manager. "Well, she's traded out a lot of airtime over the years for plastic surgery. If we can convert that into a paying account, they'll be our top advertiser." He then noted, "She also has a habit of giving away TVs to major accounts, and apparently she came into a recent sales meeting announcing to several of the female sellers: 'Girls, the TVs ran out, looks like you'll have to give the clients blow jobs instead!'" While Emmis was a freewheeling, fun culture, it was never *that* freewheeling, and I was mortified by the story. Clearly, KSHE would have to undergo a complete culture change on the day we took over. First, Shelly and his program director, Bob Burch, had to go. Rick recalls his only meeting with Burch. He introduced himself and Burch picked up his newspaper and continued reading. Since Rick was to be Burch's boss if Burch stayed at KSHE, it was instantly clear that Burch was ready to move on and didn't even care to discuss the job. Burch, who had been married to Michelle Phillips of the Mamas and Papas, was well known in the rock industry; apparently, he had already lined up an opportunity in the music business in Hollywood. Besides, he knew that all the perks he was getting with Shelly Grafman at KSHE were about to go out the window. So, when Rick entered his office, Burch didn't have any interest in wasting his time pitching a job he didn't want and knew he wasn't going to get.

We viewed KSHE as the ultimate challenge in repositioning a radio station. We hired Rick Balis as our new program director and constantly hammered him about making the station "palatable." After a few months of this, Balis said he woke up in the middle of the night wondering if whatever he was doing was palatable. "Are my eggs palatable? Are my shoes palatable?" The idea was to take the rock image of KSHE and play songs that people actually knew and wanted to hear. We badgered Balis and the air staff: "Don't play the twelfth song on the Rolling Stones' album, play the two hit records." KSHE was transformed into a much more listenable station. An important point: We didn't have to fire a lot of the staff. Most people are thrilled to learn a new approach to their jobs, especially if you can demonstrate that it will make them more successful. Emmis has always been a company that believes it can work with the people it finds and make them better. One of my favorite quotes is from legendary football coach Bum Phillips, who described Don Shula's management abilities as follows: "Don Shula can take his guys and beat your guys and then he can take your guys and beat his guys!" To me, that's the essence of great leadership: getting the best out of the people you find. In most cases, this philosophy has served us well. There's also a corollary that I have constantly noted for decades: "I've never, ever met anyone who came to work every day and said, 'How can I screw up my job?' People want to be successful; we have to provide them with the leadership and the tools to find that success."

At KSHE, the fun was not only changing the sound but also changing its image in the community. When we talked to listeners, everyone loved Sweetmeat, the pig mascot. Unfortunately, advertisers had a different opinion. They quickly noted that it was hard to embrace a station with a pig with a scraggly beard and a joint hanging out of his mouth. Our challenge: reinvent Sweetmeat. So, we updated him with aviator glasses, a clean-shaven face, and a more likable countenance. We created a Sweetmeat costume and sent various interns in costume to every charity event and hospital we could find, thus making the station a new, more "palatable" part of the St. Louis community. While John Beck built the station operation, we turned Stuart loose on the marketing. For advertisers, Stuart took a page from a *Rolling Stone* magazine campaign called "Perception versus Reality." He took pictures of actual KSHE listeners, from their youth, usually fitting the negative stereotype of longhaired, revolutionary hippies who were the dregs of society. Then he showed pictures of the same people, clean-cut and important members of polite society. The common theme was that they had always listened to KSHE; it was an important part of their lives. It was funny seeing someone who looked like they were ready to bomb the federal building, twenty years later becoming a federal judge, or a woman who looked like a groupie for the Grateful Dead, now becoming a prominent surgeon. The campaign did a lot to dispel the reluctance to buy time on KSHE.

More importantly, we created a TV campaign that went to the heart of the issue. In a spot called "You're Never Too Old to Rock and Roll," we had a middle-aged man, coming home from work, wearing a suit and tie, being welcomed by his wife and daughter. As he walks into his den, he shuts the door, rips off his jacket, loosens his tie, and turns on the radio. As the

Rolling Stones' "Brown Sugar" blares, he starts playing air guitar, doing his best Stones imitation. Unbeknownst to him, his daughter peers through the door and sees him. She runs into the kitchen, and tells her mom: "He's doing it again!" "Doing what again?" the mother inquires as her daughter leads her into the den. Both watch in horror as he continues his mini-concert until he sees them and sheepishly stops his act. The tagline: "KSHE 95, because you're never too old to rock and roll."

The commercial was an absolute smashing success. It communicated that KSHE was a station for the emerging middle class, upscale St. Louis audience and that it was okay to listen and advertise on it. KSHE's ratings tripled in its first year under our ownership, all the way to a 14 share, unheard of for an FM in those days, and revenues followed. It gave us a great opportunity to learn whether we could reinvent a stagnant brand, and the results were beyond gratifying.

Unfortunately, Los Angeles was at the other end of the spectrum. Magic 106 had always been an also-ran in the market. One of my most memorable moments was visiting the transmitter site with the chief engineer. While exiting the car, admonishing me to watch out for rattlesnakes, he confided that the station was just jinxed: "This station will never compete in Los Angeles. The signal isn't as good as those on Mount Wilson and it will never get any ratings." I knew that the Flint Peak signal was slightly inferior, but it was also clear that the other stations at the transmitter site had much higher ratings, and they had identical signals to ours. As we looked at our options, Jim Riggs, who oversaw all of our research, made a prescient observation: "This market is going to be majority/minority in the next fifteen years, and if you could do something that appeals to the emerging minority population, you'd really have something." We thought about Jim's words and wondered whether we could craft a rhythmic format that would primarily appeal to English-speaking Hispanics as well as the Black market. In Los Angeles, the Black population was less than ten percent, which was dwarfed by the Hispanic population. We discussed the idea but decided that Magic's adult contemporary format could be fixed. After all, we had started our company with the spectacular success of WENS by doing the same thing. The station just needed to be modified, and we started with a new morning man, Robert W. Morgan.

Robert W. had been a mainstay in Los Angeles for twenty years and, having listened to him, we were certain he still had enough talent to improve our mornings. We also brought in Sonny Melendrez for afternoons to attract an older audience. We allocated significant resources to advertising, with billboards, bumper stickers, and especially TV spots. The centerpiece of our whole campaign was basketball superstar Magic Johnson, whom we had lured to be the spokesman for the new "Magic 106." We wrote a commercial with Magic at his locker talking about the new Magic 106 and how he never knew how much he liked Neil Diamond. (It may have strained credulity to think Magic Johnson really did like Neil Diamond, but our string of successes had let a little hubris seep in.) The key to the spot was the tagline: "I like this station so much, I'm just glad they didn't name it Kareem 106!" We thought the line was great because Magic and Kareem were Lakers teammates, and everyone knew about their partnership on the court. Unfortunately, at the last minute before we started shooting, Magic's agent decided he didn't want to rock the boat with Kareem, who had a streak of moodiness. Out went "Kareem 106," in came "Dr. J 106." Since Dr. J played 2,500 miles away in Philadelphia, the line made little sense in Los Angeles, but "Dr. J" it was.

It's hard to blame the failure of Magic 106 on a commercial; we had many other problems. Robert W. Morgan wasn't attracting a sizable audience, and the format wasn't compelling enough to persuade listeners to switch from the three other stations in the market playing similar music. While the station had a minor uptick in ratings, that was nowhere near enough to propel it into the market's upper echelons. After we closed on the purchase in March 1984, we stayed with the Magic 106 format until the final quarterly rating book of 1985. Our sales efforts had improved cash flow from essentially nothing when we bought the station to over $1.5 million, but we were certain we could do better. In September 1985, Rick, Doyle, and I decided that we needed to do something dramatic. We agreed that if the station didn't rise above the 2.4 share it was regularly getting by the end of the fall 1985 ratings period, we would change the format to the rhythmic Top 40 format we had contemplated the previous year. Rick and Doyle went to work researching the format. There was nothing like it, which made sense because no market had the same dynamics as Los Angeles. Don Kelly, a consultant from New

York, had introduced a somewhat similar format in Philadelphia, but that market had a minuscule Hispanic population. Secretly, we attended the DJ clubs around town to hear playlists, monitored what was selling in various pockets of Southern California, and then put a plan in place. The goal of the station that would become Power 106 (KPWR) was to create a coalition between young Hispanics, younger Black listeners, and hip white teenagers from throughout the prosperous suburbs.

On January 6, Steve Crane and I were at the Newark airport when Rick called with the ratings. "Well," he commented, "when we bought Magic 106 it had a 2.1 share of the market. In eighteen months, with our programming brilliance, adept marketing, and world-class turnaround skills, we got the ratings today—we're a 1.8." So, waiting in line at Newark airport, we made the instant decision to switch to Power 106. Anticipating that Magic 106 wasn't going to improve markedly, Rick had already brought Don Kelly to the market to put the playlist together. Kelly was effusive about our prospects, noting, "I think this thing will get a five share of the market." Rick chimed in and said, "Don, if you get a five share of the market, we'll give you a $100,000 bonus!" Without missing a beat, I added, "Besides the $100,000, I'll build a statue of you on Hollywood Boulevard! If you get a five share!"

One of the marketing elements we used was the station ID. Because many, especially those in the advertising industry, assumed Power had a weak signal, we played on the fact that we were transmitting 72,000 watts from our tower. While the stations from Mount Wilson (the best location in Los Angeles) transmitted with less power, their superior height allowed them to cover Los Angeles more effectively. However, by emphasizing our superior power, we projected the image of a very strong station. The late Chuck Riley, who had a voice very similar to Orson Welles, boomed at the top of every hour: "72,000 watts of music power, Power 106, KPWR Los Angeles."

It took us a week to launch the new format. When Magic 106 ended, I believe Robert W. said something like, "This station is going from a guy who has done a lot of blow to the nonstop music of Kurtis Blow [a well-known urban artist of the day]." I've talked about the experience of living in Los Angeles during the heyday of KHJ, when it seemed you heard the station at every intersection. Even at a time when radio, like life itself, was becoming more fragmented, Power 106 was skyrocketing. After our first week on the air, Rick called: "I was out all weekend, and you heard Power 106 all over the place. I think we've really got something here." The buzz on the station continued and we knew that we were onto something big, but no one knew how big. Don Kelly's premonition seemed ridiculous. Having a five share would put us into the top five stations in Los Angeles right away. When the first monthly ratings trend came out, despite only having two weeks in the new format, the station showed an immediate spike. When the next monthly came out, it spiked again. I was in Chicago, getting ready to speak to a group of bond investors, on the day our first quarterly rating book was released. Just as I was about to walk to the podium, Doyle called: "Jeff, it's a six share for the whole book." I remember my exact words to Doyle: "Don't screw with me, I have to give a speech, and if we had a six share for all three months, our last (third) month had to be nearly a ten share. That's impossible." "Jeff, you're right, we've done the calculations and we think it was exactly a ten in the last month." Absorbing this new information, I quickly joked, "Doyle, don't call me anymore; I'm too rich to talk to you!"

Steve was with me in Chicago, and we went out to celebrate after the speech. He used the line from the Michael Keaton character in the movie *Night Shift*: "Is this a great country or what?" Walking down the street, Steve confided to me, "I know we aren't that smart, is it just possible that everyone else is dumber than we are?" To which I responded, "Looks like it, it just looks like it." As a postscript, Don Kelly got his $100,000 bonus but fortunately turned down the statue on Hollywood Boulevard.

Hitting a home run with Power 106 couldn't have come at a better time. In late 1984, a number of months after our Century deal closed, our original investors determined that they either wanted to stay in control of Emmis or have us buy them out completely. Although our agreement called for us to control the company, Mickey Maurer and Bob Schloss were no longer in love with that prospect. It was clear that we wanted to grow rapidly and they didn't. In retrospect, it was a rational decision by people who wanted to take outsized gains and move on. When they first broached the subject about us buying them out, I was taken aback: "Mickey, that would cost us $10 million, where would we get that money?" Mickey's response indicated it was going to be a challenging negotiation. "Jeff, we think our shares are worth $15 million." Stunned, Steve and I set about figuring out how to find the funds—clearly, we needed a Wall Street investment bank.

Through one of our sales managers, we were introduced to Morgan Stanley's Steve Rattner, who had recently entered investment banking after a career as *New York Times* reporter and had been tasked with growing the firm's media practice. In those days, Morgan Stanley was considered the primary "silk stocking firm" on Wall Street, catering mainly to America's largest companies. However, they decided to enter broadcasting to feed their new "junk bond" business, which was a reaction to the spectacular success of Michael Milken from Drexel Burnham Lambert. Milken had revolutionized corporate banking with his thesis that the default rates of higher risk companies were not significantly greater than the default rates of the Fortune 500. By providing debt to those high-risk companies at high interest rates, he could capitalize on the fact that they weren't as risky as people believed. This glitch in the system enabled Drexel to become the bank of choice for many of the entrepreneurial companies that had never before found a home on Wall Street. As one of Milken's clients said to me: "Morgan Stanley is strictly Park Avenue. Drexel is Seventh Avenue, where all of the rag merchants reside." Despite Drexel's humble status, Milken raised billions of dollars. Like a lot of things in life, success led to excess, and the Drexel machine quickly began skirting the law and careening out of control; that led, several years later, to a prison sentence for Milken and the downfall of the firm.

Steve Rattner liked our story and quickly decided that we would be a good fit as a client. His protégé Paul Taubman handled most of the legwork on our account. They determined that not only did we need to raise money to buy out Mickey and Bob, but we also needed to raise funds to prepare us for further growth. Morgan Stanley proposed a $50 million bond offering, priced at 14⅝ percent as well as raising equity of nearly $10 million. While the 14⅝ percent seems like usury today, it was a hallmark of the era, and projections of our growth indicated that we would be able to service the debt. The firm's merchant banking group, led by Chas Phillips and Peter Castleman, bought a significant portion of the equity, and family and friends like Dick Leventhal, Greg Nathanson, and David Letterman purchased the remaining shares. While the pressure of having to buy out Mickey and Bob seemed enormous at the beginning of the process, in the nine months it took to reach a deal with them, it became clear that we would find the funding as it evolved. For Mickey and Bob, the $85,000 apiece they put into the deal paid off handsomely. With over $1 million in dividends that we distributed in the four intervening years and their final payoff of $22.3 million, it was a remarkable investment. While negotiations were strained and the deal became more expensive as it went on, we knew that without the initial cash they had provided, we would never have had the credit to do our first four deals.

Susan Hapak, a friend who taught at the University of Chicago's Booth School of Business, was aware of the tense negotiations with Mickey and Bob and the significant payout they received. She built a case study around Emmis just as we were reaching an agreement, in the fall of 1985, before Power 106 was launched. She gathered all of our financial statements, all of the Morgan Stanley funding proposals, and the agreement that, if Mickey and Bob had not been bought out, they would remain in control of the company for at least five years, despite the original deal. On the night the students discussed the case study, she had Steve and me sit in the back of the class and listen to the MBA students. Invariably, they determined that we should not take the Morgan Stanley deal. Universally, they thought Emmis had too much debt, and in the intervening years, the 14⅝ bonds looked rather ridiculous. Many thought that even though Mickey and Bob had changed their minds about ceding control, that the relationship was workable and we should just accede to their position for five years. Very few people thought putting that much debt on the company was sane. In hindsight, they were probably right. No one, certainly not Steve or me, could foresee the spectacular success of Power 106, and without its cash flow, the new financing would have been shaky at best. When the class discussed Mickey and Bob as our partners, however, we introduced a new insight. The two had not been bad; Mickey had an excellent financial mind, and neither interfered with our plans for the business. Nevertheless, we had had an agreement from the outset on how we would proceed with Emmis. Given the remarkable success of our stations (even with low ratings, Magic 106 had grown its profitability quite nicely), it was impossible to argue with our performance. We had earned the right to be in control. By changing the terms, Mickey and Bob had made us realize that if an agreement could be discarded in good times, what would happen to the relationship during the inevitable difficult times to come? Trust is the most critical part of any human relationship, and when that trust is broken, it is difficult to want to continue in the same situation. The trust factor is something that most MBA students don't consider—they usually spend all of their time running mathematical models—but it is a critical component for understanding how to run a business.

Even before we received the spectacular ratings on Power 106, we knew that we were on the right track by the end of January 1986. Finishing the buyout of Mickey and Bob and regaining full control of Emmis had been a relief. Armed with the funds we had raised, we were ready to grow aggressively, hopeful that we would have the Midas touch with everything else.

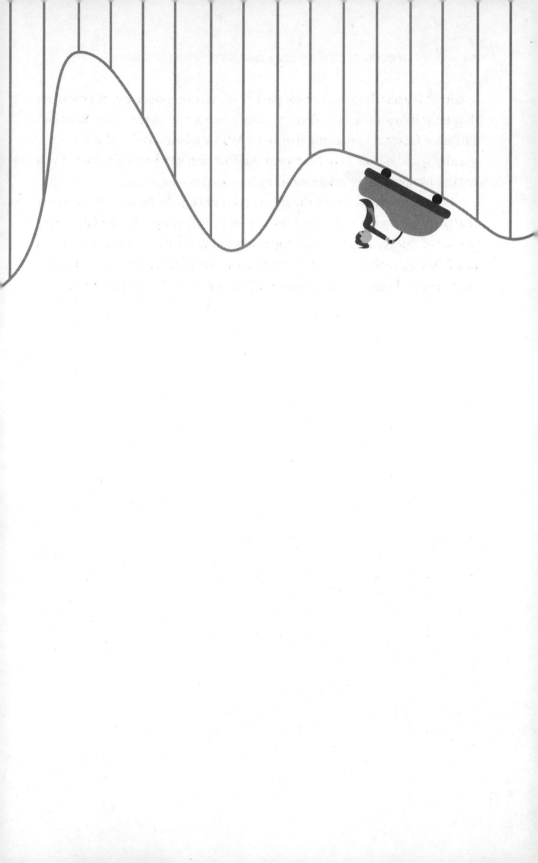

Top left: The original Hot 97 logo. *Top right:* The WFAN logo. *Bottom:* Me pitching in a charity softball game on the mound at Shea Stadium.

3

The Fine Line Between Idiot and Genius

Having proved ourselves on the biggest stages, and armed with fresh capital, Emmis was ready to grow again. So, I decided our best move would be to launch a format no one had ever done before: all-sports radio. While the format was always at the back of my mind, I didn't make it our next mission. We were all about growing our FM station group. But sometimes, opportunity strikes when you least expect it.

In early 1986, Gary Stevens, who ran the broadcasting arm of Doubleday Publishing, told me that the Doubleday family was willing to entertain offers for its radio business. I'd gotten to know Gary well—we were co-tenants at the IDS tower in Minneapolis—so it was logical for him to get in touch with me. The decision to sell was painful to Gary; he'd worked his way up from well-known New York disc jockey (during the sixties, he was one of the infamous WMCA "Good Guys") to the head of a major radio company, and now his life's work was being sold out from under him. Nevertheless, he had his marching orders and, because we were armed with cash from the Morgan Stanley deal, Emmis was high on his list.

We fell in love with the assets. Doubleday had two major FMs: WAPP in New York and WAVA in Washington, DC. Both had excellent signals, although only WAVA had any significant ratings. Also part of the package was Doubleday's sole AM station, WHN—not only America's largest country music radio station, but also the flagship of the family's Major League baseball team, the New York Mets. WHN was an unwanted addition to the deal. We had built our entire company on the notion that music was going to move to FM, and that the AM band would continue to erode as time went on. However, the allure of having FM signals in New York and DC made the whole package extremely attractive to us.

WAVA had a popular Top 40 format in Washington, DC, anchored by the talented, if erratic, morning show hosts Don (Geronimo) and Mike (O'Meara). They were highly innovative, which kept them employed even though they were a continual management challenge. WAPP, New York, had been Gary's passion project. He'd launched it as an album rock station a year earlier with no commercials for the first four months. Without commercials, the station skyrocketed to the top of the ratings. Unfortunately, as soon as the commercials appeared, WAPP's audience plummeted. At Emmis, we'd learned early on that the "commercial free" gambit always had risks. I once watched a focus group address the phenomenon. One member recalled that "when the station went on the air, I loved it and thought, this is great. Finally, a radio station that played the music I loved without all those damn commercials! It was great. Then, after a few months, they played commercials like everyone else and I felt betrayed. I immediately stopped listening." The rest of the focus group nodded in agreement. I always imagined that when WAPP went down the tubes, Nelson Doubleday decided he'd had enough of radio and told Gary to unload the business.

We reached a deal in the spring to buy all three stations for $56 million. While it was another milestone for our rapidly expanding company, the deal came at a time of great personal upheaval for me. My marriage was failing, and for the first time I had to balance the needs of a growing business with the needs of my two young children; this perpetual trade-off was as daunting to me as any problem I'd ever faced at Emmis. I've always found that in the toughest of times, it helps to lose yourself in an activity that takes your mind off the challenges that, at the moment, feel impossible. During my personal crisis, I was able to immerse myself in building up the New York and Washington FMs. WHN, despite being America's largest country music station, was not on our radar. Sure, it had the most country listeners in America, but that was strictly a function of the size of New York. In terms of its ranking in the market, the station was clearly a marginal player. And while the Mets provided a nice boost in audience, we never thought we could make WHN a major player in the city. New York wasn't exactly Nashville, and while conventional wisdom at the time held that country music was the one format that would be immune to the fidelity of FM, and thus able to survive on AM, we were certain that was wrong. Just as we had believed five years earlier that the adult contemporary and Top 40 formats would cross over to FM, we thought that the more change-resistant country listeners would ultimately make the switch to FM as well.

WAVA had a solid position in the DC market, so it only needed some tweaking. WAPP, on the other hand, was clearly struggling in New York, and we ended up focusing almost all our energy on figuring out what to do with it. At a dinner at a Midtown steak house, a number of us gathered for our final decision. In typical Emmis fashion, it was a raucous discussion, with various format alternatives being tossed out, debated, and then ultimately dismissed. By then, our Los Angeles station, Power 106, was an icon in American radio. Because we'd created Power, logic would dictate that all we had to do was replicate the format in New York. However, we understood Power's success lay in the fusing of the Hispanic, Black, and hip white subcultures of LA, and those were constituted differently in New York. The Black community there was far more dominant than in LA, and the Hispanic population was largely Puerto Rican, with a considerable mix of other Caribbean émigrés. Culturally, these groups were miles apart from the largely Mexican-based population of Southern California. We knew that to replicate the success of Power 106 at the other end of the country, we would have to build an entirely different audience coalition, one that was responsive to New York. We decided it was worth the effort, and Hot 103.5 (WQHT) was born.

During all this work on WAPP, Steve Crane and I found ourselves having a late-night snack in a nearly deserted diner on Seventh Avenue, near our hotel. Two things were notable about that evening. One was that Tony Bennett was a few tables away. The other was that Steve and I discussed the birth of all-sports radio in America. Steve asked what we were going to do with WHN. Half musing, I replied that country music didn't seem to have much of a future on AM, and "if you can't play music, you're left with information, but WABC and WOR own talk and WINS and WCBS own news." Reading my mind, Steve added, "Well, that pretty much leaves sports or weather." I mentioned that a few people had tried all-weather stations on smaller AMs and they were a disaster, but sports was another story. While ESPN was in its infancy on cable TV, no one had ever put on an all-sports radio station. I'd been harboring the idea for over twenty years, since daydreaming about it in a class at USC—perhaps the time was finally here. As I told Steve, "If we're ever going to do it, New York is the place, people here talk about sports all day and night." I pointed out the value of carrying the Mets: with a baseball team playing 162 games a year, we already had a lot of sports fans who knew our station. I discussed my shopping center analogy: having the Mets was like having a large department store that would bring in tons of traffic to the mall. As I became more animated, Steve realized how much the prospect excited me. The format would provide a great opportunity for WHN, which had clearly been the stepchild of the Doubleday stations. Steve and I continued the discussion for a while, and I decided to broach the subject with our programming wizard, Rick Cummings, and our operations czar, Doyle Rose.

Since WHN was way down on the priority list, it was a short conversation; both of them summarily dismissed it, each in his own way saying: "That sounds like a really stupid idea." However, now that the subject was out in the open, I was like a dog with a bone. Steve, by the way, loved the idea, but he wasn't seen as a programming guy, so generally he deferred to Rick, Doyle, and me when it came to product ideas.

When the Doubleday deal officially closed in the fall of 1986, we were still fully occupied with our FM revamps, so we agreed to postpone any discussion of an all-sports format for at least six months. Meanwhile, I got to know the Mets general manager, Frank Cashen, and his assistant, Al Harazin. A former sportswriter, Frank had worked his way up in the Orioles organization and had been a major factor in that team's dominance in the latter half of the seventies. When Nelson Doubleday and Fred Wilpon bought the Mets in 1980, Frank was their first major hire, and he became the architect of the Mets of '86. Since my first summer job during college had been as a sports-writer, I instantly bonded with him. Short, stocky, and always dressed in a suit and bow tie, he was unpretentious, but a great student of the game—the antithesis of the prototypical baseball executive. Because the team's radio rights were being transferred from essentially an in-house entity to a third party, Frank initially was concerned that our relationship might be contentious, but he quickly saw encouraging signs of collaboration. More importantly, in our first months as the owners of WHN, Frank began to understand that our entrepreneurial approach would be helpful to the Mets.

Al was more of a financial expert than a baseball wizard, which caused significant problems six years later when Frank retired and turned the reins over to him; Al ended up lasting only a year as the Mets GM. As a team, how-ever, Frank and Al's complementary skills worked exceedingly well, and I thoroughly enjoyed working with them both. It was my first experience with baseball executives, and the relationship would prove tremendously helpful a few years later when Emmis explored buying a baseball team.

In 1986, our first year owning WHN, Frank's labors with the team bore fruit: The Mets became world champions, winning in a remarkable seven-game World Series against the Boston Red Sox. Because our station was the team's flagship, we had both a suite at Shea Stadium, where we entertained excited clients, and a number of prime seats at field level. One of the most memorable moments of my career came during the legendary sixth game of the series. Any baseball fan will remember that the Mets were down by two runs in the bottom of the tenth inning, with two outs and nobody on base. Remarkably, before the last out, the scoreboard flashed: "Congratula-tions to the Boston Red Sox, 1986 World Champions." It was up for maybe three seconds, but a lot of us noticed. We laughed and agreed that somebody on the scoreboard team was going to be in a lot of hot water for running that three minutes early. We were seated right behind home plate, near a very excited group of Red Sox players' wives and family members who were enjoying a premature celebration. Unfortunately for them, the Mets went on to score three runs, capped by Red Sox first baseman Bill Buckner's error on a Mookie Wilson ground ball; that forced a game seven, which the Mets won, 8–5.

By the spring of 1987 we'd made notable progress on both WAVA and WAPP, so it was time to revisit the issue of what to do with our country music station. Not that I was going to decide unilaterally; I'm a big believer in testing ideas in the marketplace, and in this case the marketplace was Emmis's management team. I called a managers' meeting and lobbied hard for all sports: I conceded that doing something no one's ever done before is a lot more difficult than doing something familiar, but I argued that if you just do what everyone else is doing, you'll never create anything special. Despite my fervor, I wasn't getting any traction, and after a long debate, our senior leaders voted down the all-sports idea. Joel Hollander, our sales manager who later went on to head CBS Radio, was a vigorous proponent of the format, as was Steve. Our other managers, led by Rick and Doyle, not so much! As the meeting broke up, a dejected Steve, standing with Joel, asked me what I wanted to do. I answered: "This deal is dead—you can't lead where others won't follow." I've always believed that leadership means having to convince your team of the wisdom of your ideas. If you can't, the idea will never work. So, I walked away from the meeting thinking that sports radio was dead and buried.

The next day, Rick and Doyle walked into my office: "We still think this idea sucks, but we owe you one. You care about this thing and we're hitting on all cylinders with everything else, so we'll give it a try. However, we've got to find someone to put it all together. We don't want to waste our time with it." Not the monumental change of heart I'd hoped for, but good enough: all-sports radio was back on. Now, we just needed an executive to head up the effort. Since we were inventing a new format, it was impossible to find anyone with all the skills we needed, so we picked someone who at least knew sports. John Chanin, a sports executive with the ABC radio network, fit the bill—he knew everybody in sports who had any ties to radio—and he was tasked with putting the station together. John's most lasting contribution was coming up with the name "The Fan." Actually, even that wasn't his contribution; the idea came from his wife.

While we found John to be a kind, likable man, he came from the world of network television and radio, which was light-years away from the business of running a radio station. Perhaps a few quick stories about networks in the mid-eighties will explain where John was coming from. At that time—long before streaming video, and at the dawn of the cable industry—the three television networks (ABC, CBS, NBC) reigned supreme. With their dominance came cash flow growth of at least 20 percent per year. One thing I can guarantee is that when a business grows by that much annually for two decades, excess is everywhere. On one of my first trips to the NAB convention, I was getting ready to walk to a cab line when I saw a friend, a low-level executive at ABC, make a beeline for a waiting limousine. I was astonished. Another friend beside me explained, "Everybody at ABC has a dedicated limo out here!" Rumor has it, the day Capital Cities closed the 1985 deal to buy ABC, the current ABC executives walked out of their office building to a line of idling limos, waiting to take all of them to another meeting. When the ABC leaders beckoned Cap Cities' chairman Tom Murphy and CEO Dan Burke to join them, the remarkably thrifty Murphy and Burke said, "We'll walk." I'm certain that what Murphy and Burke saw in ABC was the excess of the network lifestyle, which they would've considered the lowest of the low-hanging fruit. I don't know for sure how much of that excess Murphy and Burke instantly took out of ABC, but it had to be many millions of dollars.

In fairness to John Chanin, he was the product of that lavish environment, and his vision for WFAN was consistent with his experience. He built a newsroom that replicated what he'd had at ABC, filled with producers, writers, reporters, anchors, and other assorted staff members. One story that made the rounds was that one of John's high-priced editors needed to hire someone to come in and splice tape for him. Apparently, he was stunned to find out that we had editors at our stations working for half the price who could actually splice their own tape. As Rick observed, "We knew it was too many people, and too many expensive people, but we weren't exactly sure how to fix it." After all, we were building WFAN on the fly, trying to get it off the ground; it was such a monumental undertaking it took us several months to realize we had created an unwieldy mess. And because none of us knew exactly what we wanted the station to be, we deferred to John's game plan: well-known national personalities as hosts, intermixed with news updates four times an hour.

As we assembled our on-air staff, we actually talked about putting Don Imus in the morning slot. Imus, who had a passable knowledge of sports, had built up a sizable audience of upscale males on his WNBC morning show. Since no one had ever done sports radio before, we were worried that even sports fans wouldn't want to listen to the format in the morning. If we had someone like Imus, who could also talk about topics outside of sports, our morning show might have a broader appeal. There were two problems with the Imus idea. First, he was under contract to WNBC, and second, he was in the midst of a series of rehab issues, which was keeping him off the air for long periods of time. Realizing we still wanted someone to make a splash in mornings, we ultimately chose Greg Gumbel. Greg, who has had a spectacular career at CBS TV, was knowledgeable and utterly likable. Yet, to our dismay, his talents didn't match the format. He was a charming in-studio television host (which he did for many years at CBS) and a gifted play-by-play announcer. But carrying a four-hour sports talk show wasn't his forté, and we had the miniscule ratings to prove it. Greg's laid-back style, perfect for NFL pregame shows, was in direct contrast to the more in-your-face nature of sports talk radio.

Jim Lampley, who has also had a great career at ABC and HBO, had the midday slot. His keen wit and ability to engage with callers and guests should've been a big success at WFAN, but John Chanin's early strategy completely interfered. Every time Lampley would get rolling with a compelling interview, one of those frequent sports updates would interrupt the flow of his banter. Partly because of that, and partly because Lampley was busy lining up television gigs, he was never fully committed to the radio station. He'd have networking luncheons that ran late and he'd be racing to make his 1:05 PM start time. Often, we'd have to run the three-minute station identification and introduction to give Jim just that extra bit of time. Once he dashed in from lunch without any time to go to the bathroom (and he had to go desperately). As he launched into his opening monologue, he signaled to his producer to get him a cup. And he took a leak while he was riffing away, and the audience was never the wiser! After a few months with us, Jim had a great opportunity to move to Los Angeles, where he continued the WFAN midday show by satellite for another few months. Finally, we mutually agreed to call it quits. Jim, who has remained a friend for many years, laughingly referred to the early days of WFAN as "the Vietnam War of Emmis," and it was an incredibly accurate assessment, widely shared in the New York market.

To make matters worse, our major talent acquisition was Pete Franklin, known as the most successful sports talk host in America. He had owned the airwaves in Cleveland, where his drive-time show was an institution. Hiring Franklin was a major coup for us, and the newspapers touted it as an indication that WFAN was primed to become a major factor in New York radio. The notion of the caustic Franklin going toe-to-toe with acerbic New Yorkers created quite a buzz when he signed on. Articles heralded the arrival of our savior. We'd all have to wait a bit, though; right after we hired him, he suffered a heart attack, which postponed his debut by several months. The delay actually helped build the anticipation for his arrival; so much so, we let ourselves believe things would turn around. Instead, Franklin laid a Godzilla-sized egg in the Big Apple. The show never worked. He hated the listeners, and those listeners he did have apparently hated him, too. It was one of those things you can never explain. He was the king of all sports talk, and we assumed his scathing wit would be a perfect fit for a town with sixteen million sports fans known for their biting sarcasm. On the contrary, Franklin—mild-mannered when off the air—spent most of his time calling his listeners and many of his guests schmucks. One lesson I've learned is that never in the history of the world has a schmuck liked to be called a schmuck. Franklin's program turned out to be just another in the litany of problems we had in our first six months on the air.

Because of John Chanin's expansive vision, WFAN was a very expensive format to operate, and our meager audience and negative buzz meant that revenue was miniscule. After about six months in business, I was walking down the street with Joel Hollander, our first sales manager. Sarcastically, I asked, "Joel, there are sixteen million people in the greater New York area. Wouldn't you think at least a few of them would want to buy some ads from us?" Joel later proved his mettle not only as a great sales manager, but also as a general manager and ultimately president of CBS. Nevertheless, he reminds me to this day that my biting remark was the low point of his career. Coming from me, the guy who always had positive and uplifting things to say, that comment was a terrible shock. As Joel later told me, "When Jeff Smulyan, who never says anyone sucks, tells you that you suck, you must really suck!" Unfortunately, when failure settles in, the challenge for every leader is to build up their troops, rally them, and get them ready for the next battle. And I absolutely violated that maxim that day with Joel. Knowing its effect on him has prevented me, as time has gone on, from doing it to many other people.

It was no secret at Emmis that WFAN was my baby and I cared passionately about it. During our first week on the air, I took my kids, along with my best friend, Gary Kaseff, to spend a week at a rented house in the Hamptons. Normally a great place to relax, this resort community also received our AM station's signal perfectly. So much for the pool or the beach—I was hunkered down listening nonstop to WFAN, constantly making notes. While the launch had its problems, I also realized that we were doing something no one had ever done before and understood it would take time.

My most lasting memory of that week's programming was a commercial for discount funeral services. It seemed to run at least twice every hour, and it was one of the most depressing, annoying ads I had ever heard. When I returned to New York, I commented to Stuart Layne, who by then was running Hot 103.5, "I don't know how much they're paying us for those discount funeral spots, but it can't be enough. We've got to get rid of them, they're awful." The spots were killed, but Stuart didn't have the heart to tell me that we weren't getting paid anything because they were PI (per inquiry) spots, meaning we weren't paid for the commercial unless the client actually got paying customers from the ad. It's invariably the lowest form of income any station can generate, and my guess is we made absolutely nothing. The best part of the story is that the guy who owned the discount funeral business was the brother-in-law of one of our salesmen; he ran the commercials to help his relative get a little notoriety during our first week on the air. Stuart later admitted, "If we'd told you all of that at the time, you would've either died or killed all of us!"

Of course, among our senior managers, the WFAN debacle was irresistible fodder for the usual Emmis teasing. It seemed like every day, someone would say in a meeting, "Well, it's five thirty, we've just lost another $25,000 today at The Fan!" I had a hard time joining in the fun—I was totally, emotionally invested in this station, and clearly out on a limb. Steve Crane, who also loved WFAN, kept my spirits up, and because everything else at Emmis was going well, WFAN was more frustrating than a source of major anxiety. One of my oldest friends, John Dille, who ran Federated Media for decades, called me a few months after the launch of WFAN. He'd just been to New

York and had sampled the station. His verdict: "Jeffrey, I used to think you were a pretty smart fellow, but I just listened to WFAN and I think it's a really dumb idea!"

We did get some things right at WFAN, although even those required a bit of tinkering. Our first day on the air, I listened in horror as Suzyn Waldman attempted to read a sports update. She was terrible, stumbling over words, her inflections off, sounding as though she had never read a script before. Over the years, I've learned to moderate my opinions about our programming; I'll write down the observation and wait for my emotions to subside before passing it along a day or so later. But on Day One of WFAN, that wasn't going to happen. I stormed into Rick's office and told him that Suzyn was the worst anchorperson I had ever heard, and we had to get her off the air. Fortunately, for me and for Suzyn, my colleagues agreed. Her real talent turned out to be reporting: She became a beat reporter on WFAN covering the Yankees and proved to be one of the best ever. After a few years on WFAN, she became revered and today does color commentary on Yankees radio broadcasts.

Despite our beginnings, I became one of Suzyn's biggest fans. In fact, a few years later, when we owned the Seattle Mariners, I was talking to her in the press box at the Kingdome. I asked her opinion about the best young minds in the game. We were ready to replace our manager, Jim Lefebvre, and I knew Suzyn knew baseball as well as anyone. Her response was immediate: "Buck Showalter is the best I've seen. He's going to be a great Major League manager soon." There's a wonderful postscript to this story. When we didn't renew Lefebvre's contract, the first person we contacted was Buck Showalter, who, along with the rest of the Yankees' coaches, had just been fired in one of George Steinbrenner's regular purges. Showalter flew out to Seattle to talk to us and it ended up in the New York papers. I've heard that George told his people that if the Mariners were interested in Showalter, then he must be pretty good. Steinbrenner summoned Showalter back to New York and rehired him, not as a coach but as the new manager of the Yankees! Thus started Buck Showalter's long and very successful managerial career in Major League Baseball.

My favorite part of the WFAN launch was doing the top-of-the-hour highlights. Radio stations invariably try to have a catchy ID for their legally required identification at the top of every hour. For Hot it was, "From the top of the Empire State Building, Hot 103.5, New York City," with the same booming voice of Chuck Riley that we had used for Power, "72,000 watts of music power, Power 106, Los Angeles." For WFAN, we had a different idea. We would play a memorable moment in sports, and then use the tagline, "For all of the great moments in sports, WFAN, New York." We compiled audio from hundreds of great moments. Since I was in charge, we started the station with my favorite: Bobby Thomson's home run to win the pennant for the New York Giants in 1951. Almost every sports fan alive gets chills when Russ Hodges screams, "The Giants win the pennant! The Giants win the pennant! The Giants win the pennant!" I loved the concept and it became an unforgettable identifier for the station. Of course, as Rick pointed out, when you run one of your hundred moments every hour, twenty-four hours a day, people can get tired of them rather quickly. Nevertheless, it became a tradition.

The other thing Emmis did really well was television commercials. To this day, I think they're some of the most creative projects I've ever been involved with. Our most notable started with a camera zooming in on the back of a car, clearly on a lover's lane. The back window was fogged up, but the audio came on with a man and a woman going back and forth: "I love it . . . Ooh, it's wonderful, more, please more. This type of dialogue continued for about ten seconds. Finally, the camera panned to the front of the car, where, instead of two teenagers locked in an embrace, an older man was sitting on one side of the front seat while his wife was sitting as far away as possible on the passenger side. Then the voice-over announced, "Yankees 4, Orioles 2," and the couple moaned; "Mets 7, Dodgers 1," more moaning; "Cubs 2, Reds 1," still more unbridled fervor. The voice-over continued, "Finally, for those with a passion for sports, WFAN, the world's first all-sports radio station." After a few more scores, the couple returned to their moaning and groaning. I've always thought it was one of the most entertaining commercials I had ever seen.

Some of our marketing was so edgy, we couldn't use it. We shot one commercial that started with a creaking sound, then a cross rose slowly from the ground until it stood straight up. On the cross was a referee, obviously being crucified. Over that, a voice intoned: "There are only two things a New York sports fan wants; the other is WFAN, the world's first all-sports radio station." After we previewed the spot, somebody commented that if we didn't discuss it with the Archdiocese of New York, we were going to be in big trouble. We did, and they promised a widespread boycott if the commercial ever went on the air. It was brilliant, but we had pushed the envelope too far.

Thereafter, we avoided the religious imagery and developed a commercial that became our all-time greatest envelope pusher. It started with a jockstrap on a black background. Then it slowly expanded with appropriate stretching noises. As the jockstrap reached its full length, the voice-over came up, "Finally, expanded coverage for the New York sports fan, the world's first all-sports radio station, WFAN." We knew the spot could never run in prime time, but the cable companies were happy to take our money and run it on late-night cable. The spot became a cult classic, and two years later, while driving down a freeway in Dallas, I was astounded to see a fully erect jockstrap on a billboard, using our tagline: "Expanded coverage for Dallas sports fans, KTCK, all-sports radio." People were even stealing our erect jockstrap!

Our marketing was definitely getting buzz, but it wasn't delivering improved ratings. As we had learned from experience, great marketing will just expose a bad product sooner, and that's what seemed to be happening with WFAN. Jim Riggs, our research head, discovered that we were failing to attain one of our earliest goals: to become the place sports fans went for their information. Before WFAN, almost all New Yorkers were conditioned to get their sports updates at fifteen and forty-five minutes after the hour from the all-news stations, WCBS and WINS. After our first nine months of operation, Jim's research indicated that most listeners were *still* going to WINS and WCBS for the latest news in sports. That was the behavior we had to change to have a shot at success. We needed to be New York's sports authority.

Near the end of 1987—less than six months after WFAN's launch—we decided we'd have to rethink the entire approach of the station, and that meant replacing John Chanin with a program director capable of making WFAN more New York–centric and less constrained by constant sports updates. Once again, no one we talked to had all the requisite skills. We selected Mark Mason because he'd been a news programmer for WINS, so at least he knew how to program a station for a New York audience. Although

WFAN was a mess, we were able to lure him for two reasons: most people in the industry loved the idea of coming to work at Emmis, and Mark realized he could be a hero if he figured out how to fix our station. Mark didn't know me yet, but he was already following one of my favorite maxims for managers: "Go somewhere where there's a chance to fix something that's broken. That's how you become a hero quickly." Or, in other words: "You can't commit suicide by jumping out of a basement window." Since WFAN was in the sub-basement of the Kaufman Astoria (Movie) Studios in Queens, that statement was both literally and figuratively true! Mark understood that a complete focus on New York sports was essential, and that the information elements had to be scaled back to avoid impeding the flow of the talk shows. It didn't take long for us to realize hiring Mark was a wise choice.

In early 1988, just as we were beginning to revamp WFAN, a whole new wrinkle appeared: NBC's radio stations suddenly became available. Randy Bongarten, president of NBC Radio, was handling the sale. Randy's story was one of the most amazing in radio. As a wunderkind in the industry, he'd shot up through the ranks of General Electric (GE) Radio and by his early thirties was named its president. GE Radio wasn't large but it owned a prestigious group of stations. Unfortunately for Randy, Jack Welch became CEO soon thereafter, and his mantra, "If we're not first or second in any business, get out of it," applied to radio. So, as the newly named president of GE Radio, Randy was tasked with selling his stations. He completed the sale and, out of a job, headed to New York City, where he promptly landed at NBC. After a few years, Randy had again shot up through the ranks and was named president of NBC Radio. Just when you think lightning can never strike twice, you learn the next chapter of Randy's story. Jack Welch led GE's takeover of NBC, and shortly thereafter, Randy got the same speech, with the same result: sell the radio division. And that's what brought Randy to us.

For Emmis, the chance to buy the storied NBC radio stations within seven years of starting our company was the ultimate feather in a cap that was accumulating feathers quickly. With Morgan Stanley as our financial advisor, we quickly put together a $122 million deal, which brought us NBC stations in Boston, Chicago, and San Francisco, as well as the two New York flagships, WYNY-FM and WNBC-AM. If our success with our first stations hadn't cemented our reputation, the NBC purchase clearly vaulted us to the

THE FINE LINE BETWEEN IDIOT AND GENIUS

top of the industry. And with the addition of the NBC stations, we became the largest privately held company in radio. Articles called us the next "Cap Cities," comparing us to the legendary radio/TV group that had recently bought ABC. Several noted that our people-first culture made it natural that NBC would choose us as a new home for their people.

Now, I've been in countless bidding processes over the years, and it's true, Emmis has a reputation that's often helped us win bids. We like to kid that we're usually the favorite to win a beauty contest because most sellers like our culture and reputation. However, I've cautioned my team that being a preferred bidder doesn't get you very far. My maxim has been: "If the other side likes you and wants to do a deal, you have a chance to win if your bid is slightly lower than other parties. For example, if you're bidding ten times cash flow for a station and the other bidders are at 10.5 times, the seller may choose your slightly lower bid. However, if the other bidder is at eleven times cash flow, you'll lose every time, even if the other bidder is Joseph Stalin!" For better or worse, popularity doesn't count for much in buying businesses.

Randy later teased me that, "Yes, we liked you and your culture, but we also knew you were paying near the top for stations, and you had your financing in place, and we liked both of those a lot better than your stellar personality!" With that crisp assessment, Randy proved he would fit right into our culture. So, it was no surprise that after we acquired the NBC stations, Randy joined our growing group as a senior vice president. He was a terrific leader, especially in helping us to absorb all his former stations.

In those days, the Federal Communications Commission (FCC) didn't allow a company to keep more than one AM or one FM in any market; it was a no-brainer for us to sell our current FM 103.5 and AM 1050 frequencies and move our stations to NBC's better signals. WQHT's switch from 103.5 to the NBC's 97.1 frequency boosted the new "Hot 97" to even greater success. To market the switch, Stuart Layne, now running WAPP, decided to hire Vanna White to flip the numbers on the station from 103.5 to 97.1—the event garnered impressive publicity.

For WFAN, the switch was even more of a boon. The WNBC frequency, 660, was a clear-channel signal, meaning you could hear WNBC thousands of miles away, and in the New York metropolitan area, the station had a near-perfect AM signal. WFAN's signal on 1050 was just as powerful as WNBC's on 660 (both 50,000 watts), but WFAN encountered interference at night so it had to cut its power to 10,000 watts, which reduced its coverage significantly.

Not only did the WNBC purchase give WFAN a much greater audience reach, it gave us a shot at picking up the contract of one of the truly brilliant personalities in American radio: Don Imus. Now we could go back to our first instinct and see if Imus could transition to sports and do for WFAN what he had done for WNBC: attract a passionate fan base made up of the coveted male 25–54 demographic.

Full disclosure: Long before I became his boss, I was a big fan of Imus. Years earlier, I had bought an album of his original comedy bits from Cleveland, *Ten Thousand Hamburgers to Go*, and I'd followed his career ever since. Like many in our industry, I knew about Don's churlish nature, and that he'd been drifting in and out of rehab for several years now. But if I was going to hire him, I'd need to know exactly what I was getting into.

My best source of intel was Randy Bongarten, who'd managed Imus at NBC for the past five years. In addition to explaining the daily challenges of life with Don, Randy gave me a key bit of insight into Imus's psyche. Early on at NBC, Randy had managed both Imus and Howard Stern, a norm-breaking shock jock, and he described their differences: "With Howard, what you get on the air is the polar opposite of what you get after his show. On his show, you think he's this out-of-control guy, who is always coming close to jeopardizing your license with his latest antics. Off the air, it's totally different. He'll talk about the goal of every segment, explain why he thought it could go up to a certain line, without crossing over it, and how the process could be improved. It's hard to believe, but Howard applies a very intellectual approach to what appears to be a completely out-of-control talent." (To be fair, when Mel Karmazin later employed Howard, his company paid millions of dollars in fines to the FCC when Howard crossed over a number of those lines.) In contrast, Randy noted, "Don off the air is exactly what you get on the air, an extremely talented, extremely difficult personality. Managing him on his best days is always challenging, because he's going to do whatever he feels like doing. You don't coach Don so much as you try to keep him on the rails."

After dozens of other "scouting reports" from people who'd worked directly with Imus, we decided we wanted him, even though managing him

would be difficult. Not that we were intimidated about bringing him in—
we prided ourselves on managing challenging personalities—but we knew
he'd probably break the mold. So be it. I picked up the phone and called
Imus's agent, Mike Lynn. He and I knew each other—Mike had been the
agent for Robert W. Morgan at Magic 106 in Los Angeles. Over the years
we'd had many spirited conversations about how to deal with Robert W.'s
escapades. Now we discussed the fact that WNBC was going away and
Imus's new home, if he wanted it, could be WFAN. I went to Mike's New
York office to finalize the agreement, and during our meeting he asked how
I thought WFAN would do going forward. I answered, "Let's see, we have a
radio station that is losing record amounts of money; Don Imus, who has
spent most of the last few years in rehab; and the Mets, who appear to have
set the Major League record for drug and alcohol abuse. What could possibly
go wrong with that combination?"

Our bankers were also concerned about WFAN's prospects. At a financing meeting, one of them inquired, "You guys are hitting on almost all cylinders, but WFAN is a mess. How long do you think you'll keep doing it?" If our
finances had been somewhat precarious, this question would've been more
of a mandate than an inquiry, but the success of the rest of our portfolio gave
us more leeway. However, I replied, "We're committed to this and we want
to see it through, but we're not crazy. If we don't see any progress in the next
year, we'll cut our losses." This has always been my philosophy about business and life. Try as hard as you can, put the most rational plan in place with
the best team, and go for it. You never, ever succeed unless you take risks, but
there are some times when success isn't possible.

So, with the tepid support of our bankers, and the deep-rooted skepticism of my management team, "Smulyan's Folly" (as WFAN was known)
entered a new era with the addition of Imus in the morning, the much better 660 signal, and Mark Mason's programming changes. We had the courage to buck conventional wisdom—that we should pull the plug and sell the
660 frequency—but with the odds we were facing, it felt like I was following
another of my favorite sayings: "Never shoot yourself in the foot when you
can point the gun straight at your head!"

Never had I felt that gun closer to my head than when we had Imus
announce the imminent launch of his show during a Mets play-off game at

Shea Stadium. He told the crowd that he was "going to work for these idiots at WFAN, as the station switches to 660 tomorrow. Of course, they haven't figured out that I'm one drink away from blowing the whole thing up!"

It turned out he was just blowing smoke that night. Rehab had done its job, and Imus, committed to his sobriety, was more focused and energized than he'd been in years. He was at the top of his game and elevated everyone at the station around him. True, on his best days he was a curmudgeon, and on his worst, a run-of-the-mill asshole. But on-air he was magic. While he continued to engage his non-sports listeners with humorous general-interest talk, he also had fun with the core audience. On his occasional forays into sports, he would constantly mock "the morons" who spent their lives worrying about stupid games and stupid players and stupid owners. In the same mocking, entertaining manner, Imus promoted the rest of the station endlessly—a real team player, albeit with his own particular spin. Take his sign-off, for example. Every day, he delivered one of the most memorable closings I've ever heard: "This concludes the entertainment portion of today's programming. For the next twenty hours you will hear mindless drivel about sports from mindless listeners and mindless hosts. Join us for more real entertainment tomorrow morning at six." Listeners loved it and everyone at the station thought it was hilarious.

As for me, I became great cannon fodder for Imus. He regularly referred to me as "the hillbilly from Indiana with the Rolex." Since at this point I was rarely in New York to listen, I had no idea that he relished chronicling my life. One night in Seattle, during our ownership of the Mariners, Paul Newman visited the Kingdome with his agent. Upon being introduced to me, the agent exclaimed, "I know all about you. I know who you date; I listen to Imus every morning and I feel like we're old friends!" While Paul Newman didn't say whether he was also an Imus listener, he laughed at the story and joined in our brief discussion. I've never been star struck, but Paul Newman was one of my idols, and *Cool Hand Luke* and *Butch Cassidy and the Sundance Kid* are two of my favorite movies of all time. So, I owe Imus for that. In fact, I didn't mind what he said about me—I was a fan, and I was also mostly outside New York so I didn't have to live surrounded by his listeners. Later, when Mel Karmazin took over Imus's contract, supposedly he got a written commitment from Imus that he'd never mention Mel's name. Living in New

York, the thin-skinned Karmazin had no interest in being pilloried every day by his newest, high-profile talent. To get around the ban, Imus for years referred to him as "the Zen Master."

Thanks primarily to the addition of Imus—with a boost from the switch to the 660 frequency—everything at WFAN was clicking. With the exception of Pete Franklin. He was angry about everything, and vented to his listeners about his horrible working conditions. We were stuck in a sub-basement, saddled with a ten-year lease the Doubleday stations had bequeathed us, and Franklin's dinky little office was next to a bathroom that overflowed and would flood his workspace. He went on a tirade about how urine that over-flowed outside his office was now leaking in, and he just wanted an office that didn't reek of urine. He went on and on, begging to be fired rather than go through all the indignities. Since he had never achieved significant rat-ings, we felt we could oblige him.

We had a few potential replacements waiting in the wings: Chris Russo had been filling in doing sports reporting for Imus's show. He had a frenetic style with a high-pitched voice and the result was a unique character who was highly relatable to the New York audience. Imus called him "Donald Duck on steroids" and helped promote the nickname Chris had received from the *Daily News*'s Bob Raissman: "the Mad Dog." Mike Francesca, affec-tionately known as "the Sports Pope," was incredibly knowledgeable about everything and everybody in the New York market. When WFAN launched, he was a producer at CBS sports with an encyclopedic knowledge of his job. He wanted to be on the air in the worst way, and after being continually rebuffed, we finally gave him a weekend time slot. Once he was on the air, everyone realized Mike was a real talent, and it was clear he was destined for bigger things. Both Russo and Francesca were vying for their own time slots, but Mark Mason, in a flash of inspiration, decided a team would pro-vide more continuous and amusing banter. By the fall of 1989, he'd thrown Francesca and Russo together to replace Pete Franklin in the afternoon slot. It didn't matter that neither one wanted to do a two-man show, or that they didn't particularly like each other; Mason insisted on the shotgun wed-ding. Stories have been written about how, during their first three months together, Francesca and Russo wouldn't talk or even look at each other when the microphone was off. But that was immaterial because on the air, they had instant chemistry. Both were opinionated New Yorkers, the antithesis of polished announcers, and they had not only a remarkable depth of knowledge about sports, but even a greater passion about their beliefs. Mike and the Mad Dog argue violently about whether the Mets' bullpen was capable or whether the Jets' coaching staff was competent was some of the most entertaining radio I've ever heard.

The "Mike and the Mad Dog" show exploded in the ratings, hitting number one in the key male 25–54 demo by its second rating book. Meanwhile, the newly energized Imus made his program the place to be for authors, politicians, entertainers, and even the occasional sports figure. It seemed that by the end of his first year on WFAN, Don had the hottest, most powerful morning show, not only in New York, but in America as well. And we had become New York's sports authority: When Jim Riggs had studied the stations that sports fans went to for information in 1988, WFAN lost to WCBS and WINS by an overwhelming 85–15 margin. One year later, the same research indicated that New York sports fans preferred WFAN by a 90–10 margin. And that was despite the fact that, to focus more on the personalities, we'd cut down our updates by over a third. The Fan was becoming the station we'd hoped it would be: a destination for knowledgeable sports fans to debate fanatically about the teams in New York that everyone cared about.

With the new ratings, revenue shot through the roof. WFAN went from the station no one could sell to advertisers to the hottest buy in the market. I've always said, the line between being a genius and an idiot is very fine. For two years, I'd been an idiot for trying to found all-sports radio. After two years, I'd moved firmly into the genius camp. As you can imagine, my managers never heard the end of my brilliance. When sales rocketed skyward, I turned the tables and told them how much money WFAN had made that day. But I was always aware that I could go from genius to idiot just as easily—it's happened to me many times. If you take risks in your life, you're bound to be on both sides of the equation; it's just important to realize that no one is infallible, and that anyone who doesn't understand how fine the line is has probably never managed anything of consequence.

Even with great success, you always face challenges running something as complex as WFAN, and the most daunting dilemmas usually landed on my desk. One day in 1991, when I was in Seattle, my friend Marty Franks, head of government relations for CBS, called me: "Jeff, my owners have a major problem, and it revolves around you." Hearing that the owners of CBS, the Tisch family, had a problem that involved me was clearly not going to be good news, so I slumped in my chair to hear the details. The Tisch family, in addition to owning CBS and a myriad of other enterprises, had just bought a 50 percent stake in the New York Giants football team. They'd been able to convince the legendary Mara Family, the original owners of the team, to part with half their franchise for estate tax purposes. Unfamiliar with the significant exposure that comes with owning a professional sports team, the Tisch family hadn't appreciated what it meant to become the subject of Don Imus's ire.

The Giants had picked up the contract of Zeke Mowatt, a talented tight end who'd been unceremoniously dumped by the New England Patriots. Mowatt's problem was not on the field but in the Patriots' locker room, where he'd allegedly decided to expose himself to a female sportswriter. The Giants decided to pick him up in a move that Imus roundly criticized. He berated their decision with a regular comedy bit in which Mrs. Tisch and her daughter, as the new owners of the team, decide to visit the Giants' locker room. While they meet the players, Mowatt jumps out and exposes himself, causing pained shrieks from the women. Imus played the parody repeatedly—he loved it. The Tisch family did not. They insisted that Marty Franks file suit to revoke WFAN's license because of Don Imus's outrageous conduct. Marty told Bob Tisch that the owner of WFAN, Jeff Smulyan, was a friend, and rather than go to war, he could call to see if I could help the situation. Bob agreed.

By 1991, I had worked with Don for nearly three years. While mostly he dealt with his program director Mark Mason or general manager Scott Meier or Doyle and Rick, I had visited the station and gotten to know him. He knew that I'd been a fan of his for years, and our relationship was cordial. Still, no matter who you were, asking Imus to stop a routine was strictly a coin flip. I told Marty, "I'm certainly willing to go to Don. However, it's absolutely impossible to know how he'll react. He'll either agree to lay off of the Tisch family and the problem will be solved, or he'll go ballistic that they tried to pressure me and will attack Bob Tisch every day for the next hundred years, or until Bob succeeds in having our license taken away (which Marty knew was highly unlikely for radio satire)." I continued, needing to hammer one point home: "Marty, I hate to say it, but, based on my daily existence in Seattle, your clients are too thin-skinned to own a sports team, and this is going to happen again and again, in many other forms. But as for Imus, it's your call, and I'll do whatever you'd like." Marty contacted me the next day to say he'd like me to call Don. I was grateful that I'd never before tried to interfere with Don's show or ask for a favor. He had a good relationship with Emmis and apparently considered it a good place to work. When I spoke with him, I let him know that I was on baseball's television committee, which was in the middle of contentious negotiations with Tisch's CBS network. Don also knew that not only was the radio industry going through challenging times by 1991, but also that I was going through a well-publicized set of personal attacks in Seattle, over my ownership of the Mariners. (See the next chapter for blow-by-blow details.) I think it was one of the few times that Don ever pitied anyone, but for whatever reason, he decided to lay off the Tisch family from then on.

By 1992, WFAN was one of the greatest success stories in American radio, ultimately becoming America's highest-billing station. Imus was voted onto a number of "most influential Americans" lists after his humorous interview with Bill Clinton in early 1992 was widely credited with turning around Clinton's fortunes in the New York primary. As for Mike and the Mad Dog, they became icons as well. They reinvented the idea of sports talk and developed a cultlike following throughout the tri-state area.

WFAN spawned a national frenzy for sports talk, with five hundred stations launched after our station began resonating with New Yorkers. It also changed the nature of sports commentary. Unlike ESPN, sports radio is local, and its commentators and callers provide a nonstop analysis of players, managers, owners, and everyone else in the sports ecosystem. This created a major change for everyone in sports. As one friend told me, "Before sports radio, if you got attacked in a column in the newspaper, you read it, put it down, and moved on with your day. With sports radio, you can get destroyed all day long. Every time you turn on the radio, someone might be belittling your performance. It's changed how we live our lives."

As an ironic aside, my friend Jerry Reinsdorf, who has owned the Chicago White Sox and Bulls for many years, was in Seattle during our ownership of the Mariners. One of the sports talk hosts was criticizing something I had done, carrying on a rather lengthy tirade about my lack of intelligence. Jerry heard it while driving through Seattle and commented, "I'm not a religious person, but to think that the guy who invented this God-forsaken format, which has made every owner in sports miserable for years, is now a team owner himself and is getting ripped by the format he invented, does my heart good. It proves there really is a God after all!"

Top: My favorite part of baseball was being with Ken Griffey Jr. Here is Kenny, flanked by me and Gary, before a game one night. *Bottom:* At our farewell lunch, our staff provided Gary and me with a dartboard, with pictures of Senator Slade Gorton and County Executive Tim Hill affixed to the board.

4

From Genius to Idiot

To start the Mariners story, we have to go back to 1989. By that time, Emmis had conquered just about everything possible in radio. We had grown spectacularly over the decade, from having a single station to owning stations in almost every major radio market: New York, Los Angeles, Chicago, San Francisco, Boston, Washington, Houston, St. Louis, Minneapolis, and our home market of Indianapolis. We wouldn't be allowed to buy too many more of these major-market stations, because, as noted, back then you could only own one AM and one FM per market. Our stations were also top performers in most markets, so we didn't have much to do there. We were hailed as turnaround wizards, almost always buying failing stations, and through incisive strategy, great people, and a bit of luck, generally hitting the ball out of the park.

In effect, we were peaking in radio, so it was time to look outside that space for our next challenge. With the success of WFAN and our relationship with the New York Mets, the Emmis team had gotten to know a number of people in Major League Baseball. I've always loved sports, especially baseball, and like many other kids of my day, I dreamed that someday I would replace Willie Mays as the centerfielder for the San Francisco Giants. Unfortunately, at an early age, I realized that some genetic limitations that had been passed down from my ancestors in the Old Country were going to interfere with my dreams. In fact, I'm pretty certain that the last great athlete in my family was run over by an ox in 1823 in Minsk! Therefore, at some point I subconsciously began to drift to the old adage: "What do you call a Jew in Major League Baseball? The owner."

As we vigorously debated the merits of buying a baseball team, we all at one time or another brought up our love for the game. Nevertheless, I can state fervently that my motivation wasn't based solely on my passion for baseball; it was also based on a theory I had developed about the coming value of baseball as television content. In the early days of cable TV, I had thought that sports, and especially baseball with its 162-game schedule, would be an incredible programming resource. My college roommate Greg Nathanson, who has been an investor and board member of Emmis for many years, has always said, "Jeff, you spot trends earlier than anyone I've ever known. Unfortunately, capitalizing on them usually requires collective action to succeed and that's almost always impossible, so your ideas don't work out." That's another way of saying that sometimes the pioneer makes it to the promised land, but sometimes he dies along the way with lots of arrows in his back.

One of our friends in Major League Baseball indicated that Seattle Mariners owner George Argyros was interested in selling. The consensus was that George was a brilliant real estate developer, but his marketing skills left a lot to be desired. As a result, the Mariners were in desperate need of the expertise we had to offer; at the time, everyone looked at us as marketing wizards and turnaround experts. We started investigating a possible Mariners buy and fell in love with the project. I had visited Seattle as a teenager and thought it was America's prettiest city. It was also in the early stages of transforming into the boomtown that, over the past thirty years, has exploded. And, bottom line, I thought we could make it work. I'd had more success in a decade than I could've ever dreamed of: One day you're starting a company with $40,000 of savings and another $40,000 of borrowed money, and it feels like almost the next day, people are telling you that you're worth hundreds of millions of dollars. Although one of the Eleven

Commandments of Emmis is "Never get smug in life," it's hard to follow that dictate when you've had a decade like we had in the eighties, going from success to success to success.

It's not that we were relying on the Emmis "magic touch." Having thoroughly studied the economics of baseball, we believed we could dramatically improve the Mariners' ticket sales, advertising, and local broadcast and cable revenue. My management team and I were also convinced that national television and advertising revenue would continue to grow. We analyzed the Mariners the exact same way we analyzed an underperforming radio station, examining potential revenue in the market and how we would increase each area. We figured if we could make the Mariners slightly better than a distant fourteenth in American League revenue, we could generate enough to service our debt and earn a nice profit. It was going to be a marketing challenge, but we were excited about all the ways the franchise could be improved. While buying a professional sports team is usually deemed an "ego play," for us it was anything but. Sure, everybody at Emmis loved baseball, but we thought the ability to make the Mariners a competitive Major League team was a compelling economic opportunity. I'm certain that if we hadn't had such a string of successes with all of our radio stations, we would've been much more skeptical about the purchase. However, in 1989, we were on top of the world, and most thought that if the Mariners could be made viable, we were the group to do it.

During our negotiations with George Argyros, we were introduced to Major League Baseball's ownership committee, which then and for many years thereafter was headed by the owner of the Chicago White Sox, Jerry Reinsdorf. Jerry and I had some mutual friends, and our working relationship developed into a close friendship. I had never really had a "big brother" in the radio industry, but that's what I gained with Jerry. During my days in baseball and in the years since, he's been someone I've relied on for advice—and, like all of my close friendships, ours has been based more on friendly needling than anything else. As Jerry would say, "I've given Jeffrey plenty of advice over the years; I just don't ever remember him taking any of it." When Paul Volcker, former head of the Federal Reserve, was doing a study of Major League Baseball, he interviewed me, among many owners, to deepen his understanding of the game. He asked who I thought was the most knowledgeable owner and whose advice I relied on, and I instantly answered, "Jerry Reinsdorf." Volcker responded, "Jerry seems to be the answer I get a lot more than any others."

Early on in our relationship, I learned to rely on Jerry's instincts when it came to almost any aspect of the game. It was clear from the start, that, given the league's analysis of our ownership group, we would be welcomed. Only later did I learn of their actual assessment of us. We were viewed as aggressive young owners with the marketing skills that baseball wanted. The ownership committee even noted that, "if these guys can't turn around the Mariners, it will prove the point that the franchise is hopeless and we'll send the team to Florida." A flattering assessment, which I didn't know about until years later. At the time, however, Jerry summed up baseball's position on us with the quick statement: "You will definitely be approved to buy the Mariners; however, I'm not sure you should want to own the Mariners!"

After a lengthy negotiation with Argyros, and with the league's approval, we finalized the purchase of the Mariners in September 1989. I'm not sure I was fully prepared for what came next, but it was a whirlwind. The day the deal was announced, TV camera crews were outside my office and my home. Everywhere I went, there was a microphone in my face.

Seattle's first response to our purchase was to assume that we were buying the team to move them to Indianapolis. Years earlier, some friends had made a serious attempt to bring baseball to Indianapolis, and I had been peripherally involved. After studying the economics of the game and Indianapolis's limited disposable income and limited regional TV opportunities, I became convinced that the game would never work in my hometown. I strongly felt that way the day we purchased the Mariners, and I feel the same way today. One of my favorite sayings is: "All of life is a math question." In this case, the math didn't and still doesn't work. I'm thrilled we have the Pacers and the Colts; the economics of both sports are better than baseball for a smaller city.

I'm not sure if I succeeded in my initial attempts to prove to the people of Seattle that we were serious about staying, but I was certain my actions would convince them over time. In one of my first interviews, I noted that I didn't know if we could make it work, but we had a solid plan, and I was certain we would put together a great group that had the chance to succeed.

I promised that no one would work harder than we would, and years later, I'm proud to say that our statement was accurate.

So, how did I start out as a genius and turn into an idiot?

I could give you a thousand reasons why I got a bad deal in Seattle, why another thousand things that happened to us were ridiculously unfair, and that there's no way that I deserved to end up a pariah—but that would just be me, rationalizing. Blaming the outside world. We all do it, even though it's not helpful. With the Mariners, I was ignoring one of my major tenets: that when you face a problem in your life with anything—your business, your wife, your kids—the first place you look for the source is . . . in the mirror. But for so long with the Mariners, I was looking elsewhere. Finally, I stood in front of that mirror and took a good hard look. Was everything that happened to us in Seattle unfair? Maybe. Were we the victims of bad luck? Probably. Was the community largely indifferent to Major League Baseball in those days? Definitely. I really didn't understand the dynamics of the Seattle market; that I didn't do more analysis was a major failing. We did massive homework about baseball, and there really weren't many surprises about the operation of the team, but comprehending the history of the community was a course I didn't take. Now, after a few years, I could've taught that course, but by then, it was too late. And, most importantly, at the end of the day, I wasn't financially capable of funding the kind of losses that the Mariners had been sustaining for years; without a turnaround, we could not afford to own the team for more than a few years. Sure, the radio business had gone to hell, and taken our cash cushion with it, but that wasn't the determining factor. The painful lesson I learned from my days in baseball was that, to meet the challenges of owning a team in Seattle in that era of the game, you really needed to be a billionaire (and I certainly wasn't). Of course, to own the Yankees or Dodgers in that era, all you needed was to run a moderately successful paper route. Wildly different economics, wildly different markets.

So, if I wasn't a billionaire, what was I? Well, according to Rick Cocker and Bob Gogerty, the public relations wizards we inherited, I was the perfect antidote to eight years of George Argyros. George was a conservative Southern California real estate developer. He also took great pride in being viewed as a penny pincher who wasn't going to invest in the team. In Seattle or anywhere, that's three strikes, and Seattle was as happy to be rid of George as George was to be gone from Seattle. Having decided I would be the perfect alternative, Cocker and Gogerty sent me out to every Rotary Club, Kiwanis Club, and chamber of commerce event throughout the Northwest to tout the "new" Mariners. I was self-deprecating, open, and politically more aligned with the progressive Northwest (we'll leave out Northern Idaho). I've always loved speaking, so it was never a chore to talk about our passion for baseball and our dreams for the franchise.

Initially, the reviews of our group were extremely positive. I brought in my closest friend, Gary Kaseff, a successful Los Angeles attorney, to become team president. We were the perfect combination. Gary was a fanatic about details and one of the best managers you could find. He was Mr. Inside, and I was Mr. Outside. I led the team that built the plan, laid out the vision, marketed the plan, and motivated the troops. Gary's job was execution. In addition, Stuart Layne, who had run Hot 97 in New York and was a wizard at marketing, joined us. John Thomas, who had led our sales effort in Minneapolis, also came in, to oversee ticket sales. It was a young, energetic group, and probably as good a management team as I've ever led. We looked at the franchise from every angle, trying to change the perception of a team that had never had a winning season and was viewed with indifference by the population, not to mention the local government and the corporate community.

Seattle's indifference to baseball was largely a function of their never having to unite to persuade a team to come: They essentially won theirs in a lawsuit. When the original Pilots were awarded to Seattle for the 1969 season, the city constantly battled with Major League Baseball over stadium renovations. I've heard that when the league's stadium operations team arrived in Seattle in mid-1969, the Pilots' first and only season, they discovered that the planned renovations to Sicks' Stadium hadn't been completed (or in some cases, hadn't even been started). Furious, they demanded to know what had happened to all the pledges Seattle had made. City leadership treated them with polite, but complete, indifference. The years of animosity between baseball and Seattle had officially begun. The ownership group, led by the Soriano family of Cleveland, had endured losses well beyond their initial funding and were ready to bankrupt the team after the first season. Because of their growing hostility toward the city over these stadium issues, the ownership committee secretly voted to allow Bud Selig's group in Milwaukee to buy the team. Nothing was mentioned, and at the end of spring training, the team headed to Milwaukee to start the 1970 season, stunning the people of Seattle.

A lawsuit was filed, spearheaded by county district attorney Slade Gorton. Several years later, Gorton discovered audiotapes of league meetings with incriminating statements about Seattle, and apparently other topics. Gorton, realizing that he had baseball over a barrel, was willing to settle and pledge not to release the tapes if Seattle were given a franchise in the next expansion; that occurred in 1977 when the Mariners and the Toronto Blue Jays joined the American League. The problem with this scenario was that no one in Seattle was invested in the team, and the community never embraced it the way other communities had with theirs. It was a fact of life in this city that I had never fully understood until I was the owner.

Several people in baseball swore that "Seattle is jinxed." Hence, I had Jerry Reinsdorf telling me that "we'd love to have you in baseball, but I'm not sure anyone would want to own the Mariners." I didn't listen, partly because when you think you're capable of anything, you'll try anything.

We transformed every part of the franchise, trying to make the game experience fun and entirely different from what Seattle had ever experienced. One of our running jokes was that if you were marketing the Red Sox, your marketing campaign was: "The Red Sox season starts April fifth, get your tickets now." In Seattle, we knew that approach would be met with massive indifference, so we did a TV campaign that tackled the problem head-on. The commercial opened with an old clip from a silent movie showing a group of peasants milling around, obviously looking forlorn. The voice-over intoned, "It's time for another Mariners season!" The peasants look increasingly forlorn and the voice-over went: "They suck." The narration continues with a pitch about a new attitude and new owners; at the end, the peasants rally and seem to be excited about baseball. Jim Copacino, then working at McCann Erickson, created the campaign and continued to create brilliant marketing for the team for many years. He was regularly recognized for his exceptional work, and that helped change the perception among the fans. We tried all sorts of fun events in the stadium, including music clips for various game situations. Of course, we had fun going over the line, too. When Luis Polonia came to bat, we played, "She was just seventeen, you know what I mean . . ." clearly a reference to a recent statutory rape charge. When we mocked Mark Langston over his decision to spurn our free agency offer to sign with the California Angels using the song, "Act Naturally," Langston exploded. He'd accepted owner Gene Autry's offer partly because Autry told Langston and his wife that they would get movie offers. Obviously, the lines from the song "They're going to put me in the movies, they're going to make a big star out of me" set Langston off. I think it's the only time a Major League pitcher flipped the bird to the other team's marketing office.

We were the first team in sports to do old movie clips, using John Belushi's "Was it over when the Germans bombed Pearl Harbor?" from *Animal House*, which we played when we were a few runs behind going into the bottom of the ninth inning. We'd do the same thing with Gene Hackman's speech from *Hoosiers*; when the clip ended with the players banging on their seats, our fans would be bashing on their seats as well. And we'd use old TV clips, too, like Mr. Ed (the horse) running the bases at Dodger Stadium, for entertainment early in the game. We had no idea we'd need any rights until the day Gary got a call from Universal Studios—but instead of being in trouble, we'd impressed them with our novel idea, and they gave us the rights for free.

We also promoted singles nights, when we picked one homely guy and two more attractive guys and had the fans vote on who got the date with the girl—naturally, the homely guy won every time. One night, we did a top-ten list of best pickup lines heard at the ballpark. Unbeknownst to me, the top one was: "I'm Jeff and I own this team!" I have to admit, it was funny, and while I was not thrilled that they did it, the line ended up in *Sports Illustrated* and several other places. I should also mention that at the time I was definitely single, which was noted widely during my days in Seattle.

While we were having a blast with all our promotions and antics, Gary and I worried that one of our stunts would cross a line and get us into trouble with Major League Baseball. After all, I was a guy coming from rock and roll radio, a world with few boundaries. We joked that, compared to the owner of the San Diego Padres, Harvard-educated Tom Werner, we were clearly the troublemakers. Tom, one of the nicest, most hardworking people in entertainment, had earned his fortune producing award-winning television programs. So, it seemed out of character for Tom to ask the outspoken and often crude Roseanne Barr, star of his hit TV series, *Roseanne,* to sing the National Anthem at a Padres game. Roseanne screeched her way through the song and also grabbed her crotch at the end. The stunt created a national furor, casting a pall over all of baseball. The next day, Gary and I joked, "What are the odds that instead of us embarrassing the National Pastime, it was Tom. Go figure! We could have made a lot of money betting against that!"

Our first opening night, it appeared that all of our hard work had paid off. We had a sellout crowd and there was an incredible electricity in the ballpark. Fay Vincent, then the commissioner of baseball, told me that he wished he could steal our marketing magic for the Atlanta Braves, who were then playing before meager crowds. I remember telling Fay, "The Braves are available in eighty million cable homes every night; I should have their problems!" When we walked into the ballpark, Gary Kaseff turned to me and said, "This is incredible, what a night. I don't care if we don't win, I just don't want us to get killed tonight." Unfortunately, Gary didn't get his wish. Rickey Henderson hit the first pitch of the night into the left field bleachers and the Oakland A's routed us 15–3. The new era of Mariners baseball looked a lot like the previous eras!

Our team had a number of great young players, led by my favorite, Ken Griffey Jr. Having Kenny on the team was the greatest joy of our ownership tenure. He was just nineteen in our first year, and he gravitated to Gary and me, coming into our seating area under the stands before almost every game, where we would joke about various aspects of the game. I've always thought Kenny was the best baseball player I've ever seen; if not for the injuries he suffered later in his career, I think he would have broken every record in baseball. There's no doubt that the absolute highlight of owning the Mariners was watching Kenny every night. As someone who believed Willie Mays was the best baseball player who ever lived, I was certain that Kenny was going to exceed him. I'm not a big memorabilia guy, and I haven't saved a lot of mementos from my baseball days, but I cherish a few. One is a picture from Spring Training with Kenny; his dad, Ken Senior; and Willie Mays. The other is the lineup card the team presented me from the first night that Ken Senior played in a game with Kenny, the first (and only) time it had ever happened in baseball history. Junior thought of Gary and me as older brothers who could joke around with him before every game. He also, like everyone else, loved to tease me. When my nine-year-old son, Brad, was in town, Kenny knew that I didn't want him running around the field, because it wasn't appropriate for the youngsters in the stands to see another kid running the bases with Junior. Naturally, whenever Brad was with me, Kenny would grab him and run around the field, delighting in knowing that he was breaking my protocol.

The night after Kenny had made what is still considered the greatest catch in baseball history—running full speed and catching up to the ball while digging his cleats into the padding on the centerfield fence—Gary couldn't resist giving Kenny grief. If you're a baseball fan, you've seen the catch countless times, and every time you see it, you still can't figure out how he did it. Catching a ball while running at full speed up the wall seems physically impossible. That next night, Gary sternly told Junior, "Kenny, you ripped the wall up when you made that play last night and it's going to cost us a lot of money to fix it, so we're going to have to dock your pay to pay for it." Without missing a beat, Kenny said, "Get the money from ESPN; they're going to be running that clip for a long, long time." Kenny was right. I still see that clip thirty years later. One day, in an interview, someone asked me how we could afford to pay Kenny when he hit free agency. I quickly replied, "Oh, we'll find the money to pay Kenny; he's just going to have to get used to playing with twenty-four high school players."

When we brought Ken Senior aboard, it was another terrific moment. He was in the twilight of his career and loved that we were able to sign him and fulfill any father's fondest wish, being able to play with his son. And Junior felt the same way—family was everything to him, and he was forever grateful that we gave the Griffeys a chance to shine on the same field. Kenny seemed to have the ability, throughout his career, to celebrate Father's Day by hitting an inordinate number of home runs. Of course, he joked that when he hit a home run on Father's Day, it was to honor his dad—and that meant he didn't have to buy him a present!

It didn't happen overnight, but having Ken Senior around also matured Junior. In my career, I've known two of the greatest athletes, Peyton

Manning and Ken Griffey, and they were polar opposites. Peyton became one of the best ever because he outworked everyone. No one could match Peyton's preparation, and that took him to the Pro Football Hall of Fame. Kenny in his early years drove everyone crazy with what was essentially a lackadaisical attitude. However, his supernatural talent constantly made up for any lack of preparation—how do you get a ballplayer to study opposing tendencies when he could hit anyone at any time? As Kenny's career advanced, he developed the ability to become more of a student of the game, and that, along with his innate ability, took him to the Baseball Hall of Fame as well.

We also had a great young nucleus of players who would later give Seattle its first playoff berth: two more future Hall of Famers, Randy Johnson, and Edgar Martínez, as well as Jay Buhner and Omar Vizquel. It was clear we were on the rise, but we were still a sub .500 team in our first year.

Nevertheless, with the excitement of Griffey and a clearly reinvigorated ballpark experience, we were making inroads in Seattle. Despite the incredible number of things to do, fun permeated the front office and the entire organization. People responded, and countless articles were written about the new Mariners and about how we had made baseball fun, even in the tomb that was our home stadium, the Kingdome. One article called me a Renaissance man. Gary had a lot of fun with that: "Would the Renaissance man like tuna today, or just a burger?" or "You'd think a Renaissance man would have a better idea of how to manage our sales effort." Everywhere we'd go, people wanted to talk to us, to drink from what they thought was our vast fountain of knowledge. The Seattle Times assigned a reporter and photographer to cover me for several weeks, which ended in a Sunday magazine where the cover image was me pictured on a Wheaties box. Inside, they had superimposed a Superman costume on me (taken from a KIRO TV profile). I seemingly could do no wrong. If you happen to reach that point in your life, don't get too used to it—like I did. At the time, I was dating Monica Hart, an anchorwoman on KIRO, Channel 7. Monica was one of the kindest, nicest people I've ever known. She had been a cheerleader at the University of Washington and a former Miss Washington. It seemed like wherever we went, people followed us around, and we became a favorite topic of morning talk shows and newspaper columns. Again, heady stuff, and in spite of the monumental task of turning the franchise around, we were having fun every day.

It's impossible to describe what becoming a public figure is like. Gary, the most observant person I know, made a point to walk behind me whenever we entered a restaurant or other public setting. "It's creepy," he noted. "Everyone looks up at you, stares at you." I was reminded of the playful warning I got from another owner after we were approved to buy the Mariners: "You're a public figure now; never, ever pick your nose in public!" I didn't take that one seriously, not until years later, when George W. Bush was running for president, and someone circulated an old TV clip of him sitting at a Texas Rangers game, picking his nose while sitting in the front row!

I was just a minor public figure, but quickly, people knew me in Seattle. For those who gain significantly more fame, it's much more of an ordeal than an annoyance knowing that everyone is always looking at you. For those who become superstars, it becomes a lifetime of being on display. Of course, our obsession with celebrity has turned into a massive industry. One day, while at a spring training game, I was watching the usual parade of kids leaning over the railing, begging for Ken Griffey Jr.'s autograph. I asked one, "Is Kenny your favorite player?" The boy, no more than nine years old, nonchalantly answered, "No, but I can sell his autograph for forty dollars to the guy outside." Autograph vendors in this multibillion-dollar industry would recruit young kids to beg for autographs, because players were far more likely to sign for a child than for an adult. Given these antics, it's not surprising that celebrities don't love being interrupted at a dinner with their families, by people hovering over their tables and asking for just a quick autograph (or today, a quick selfie).

For Kenny, the mania for autographs was the least of his worries. One night in Texas, he was almost crushed in an elevator by a mob of fans seeking to get near him. The hysteria is real, and it has caused athletes and entertainers to go out in public with elaborate disguises or to avoid public places altogether. When David Letterman was on the Emmis board, he put on an elaborate disguise just to walk from NBC's headquarters to our meeting two blocks away! Then again, at times, the athletes don't help matters. One day, Kenny came into the office complaining about being accosted constantly while driving around Seattle. People honked, waved, slowed down in front of him and constantly yelled at him from every intersection. Our staff pointed out: "Kenny, you could avoid a lot of that if you didn't have a Mercedes convertible with 'The Kid 24' on your license plate!"

My boyhood friend Steve Paul, who was one of our Mariners attorneys, visited Seattle often. On every visit, he had to endure my nightly postgame autograph-signing sessions with fans before we could head out for a late-night snack. One night he sighed, "Any society that wants your autograph is one that cannot endure for very long!" Touché. After my experience, I'd say that anyone who becomes a public figure finds it an enthralling experience for about six months. But if you're beguiled for more than six months, you're probably a psychopath!

For all the fun and excitement we were generating, the Mariners were still losing a lot of games. One day, when I was back in Indiana, Gary and I were on the phone, both trying to cope with losing night after night. We agreed I should call Bud Selig, who had owned the Brewers for over twenty years, and get his advice. It led to one of my favorite stories of all time.

Bud said, "Jeff, let me tell you about losing. When I was in my first year in baseball, our family was still in the automobile business. My dad asked me to lunch and I said I couldn't eat. He asked me why, and I told him that the loss in the ninth inning the night before had destroyed me. He pulled me aside and said, 'Buddy, you have to have perspective in life. A month from now, only you, the pitcher, and the manager will remember last night's game. A year from now, all three of you will have forgotten. Your life must have perspective!'" Then Bud admonished me, "Jeffrey, never forget perspective."

I took Bud's lesson to heart and passed it on to Gary. A few weeks later, we were playing Bud's Brewers in Milwaukee County Stadium. I was sitting with Lee Pelekoudas, our assistant general manager; Steve Crane; and a few other people in a rickety box adjacent to Bud's box at the stadium. In the ninth inning, we were trailing the Brewers 4–1 when they brought in their closer, Dan Plesac. At the time, Plesac was one of the best relief pitchers in the major leagues. I asked Lee: "When was the last time we hit Plesac?" Lee calmly replied, "We've never hit Plesac, we never will hit Plesac, this game is over."

However, we staged a furious rally, driving the ball all over the park. With every hit, I heard banging on the walls coming from Selig's box, usually accompanied by low moans. When the game was over, we'd scored seven runs and easily beat the Brewers. Afterward, I saw Bud, or at least the smoke rising from his head. I started to speak, but he brusquely walked away, still fuming.

The next day, we were playing in the afternoon and I stopped by Bud's office. Recovered, he was much more congenial than the night before. I casually said, "Bud, what about perspective?" He said, "Jeffrey, there is no perspective in life when the son of a bitch can't get his slider over the plate!"

That story became well known in baseball. At an owners' meeting a few weeks later, Bobby Brown, league president, laughed and said, "Jeff, this game is 130 years old, and there has never been a person in this game with less perspective than Bud Selig." As Bud started laughing and nodding in agreement, Bobby continued, "Wally (Haas, the Oakland A's owner), why don't you tell Jeff about the night when you were sitting in Bud's box and he almost decapitated you by throwing an ashtray during an A's rally?" Wally laughed and said, "I never saw a throw like that; the Brewers could have used him in the bullpen that night!"

So we got used to losing, with or without Bud's advice. The team showed signs of life, and we were still in our heady days of people loving our new approach to baseball. But there were ominous signs. On a trip to Toronto, I got a stadium tour from Paul Beeston, president of the Blue Jays. The Sky-Dome was in its second year and was viewed as one of the wonders of the sports world, with its retractable roof, hotel rooms overlooking the park, and suites and amenities that made me incredibly envious. (We had the great thrill of playing in Toronto the night two fans decided to open up the hotel curtains and have sex in front of the window during the game. While that story made international headlines, I have to confess that I missed it. I was too worried about who we were going to bring out of the bullpen.)

When Paul gave me the tour, I saw all of the different ways the Blue Jays could generate revenue. After we finished, I was watching the giant scoreboard, which stretched across most of the outfield, and saw a long video from Seattle-based Microsoft. It was lavishly produced and much longer than the short videos you normally see in a stadium. I asked Paul how much the company had paid for the ad, and he called his office and replied that the ad was part of a package Microsoft had bought, and they were paying the Blue Jays $350,000 per year. My jaw dropped and I called Gary. "How much does Microsoft spend with us in a year?" He called back a few minutes later and said, "They buy four season tickets and have a hackers' night promotion for some of their employees. Grand total, $14,000 per year." When I came back to Seattle, I asked the Microsoft people: "How could you spend $350,000 per year on baseball in Toronto and $14,000 a year in your hometown, when your headquarters is exactly eight miles from our ballpark?" The answer was terse: "Baseball matters in Toronto. Nobody cares in Seattle."

Of course, when you played in the Kingdome, you developed a case of ballpark envy whenever you went to the newer parks in baseball. We were one of the first teams to play in Camden Yards, the stadium that defined the modern baseball experience. Larry Lucchino, then the president of the Orioles, gave Gary, his son, Eddie, and me and my son, Brad, a tour of the entire stadium. We marveled at the design and all of the amenities in the park. When you see the places where teams can generate revenue in a new facility, you get depressed realizing that they'll use their enhanced profits to compete with you when you need to attract and pay for your roster. As we finished our tour, we were standing in centerfield, looking out over the shining new park. I asked: "Larry, let me get this straight. You have no money in this park, everything was paid for by the city of Baltimore and the state of Maryland, correct?" "Yes," he replied. I continued, "And you're in a pissing contest with them over what to name the place?" "Yes, they want to call it Camden Yards and we want to call it Oriole Park. We want it to be Oriole Park and we're going to fight about it." To which I replied, "If Seattle built something like this for us, they could call it Yankee Stadium and I'd be thrilled to play there every day." To which Gary instantly responded, "If Seattle built something like this for us, they could call it Alcatraz and I'd be happy going in every day!"

Back in Seattle, no one was going to give us a new place to play; sometimes they didn't know where we played in the first place. One of my more remarkable encounters occurred at a dinner in Tacoma, where I was speaking to a group of accountants. Tacoma happens to be twenty-five miles from Downtown Seattle and is a significant part of the metropolitan area. Before dinner, I was speaking to the president of the organization, and he remarked that people in Tacoma loved getting on the train downtown to go to the Kingdome to watch the Seahawks play. The train trip avoided the traffic on the I-5 and created a charged atmosphere to get people ready to enjoy football. He said, he thought we should talk to Amtrak about doing that for Mariners games. I told him we'd been talking to Amtrak as well as to the ferry system (to get people from the outer islands) about doing just that. (I didn't bother to tell him that we had largely been met with indifference by both entities.) Then he explained, "Of course, the thing that makes the train so great is that it leaves you off right at the stadium. What's the closest train station to where you play?" I replied, "Well, it's right there." He countered, "No you don't understand, when we go to the Seahawks games, the train stops right at the King Street Station, which is right next to the Kingdome, where the Seahawks play. What's the closest station to *your* stadium?" It was finally registering with me. I said, "The King Street Station; we also play at the Kingdome." He was incredulous: "How long have you been doing that?" I said, "For many years, since they built the Kingdome." His voice tailed off as he said, "I'll be damned . . ."

When a civic leader—and a sports fan—has no idea where his city's Major League Baseball team plays, you know you have a problem. That, and countless other stories, gave me an inkling of how daunting our challenge was.

However, nothing could quench my incurable optimism. Gary was getting married in 1990, and he wanted to build his dream home in Renton, so he and his wife Vickie and their two kids could relocate from Los Angeles and settle permanently in Seattle. Before he bought his lot, he asked me, "Are you sure we're going to make this thing work?" All the signs that I was willing to see told me that we were making great progress. The public liked what we were doing, the team was getting a bit better, and I was convinced we were going to turn the franchise around. After I reassured Gary with a "Go ahead, buy the lot; we're going to make this thing work," he bought the land.

While Gary was on his honeymoon in Greece, I got a major jolt that convinced me that our mission wasn't merely challenging—it might just be impossible.

In any smaller market, a sports franchise has to be ingrained in the community, with significant support not only from the public but from the corporate community and the civic government, as well. Otherwise, owning a team is a losing proposition. I've lived this issue in Indianapolis and have been involved in building the partnership with our professional teams, the Colts and the Pacers, for many years. Indianapolis is a textbook case of how a sports franchise can be rewarding for everyone involved. Sadly, Seattle was the exact opposite, which is why sports ownership there has been mired in controversy for decades. In many ways, I understand. Seattle is a remarkably beautiful city, with so many attractions, that rallying around professional sports is far down on the list. As somebody once told me, "If you're a successful businessman in Pittsburgh or Boston, or almost anywhere else, you embrace the sports team, you buy suites, tickets, and ads, and you wrap yourself around the teams. In Seattle, if you're successful, you don't like the ostentation of all of those things. If you like baseball, you'll just buy a five-dollar ticket and sit in the outfield." There was more truth to that statement than I could have imagined at the time.

The one incident that made me seriously reconsider our prospects was an early discussion we had with the City of Seattle. The SuperSonics basketball team had long wanted to build a new arena on city land just south of the Kingdome (which sat on county land). Back when George Argyros had owned the Mariners, he had blocked any overture from Sonics owner Barry Ackerley, and the project had died. Enter, Emmis. Jerry Reinsdorf, a friend of Ackerley's because both owned pro-basketball teams (Jerry owned the Chicago Bulls), called to ask if I would at least listen to the idea and keep an open mind. We met with Ackerley's people and the city planners. I told them that, as they knew, the Kingdome had only two thousand parking spaces, well below Major League guidelines, and that as long as the Sonics' arena recognized that problem and incorporated large-scale parking for both venues, we would be supportive. Everyone nodded in agreement, appearing to love our thoughts, and they went to work.

A number of months after our original meeting (and a few days after Gary's wedding), the city offered its solution: The new Sonics arena would be built across the street from us with NO parking. In addition, a ramp would be constructed over that street into our parking lots. And the kicker: the arena's contract with the city had a built-in incentive to schedule any event—Sonics games, concerts, ice shows—that conflicted with the Mariners thirty minutes before our game so that fans would get there early and siphon the parking from our lot.

When I saw the proposal, I was in disbelief. I called Bob Gogerty, apoplectic. "How could they screw us this much?" I wailed. "Well, they view you as the county's tenant, and they just care about *their* tenant. Welcome to Seattle." The arena project died because it was so blatantly insane, but the experience taught me that our notion of a public-private partnership in Seattle was probably hopeless. I called Gary on his honeymoon and asked if he'd already purchased the land for his house. If he hadn't, he shouldn't buy it, because based on what I'd just seen, our chances in Seattle had just gone into free fall. Naturally, Gary told me he had. It took him twelve more years to sell that land, long after we were gone from the Northwest. A fact he dutifully reminded me every six months, like clockwork.

There were other warning signs that I ignored or minimized, not yet willing to accept the truth of our situation. When we first bought the team, our major goal was to figure out how to make every part of the Kingdome experience more fun. A tall order—not only was the Kingdome a drab, concrete building, but unlike some other domed stadiums, it didn't have a translucent roof so that light could enter. It was fully encased in concrete, and many referred to it as a tomb. Our research indicated that fans absolutely hated the building, so we tried to make it more appealing. We first thought we'd take advantage of the concrete roof and make it a projection screen for holograms. Our idea was that when we were behind by a number of runs before the game was official (at the end of the fifth inning), we'd start special effects of thunder and lightning, creating the impression that the game was about to be cancelled. We had a list of holograms that we thought would delight anyone in the stadium. We brought the technical wizards of Industrial Light & Magic to Seattle to assess what could be done. (ILM was the special-effects company that George Lucas had created when he was building his *Star Wars* empire.) They loved the idea; however, they quickly told us that before we could even consider special effects, we had to fix the sound system. It was, as they noted, "beyond antiquated" and incapable of allowing fans to enjoy anything clever we would want to attempt.

When I went to Neil Campbell, the head of operations for the Kingdome, I was in for a rude awakening. Since the county owned the building, and its sound system wasn't functioning properly, I thought getting new speakers throughout the building would be a fairly easy request. Big mistake. There were no easy requests when it came to the Kingdome. Neil, an affable guy, decided to give me a tour of the Kingdome to explain his plight. Neil knew that our speaker request was something that was necessary and fit under the terms of our lease, but that wasn't really the problem. As we toured the building, he pointed out exposed wires throughout the stadium that, despite building codes, had never been covered. The tour went on like that for what felt like an eternity. At one point he told me we had no budget for maintaining our massive air-conditioning system. (A prophetic statement: several years after we left Seattle, the system collapsed and parts penetrated the roof, causing the building to close for months.) Neil admitted that the stadium had been "built on the cheap" from 1972 (when construction started) until it opened in 1976. In truth, the Kingdome had never been completely finished and had never had adequate funds to maintain it in the years since. Neil and I agreed that the team would put up the funds to buy the speakers but that the county would reimburse us after they got approval, which they ultimately did. However, the whole mess dispelled our notion that our landlord, King County, was ever going to be a partner capable of collaborating on groundbreaking stadium entertainment. They just didn't have the funds, or the will to raise the funds, to improve the fan experience.

Moreover, our landlord's indifference to the Mariners went beyond just lack of funding and commitment. Early in our second season, the county presented us with a proposal to build an exhibit hall adjacent to the Kingdome that was to attract small conventions and festivals. The proposal did include some minor infrastructure improvements to the main building. The county asked if we wanted to weigh in, but we decided not to get involved because the exhibit hall had nothing to do with us, and it was the lion's share of the project. We'd realized by this time that the more we stayed out of local politics, the better, so we didn't file comments.

As a result, we were stunned when the first article about the proposal ran under a headline proclaiming that a county councilman was vigorously opposed because "he wasn't going to help greedy sports teams and greedy players." We were especially astounded since we'd always viewed this politician as supportive of the Mariners. When the paper called for a comment, I responded acidly, "This proposal has nothing to do with us. Unless we decide to move our bullpen out of the Kingdome and across the street to the proposed exhibit hall, there is no benefit at all. I can't imagine why we would be attacked for this. We didn't even comment on the proposal when it was given to us, because it doesn't affect us." Looking for some kind of an explanation, I called the councilman and he said something to the effect of: "Look, Jeff, let's face it, I get more voter support when I attack you guys than when I support you."

Such was the nature of politics in Seattle; it was an odd mix of Scandinavian populism and progressivism that seemed to spread across the country from its roots in Minnesota and the Northern Plains to infuse politics in the Northwest. Years later, Randy Bongarten, who was then running our TV group, complained that when we did employee satisfaction surveys, our worst scores always came from our TV station, KOIN in Portland. Randy couldn't understand it, but I told him that there has long been a fundamental distrust of business in the Northwest and that distrust was exacerbated by the business model of professional sports.

I made one more critical mistake in Seattle and it involved my area of expertise: media. The Mariners were one of only two teams in baseball without a regional cable television deal. Local/regional cable is the engine that has powered the economics of the baseball industry for the past thirty years. Since I knew that space well, and I thought I knew the industry players, cable seemed like a great place to make up some lost ground.

At the time, the average cable deal for a market our size was around $4 million per year. Because we were on the West Coast, we had a disadvantageous time zone (when we played games back east, viewers in Seattle had to watch us at 4 PM, which isn't prime viewing time). Still, most of our schedule was played out west, at 7 PM, so the problem was somewhat mitigated. Our other issue was that we had had no history of success, so Mariners baseball wasn't foremost in the minds of people in Seattle, let alone the rest of the Northwest (Washington, Idaho, Oregon, Montana, Alaska, and British Columbia). Ironically, our most significant problem was something I initially thought would be a positive, but it turned out to be our greatest negative. Unlike just about every other television market, the sports channel in Seattle was owned by the cable system, TCI. In other cities, the sports channel secured the rights to the team, then negotiated with the cable provider, thus creating a middleman who siphoned off money from the team. No middleman in Seattle. Moreover, TCI, owned by John Malone, had almost every cable home in the market and placed their sports channel,

Prime Sports Northwest, on Channel 6, the prime real estate on the TV dial, in between KIRO, Channel 7 (CBS); KING, Channel 5 (NBC); and KOMO, Channel 4 (ABC).

At night, when baseball would normally air, TCI showed old beach volleyball games and other marginal sporting events. I even noticed that on many nights, the picture had lines going through it, as if the company hadn't even bothered to clean up the signal, because they knew no one was watching. Given their programming, I approached our negotiations with great optimism, because even though we weren't exactly the '27 Yankees, we had a great young team. Griffey was a highlight reel every night, and the fans in Seattle were noticing us as never before. (Speaking of the '27 Yankees, I got a lot of laughs one night while giving a speech, after a fan asked how far away the Mariners were from a championship. I replied, "We're just two players away . . . unfortunately, those two players are Ruth and Gehrig!")

As I entered into negotiations with TCI, I was hopeful we could bridge the gap between our zero dollars for cable and other teams in markets our size. We were never going to get the $50 million a year the Yankees were pulling down, or the $15 million to $20 million other big-market teams were earning, but Seattle was becoming a boomtown, and the market's disposable income made our rights more valuable than in other places. After lengthy discussions, TCI offered us $500,000 a year. I was stunned and angry. I told them that rather than give away our rights for those prices, I'd rather take pictures of the games and walk around downtown and show them to people.

What transpired in and around that negotiation taught me more about the economics of television than I could have learned any other way and explained how the business would grow in the next thirty years. One night, soon after the negotiations blew up, I was having a few drinks with a TCI manager and he revealed: "Look, I control almost every home in this region. They pay me thirty dollars a month for their TV, and I essentially allocate where those dollars go. I charge every home in Seattle two dollars for Channel 6. They don't know what goes into their bill, and since it's one channel I own, that's where I put some of their money. That means I have $25 million a year for that channel before I ever sell an advertisement, and I essentially have no programming costs, so why do I need to share any of it with you?" In those days, he didn't have to pay CBS, NBC, or ABC anything, so what most people were watching was free to him. John Malone, who orchestrated all of this before he sold his business to AT&T, was and is the most powerful man in the history of American television. I didn't love him then and I don't love him now, but I respect his incredible intellect. He alone figured this out, and his brilliance dictated the course of TV in this country for years. Interestingly, years later, his investment banker, Jill Greenthal, who was also my banker, convinced Malone to take a stake in Emmis. Stuart Layne, remembering the pain of our negotiations, called me in disbelief after the investment: "When they wouldn't do the Mariners deal you said if you had a gun with three bullets and you had Idi Amin, Saddam Hussein, and John Malone in a room, you'd shoot Malone three times to make sure he was dead." I merely laughed and said, "Times change."

So, regional cable was a nonstarter. On top of that, we were dealt two major financial blows during our early years in baseball. The first stemmed from a lawsuit the players union had brought against Major League Baseball, charging that from 1985–1987, Commissioner Peter Ueberroth and others in the game had advised owners that they should, "hold the line on salaries." The result was that almost no owner offered a long-term contract during that whole two-year period. When we bought the Mariners, all the experts assured us that the damages would be minimal, so when George Argyros demanded that we take responsibility for them, we naively conceded the issue. Same thing happened with the team that sold right before us—the Texas Rangers. George W. Bush, their managing partner, told me later: "Eddie Chiles (the previous Rangers owner) insisted that he would pay the first $500,000 and we had to pay the rest. Our lawyers said, this is never going to be over a few hundred thousand dollars, take that deal all day long, so we did."

Unfortunately, as time wore on, the news kept getting worse—more smoking guns were revealed, all strengthening the players union's case. At every owner meeting, the reports were updated with more grim news. At one gathering, we learned the cost was likely to be $2 million per team; the next time, it was up to $4 million. On and on it went. After one meeting, Gary turned to me and asked, "When exactly do we get the good news in baseball?" The collusion case finally got resolved in 1990, awarding the players damages in the amount of $12 million per team. George W. Bush marveled at his great negotiating skills: "Eddie paid $500,000, but because I'm so smart, I get to pay $11.5 million." We were even dumber—we owed the full $12 million. When we got the final settlement number, I asked several other owners if they would collude with me over lunch, so I could get some benefit from the deal, since all of the collusion occurred before we ever owned the Mariners!

The second blow, while not baseball-related, still helped seal my fate in Seattle. Because of the real estate crisis of the early nineties, American banks had seen many of their loan portfolios implode. With the resulting recession and banking crisis, the broadcast industry—built on leverage (debt)—had its loans reclassified as highly leveraged transactions. The designation triggered regulations that modified the borrowing restrictions on the loans. These changes plunged me into a personal crisis because of a strange provision in Emmis's bonds that created ambiguity about whether we could borrow money to buy the Mariners. What was *not* ambiguous was that Emmis could take out a loan three months after the acquisition. In one of the great miscalculations of my life, and one that would haunt me for years, I decided to allow my lawyers to ask the bondholders for permission to borrow earlier. In hindsight, that's like asking your wife if she wants to buy a new dress. The bondholders said, "Of course you need permission, but we'll waive that requirement—for a $1 million fee." I thought it was an outrageous request, and my management team agreed with me. Moreover, Bob Lindsay of Morgan Stanley, the company that was investing in the Mariners for one-third ownership, said, "Jeff, this is crazy, we'll merely lend you Emmis's share personally as a bridge loan, and in three months Emmis will be able to assume this loan and everything will be fine." Because Emmis was my company, I stupidly didn't ask for indemnification. When the highly leveraged transaction rules were enacted in the ensuing three months, Emmis never could take over the loan, and it weighed on my shoulders for years. One bit of advice: When the drafting of a legal document (like a contract or loan) is ambiguous, but you think it works in your favor, go ahead. Ask for forgiveness later, if need be, but never ask for permission.

Radio, like many fast-growing businesses, relied on leverage to produce spectacular returns, and we were the masters of leverage. Here's an important business lesson. When your business is growing, leverage is fabulous. When your business is declining, leverage will get you to the poorhouse on an express bus. Here's why: We built Emmis by buying stations that invariably had little or no cash flow. Our first station had no profits, yet we paid about $1.2 million for it, with over a million dollars of debt. After our first year, however, we had over $600,000 of cash flow so our leverage ratio (debt divided by cash flow) was less than two times. We did that over and over again in the eighties, and if we had $200 million of debt and only $25 million of cash flow, we had eight times leverage. Yet if we doubled the cash flow in two years, we could pay down some debt along with servicing our interest, and after two years, our debt might be $180 million and our cash flow would be $50 million, so leverage would be safely under four times. In that scenario, you create tremendous amounts of value, as we did all through the eighties. But when the economy goes the other way, and your business drops, your leverage ratio goes up. In the above example, if your cash flow drops to $20 million, you're spending most of your money servicing just the interest. Your leverage ratio rises to ten times and you're perilously close to insolvency.

To compound the problem, when the banking rules changed in the early nineties, the banks became very nervous. In the late eighties, many bankers had discovered media, especially radio, because of its increasing cash flows and ability to service debt. Every bank wanted to lend you money, and if you were successful, everyone curried your favor. In those days, Emmis was at the top of everyone's list. When the rules changed, those same banks fled. They couldn't grasp the notion that cash flows could decline, and many scurried to sell their portfolios and go on to businesses that they viewed as less risky. As you'll see, I've lived through this cycle a number of times in my career.

With the economy sinking in 1991, Emmis's position got a lot more precarious. While I don't believe we were ever in danger of becoming insolvent (I'm sure others will disagree), it was clear that funding a losing Major League Baseball team, which now owed a $12 million collusion payment, was stretching us to our limits. The league was giving us great accolades, people loved our operations—especially our marketing—and our standing with the average fan was dramatically improved, borne out by increased attendance. But Seattle's well-known indifference was a continuing drag on our operations. A number of friends in baseball admitted that we'd be incredibly successful anywhere else, but it wasn't going to happen in Seattle.

In mid-1991, another defining moment in my career as a team owner happened in Seattle, in a meeting I didn't attend and barely knew about. While I was back in Indiana, our bank, Security Pacific, asked to meet with Gary. The essence was, "Look, we love you guys, we think you're doing a great job. But we don't think this thing is ever going to work here. We know Emmis has problems, and it can't fund losses like it could when you bought the Mariners. We don't want to have to keep funding you if this thing keeps losing money. If you move this team, we would love to be your bank, but we don't want the embarrassment of calling your loan (that is, ordering full repayment) in another year. We don't want to fund you and yet we don't want to pull the plug. The publicity from that would kill us in Seattle. We want to make sure that Jeff isn't on some crazy mission from God to make this work if it clearly isn't." Gary said, "Jeff is obsessed with making this work, but he's not crazy. He knows if it's impossible, if we can't make it work, we'll throw in the towel. If Seattle can't find a buyer, pursuant to our lease, we'll sell the team or move it somewhere where it has a chance to be successful."

Gary casually mentioned the meeting to me, and since he'd accurately explained my position, I thought that was the end of it. No dice. A few months later, in the fall of '91, the *Seattle Times* got a copy of the memo discussing the bank meeting, apparently written by someone who wasn't even in the room. Splashed across the top of the front page on Sunday morning, the article breathtakingly revealed "Smulyan's secret plans to move the Mariners." It was an exposé that discussed every problem I had, Emmis's sagging fortunes, my infamous bridge loan with Morgan Stanley, and the team's growing losses.

While technically accurate, the coverage failed to mention that Emmis was *not* defaulting on any of its loans, that we were funding the team's losses, and that my bridge loan with Morgan Stanley, while troublesome, was not a source of immediate concern. Our problem, plain and simple, was that the franchise wasn't making any inroads. In fact, by every measurable standard, our revenue was falling further behind the rest of the American League (not to mention the National League, where teams were generally better off). But, unlike the headline blared, we couldn't just pick up and move the Mariners. That was only an option if no one locally wanted to buy the team (as required by our lease with the county for the Kingdome).

The *Times* invested in a full-blown campaign, with numerous writers assigned to different aspects of the story. Their lead sports columnist, Steve Kelley—who had written a lengthy column just two weeks before noting that the Mariners' problems were the result of corporate and civic indifference—abruptly changed his tune. At first, he'd written, "don't blame Smulyan, he's doing all he can," but after the exposé came out, he switched positions, calling me "a duplicitous Yuppie without two nickels to rub together."

Daily, the *Times* attacked every fiber of my being: the food columnist wrote that I picked bad restaurants; the TV columnist said my viewing tastes were awful. Editorial cartoons landed on the front page, depicting me as a despicable individual who was worthy of complete scorn. It went on, day after day, every story showing what a blight I was on Seattle's character.

The morning paper, the *Seattle Post-Intelligencer* (*PI*), didn't quite know what to do with the story. The paper's publisher, Virgil Fassio, had been an ardent supporter of ours and confessed to being amazed by all of the negative publicity. After a few days, the entire editorial staff, sports writers, editorial writers, general assignment reporters, and financial reporters requested a full hearing with us. Gary and I dutifully trotted down to the *PI* offices, anxious to tell our side of the story. We were greeted by a court reporter, photographers, and at least fifteen reporters who grilled us for several hours about the controversy. Gary said, "Well, just think, that came from the guys who like us!" I said, "At least they want to hear our side of the story—the *Times* won't even do that."

After we left the inquisition, I turned to Gary and asked one of my favorite all-time questions: "A hundred years ago, our ancestors came here from the Old Country. Think about what happened to the ones who stayed. They endured the czars, pogroms, the First World War, the Mensheviks, the Bolsheviks, the Communists, more pogroms, the Depression, the Second World War, the Nazis, Stalin, and then more Communists. Then think about everything our families found in the United States: religious freedom, education, economic success. And I have to ask you, based on what's happening in Seattle, would we have been better off if we had stayed in Russia?" Gary cracked up. One lesson I learned from running this gauntlet: sometimes you just have to laugh.

While I thought our treatment was wildly unfair, to be honest, I couldn't afford to keep funding the Mariners for much longer. Our projections never accounted for the revenue other teams would bring in, squeezing our ability to hang on to great players. We also never anticipated the hit from the collusion settlement, the failure to get a cable deal, or the lack of meaningful sponsorships. And, as I noted before, we never thought Seattle's civic and corporate communities would leave us so high and dry.

We had several theories about why the *Times* was running a campaign that drove home the premise that we were unqualified to own the Mariners. The most common one was that the *Times* publisher Frank Blethen, who later became famous for shooting at his neighbor's dog, just wanted a controversy to sell papers. The most likely theory floating around was that several prominent citizens allied with the *Times* were betting that they could convince baseball to kick us out, so they could be awarded the team at a bargain price. At one interview, a reporter from the *Tacoma News Tribune* asked about my fitness to own the team. In frustration, I snapped that I was on baseball's ownership committee and had offered to explain the standards to the *Times* and demonstrate why we were qualified, but they refused my request. I then uttered a line that made headlines, and I'm sure made Frank Blethen's blood boil: "Look, we're qualified to own the Mariners and we can prove it; the real question is, is Frank Blethen qualified to inherit a newspaper from his father?"

A little advice: No matter how good something feels, sometimes you just shouldn't say it. But that one felt really good.

We were determined to get through this publicity nightmare with humor. When the *PI* printed their version of the exposé, it carried a number of awkward photos. So, we decided to run a caption contest for our staff. For the one of me looking forlorn with my wrist revealing my watch, the winning caption was "Takes a licking and keeps on ticking" (based on the Timex watch ad). For the picture of Gary that overemphasized his beard, the line that won the prize was, "Look, Mom, it's the guy on the Alaska Airlines planes." (The airline had a picture of an Alaska Native, who did look somewhat like Gary, on the tails of their planes.) Despite the jokes, the personal attacks were a painful experience. Over the years, I've said, "Everybody should be a pariah once in their life," but make no mistake, it's excruciating going through it. Every day, you believe you're unjustly vilified on the front page of a newspaper (today it would be digital news sites or social media). In response, we ramped up the humor in the office and in the clubhouse. The year before, I had been walking around the Kingdome giving a tour during a game. The fans in the right field bleachers stood up to cheer me. After the game, Jay Buhner, our right fielder, playfully needled me. "Jesus, Jeff, I bust my ass all night, run into walls, and nobody gives a damn. You make one appearance and the fans cheer you. That's bullshit." After the *Times* exposé, Jay remarked, "Bet you ain't going into the bleachers now!"

During the ordeal, my friend David Stern, commissioner of the NBA, called me to ask an intriguing question: "Jeff, if someone offered you the Mariners today for free, with only two conditions, would you take them? The conditions are, the economics of baseball don't change in the next ten years, and you have to stay in Seattle all ten years." I laughed, but quickly responded, "David, if baseball's economics don't change, I would lose over $500 million owning the free team, and that doesn't include the psychic costs of living here for ten years and hitting my head against the wall every day, so obviously the answer is no." He laughed, and thanked me because he had just won a bet from a friend. What that question encapsulated for me, however, was a priceless lesson: Sometimes free is too expensive! I've applied that countless times over the years.

We were reeling from the newspaper's all-out war on us, but we were finally able to discuss our plight with Seattle's civic leaders. We were willing to open up our books and try to find any way to make the team economically viable. George Duff, head of the chamber of commerce, was trying to be helpful. He asked Herman Sarkowsky, a prominent civic leader and former co-owner of the Seahawks, to head up a committee to review our books, talk to the city government and the corporate community, and make recommendations about the economics of baseball in Seattle. The goal was to find out how much money it would take to get the team to break even, and thus, at least be competitive.

Meanwhile, in baseball, people viewed our move as a fait accompli. Given Seattle's tortured history with baseball, everyone in the game thought we should say goodbye and move the franchise to Tampa. The *Tampa Tribune* even ran a flattering column that polled the American League owners and found that "Thirteen of the fourteen American League teams want the Mariners out of Seattle and in Tampa. The fourteenth? Smulyan. He still wants to make it in Seattle." As the fall of 1991 went on, my name changed from Jeff Smulyan to "the beleaguered Jeff Smulyan," and beleaguered I was. Gary and I welcomed any advice, and Herman became a great friend as we discussed every aspect of the franchise.

During the process, our legal team believed we needed to invoke the escape clause that George Argyros had put into his Kingdome lease during another of the intermittent crises in Seattle baseball. It allowed us to break the lease if certain attendance standards weren't met and if we offered to sell the team to a Seattle-based buyer, who had 120 days to make a bid. While the *Times* organized a campaign to buy up as many tickets as possible to stop the process, it was clear to our lawyers that we met the conditions of the clause.

At the end of the year, we had to decide whether to trigger the escape clause. By this time, it didn't matter what I did; I was going to remain an outcast in Seattle. Even though lots of fans were sympathetic, the consensus was that I was just a bad owner. Ironically, the only time a fan ever berated me at the ballpark was during the '92 season. I was standing in the owner's box, and from the concourse below, a fan yelled up, "Get out of Seattle, Smulyan, this is our town!" Naturally, he was wearing a complete Red Sox uniform at the time. You can't make this stuff up.

Herman's goal was to raise $15 million in annual support to at least get us to the bottom of revenues for the American League, but his meetings with city government and corporate leaders were going nowhere. The day before we had to trigger the escape clause, Gary and I went to see Herman in his spacious office atop one of the city's tallest skyscrapers. I asked him point-blank what he would do if he were me. His answer was terse: "Jeff, if I owned this team, I would move it in the middle of the night and never look back. There's no support for you or anyone in this town for baseball."

The next day, we triggered the escape clause. After everything that had happened in the past few months, I wanted badly to move the team. I felt compelled to prove that we could make baseball work somewhere. It was no secret that everyone in the league wanted us to go to Tampa, and Tampa was dying to get us. Earlier in the process, a reporter had said, "Isn't it true you can generate more revenue in Tampa?" I flippantly responded, "We could generate more revenue in Duluth than we can in Seattle." Not a wise answer, but when you're beleaguered, you say lots of things you shouldn't.

Part of the reason we were so vilified was that no one in their right mind believed a buyer could be found in Seattle. Chris Larson, one of the original Microsoft employees, had pledged $30 million to the effort, but no one else had any interest in joining him in any significant way. Craig McCaw, the cellular pioneer, said he would help, but his commitment was limited to a few million dollars. As the year ended, Seattle was scrambling to meet the deadline to find a buyer, and most in baseball thought we would file to move the Mariners to Tampa the next year.

One interesting footnote. After the new year began, and a few weeks after we had triggered the escape clause, Herman Sarkowsky issued a press release stating that he had mysteriously "found" $15 million in annual support for the team. That's when we realized the Seattle civic leaders who couldn't find the money for us had to be trying to convince some prospect that the Mariners were viable. Gary and I marveled at the timing of the press release, considering that from the day Herman talked to us to the day—three weeks later—he issued the release, he'd spent most of his time sailing in the Caribbean. We never blamed him for the obvious fiction; he was just doing his part as a loyal civic leader. For years after we were gone from Seattle, American League president Bobby Brown would tease me and say he was headed to Seattle to look for the missing Sarkowsky money. Neither Bobby nor the new owners ever found it!

Not long thereafter, I got a call from Senator Slade Gorton. The former district attorney had parlayed his lawsuit against the American League into a seat in the United States Senate, and he was now serving his second term. Because baseball had always been his signature issue, the senator was the one determined to fix the Mariners "problem" and keep the team in Seattle. He was now pleased to report that he'd finally come up with a solution. At our meeting, Gorton was all compliments: "Jeff, you've done a great job with this franchise and no one can ever blame you or attack you. The enthusiasm you generated for the team has really saved baseball in Seattle. I've found a buyer and he will buy the team from you at a fair price." I asked if the buyer were foreign, because I knew that would be an issue. Gorton told me yes, the buyer was Hiroshi Yamauchi, owner of Nintendo.

Ironically, the year before, George W. Bush and I had represented the American League on the four-member ownership committee. At that time, we had pushed to allow some foreign ownership of baseball teams; I suggested that we mirror the broadcasting standard and allow each team to sell up to 20 percent to a foreign buyer. In 1992, the Japanese were buying up everything they could in the United States, including Universal Studios and New York's Rockefeller Center. Many American League teams were starved for capital, and the idea of minority foreign ownership had wide support throughout our league. George W. Bush and I made the case to the two National League owners, Bill Bartholomay of the Atlanta Braves and Peter O'Malley of the Los Angeles Dodgers. Bill seemed lukewarm to the idea, but Peter was apoplectic. He insisted that baseball is America's game and it will stay America's game. Period, end of story. Prophetically, I responded, "If we don't have any rules about this, you may be faced with a situation where someone wants to buy not 20 percent of a team, but 100 percent of a team, and you'll have no standard and you'll face an ownership crisis." Peter was unmoved and the idea died.

Now, in Gorton's Seattle office, I was faced with a no-win situation. If Nintendo were the only buyer, Seattle would be at war with baseball, and I would be blamed for the fallout. My support of the deal would be meaningless, and I certainly couldn't oppose it. I told the senator that it would be a heavy lift, getting Nintendo approved, but I would get out of the way and let him proceed. He was appreciative, but he quickly showed his profound appreciation in a strange way.

Within days, Gorton was attacking me in the newspaper on a daily basis saying that baseball had to approve the Nintendo deal to get rid of the scourge of Smulyan. After a few days of these attacks, I called his office. His assistant responded, "Don't take it personally, Jeff, Slade likes you. He just needs to make you the villain to get the deal approved."

A few years later, when my friend, state legislator Maria Cantwell, ran for the US Senate seat held by Slade Gorton, I made sure to do a fundraiser for her and donate the maximum allowable to support her campaign. When she defeated Gorton, I thought of sending him a note saying: "Don't worry Slade, I really like you."

By the spring of 1992, the campaign Nintendo had launched was in full force. The press portrayed the company as a huge fan of baseball. We knew otherwise. In 1989, our first year, Stuart Layne had come up with a great promotion: Have two kids stand at home plate and play a Nintendo game on the scoreboard a few minutes before every home game. We'd have prizes for the kids and a charity component. We loved the idea, everybody loved the idea, but Nintendo turned down Stuart's proposal for a $100,000 sponsorship. The next year, Stuart went back and offered the same sponsorship for $50,000 and they still turned it down. A few months later, he went back again, exasperated, this time saying, "Don't pay us anything; just let us use your video games for free." Their answer: "Look, we just don't like or care about baseball." A little-known fact: on the day they announced their purchase of the Mariners, Nintendo had never owned a season ticket, even though their North American headquarters was located within ten miles of our ballpark.

So, what led to Nintendo's sudden fervor to buy the Mariners? Slade Gorton was at the center of it. As a member of the Senate Commerce Committee, Gorton had strengthened the enforcement of US electronic piracy laws, cutting down on counterfeiting and the theft of intellectual property. To video game companies like Nintendo, that protection was worth a fortune; the company owed the senator a giant favor, and Gorton called it in when he approached Nintendo about buying the Mariners. He also assured them that they would be heroes in Seattle (absolutely correct), and that they would never lose any money owning the team (as correct as Gorton's love and respect for me). In fact, immediately after Nintendo purchased the team, Yamauchi's son-in-law, Minoru Arakawa, who ran their operations in North America, attended his first ownership meeting. From what I heard, Arakawa looked at all of the brackets around the numbers (signifying losses) and innocently asked, "What do all these brackets mean?" He had no idea they had bought a money-losing business.

When the sale of the Mariners was announced, I was in Indianapolis, but Gary was called to a meeting to learn about the group behind the purchase. While Chris Larson was going to put in around $20 million and

Craig McCaw was investing a few million, the vast majority of the money was coming from Yamauchi. Major problem: baseball still strictly prohibited foreign ownership.

Seattle had decided on an ingenious strategy to convince Major League Baseball that the deal should go through. They dubbed it "the Baseball Club of Seattle, Truly Local Ownership" and the group consisted of a number of prominent civic leaders. During the meeting, I was on the phone from Indianapolis, but Gary was right there, surrounded by a host of heavy hitters seated around a law firm's conference room. The leaders—Frank Shrontz, CEO of Boeing, and John Ellis, CEO of Puget Sound Power and Light—informed us that their group of civic leaders would be overseeing the Mariners and have a financial interest in the team, while Nintendo would remain in the background, essentially a passive investor. It was clear that this group was a front that wouldn't control anything, but I understood, and even appreciated, the strategy. I asked Frank, "How much are each of you contributing to this effort?" He sheepishly mumbled, "Twelve hundred dollars each." I was so stunned, I had to ask again: "Frank, did you say $1,200 apiece?" When he said yes, I couldn't resist twisting the knife a bit: "Gee, baseball might think you guys would have a little more credibility if you put up say, $2,000 apiece." Gary later told me that during this exchange, Frank and every other CEO would have disappeared under the table if they could.

Still, Seattle played its hand well. They hired McCann Erickson to launch a marketing onslaught throughout America, minimizing Nintendo's ownership and accusing anyone who opposed the deal of xenophobia. The campaign was masterful, convincing a lot of public officials to back the effort; Major League Baseball was faced with withering pressure to support the deal. Besides, what was the alternative: to let a duplicitous yuppie uproot the team and move it to Florida? We watched events unfold and laughed that truly local ownership was only truly local if you lived in Kyoto, where Yamauchi lived. Ironically, in all the years he owned the team, he never attended a Mariners game.

As the pressure mounted, the league relented, the deal was approved, and Seattle kept its team. Emmis was paid $112 million for our $76 million investment, but despite my being called a financial genius for making a $36 million profit, the toll on me was monumental. On the day we sold the team,

Gary and I were walking down Park Avenue and he asked me what we could have done differently to make the Mariners succeed. I admitted, "Gary, the die was cast when we bought the team. The math didn't work, we couldn't afford the losses, and even if we could, we wouldn't have chosen to continue for much longer. It was just an impossible task. But, many years from now, you'll look back on this and view it as the best management job you ever did." I believed that statement then, and I believe it all these years later. You're more creative when your back is against the wall, as it was every day in Seattle. When times are tough, that's when you do your best work. We came up with ideas that are now commonplace in parks and arenas all over America. Even our infamous mascot, the Mariner Moose, was Ken Griffey's running mate in a 1996 Nike campaign to promote Griffey for the presidency!

When it was all over, I asked Floyd Abrams, America's leading libel lawyer, to look over the case and study the *Times*'s treatment of me. As a public figure, I'd have to meet the strenuous "reckless disregard of the truth" test. After reviewing the case, Floyd called and said, "Given their coverage, you'd probably win this case, but unless you really need the money, don't spend the next ten years of your life suing them. Even if you win, they'll put the story at the back of the paper, if they print it at all. My advice, go live your life—that will be all the vindication you need." It was sage advice, and I followed it.

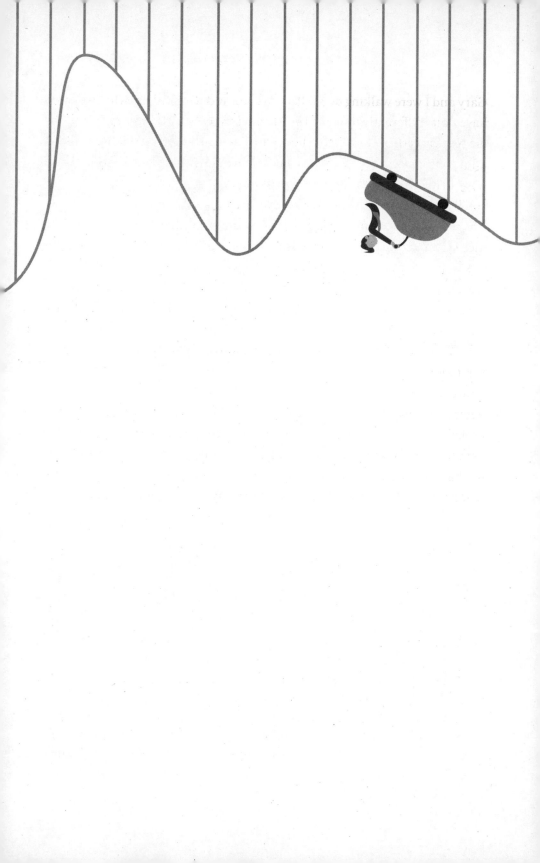

Top: At an Emmis Managers' Meeting in Palm Springs, Jay Leno entertained our folks. Here he is with my late assistant, Robin Rene, and me. *Bottom:* In our heady days in Seattle, Steve Paul proclaimed that our group was the "finest bastion of Jewish manhood." When he said it, Gary and I exploded in laughter and it led to a series of "Finest Bastion" photos. In this picture are our banker Paul Taubman, me, Steve Paul, Stuart Layne, attorney Norm Gurwitz, attorney Lenny Levine, Gary Kaseff, and my financial advisor Bruce Jacobson. We did reunion photos regularly for years with this group.

5

Rising from the Ashes, the First Time

Selling the Mariners, despite the $36 million windfall, really hurt. We had failed in Seattle and, human nature being what it is, I was determined to try again. What we had learned in baseball was that, given a level playing field (forgive the pathetic pun), we could build a terrific organization that would enable us to be more than competitive. When my tenure in baseball ended, I was gratified to learn that the commissioner of the National Basketball Association (NBA), David Stern, agreed. He called me with a remarkably flattering offer: "Jeff, I want you to take over the Houston Rockets; put whatever money you want into the franchise, we'll get you whatever else you need. I need you to fix the organization." In essence, he was offering me a controlling interest in an NBA team regardless of how much money I would put in. David ran the NBA through sheer force of will and intellect, and I knew that if he were making the offer, it was absolutely going to happen. Unfortunately, I had to turn him down, explaining, "David,

I have to fix Emmis; it's the only thing that's important to me right now." My company had been battered by the 1991–92 recession and, as a result, was overleveraged; my only mission was to restore Emmis to financial health and rebuild our holdings from there.

As I mentioned earlier, leverage is the greatest thing in the world when you're growing, and Emmis had been using it since we started. By the late 1980s, the rest of the industry had followed; radio had become a highly leveraged business known for yielding high, dependable returns for lenders, banks, and investment banks alike. For a few years, every US financial institution opened up a media lending division, and it seemed all of them found their way to our doorstep. At conventions, we were flooded with requests to meet with bankers who hoped to become one of our lenders. At one convention, I joked to Steve and Doyle, "I feel like Mick Jagger, but instead of groupies throwing their underwear at me, there are bankers throwing loans at me." We knew the frenzy was absurd, and couldn't last, but we weren't prepared for the full stop that happened in 1990. As a result of the burgeoning savings and loan (S&L) crisis, banking regulators changed the definition of highly leveraged transactions (which we had) and forced banks to disclose those loans. That disclosure would surely scare off their shareholders. Suddenly, most of the institutions that had been fighting for our business a short time ago shed their media loans and shunned the industry. In addition, the S&L crisis led to a recession that caused the radio business to suffer steep declines in profitability. Coupled with new federal rules, radio became a pariah industry overnight.

Contrary to when you're growing, leverage is the worst when your business declines. With typical Emmis bad luck, we hit the trifecta: the Mariners losses were problematic, the recession hit our overall business, and our biggest cash cows, Power 106 Los Angeles and Hot 97 New York, were experiencing severe drops in their ratings because their format—urban-flavored Top 40 music—had fallen out of favor.

Even before we sold the Mariners, we knew that we were going to have to take drastic measures. Our leverage ratios were climbing rapidly, and with expensive debt, it was clear we were perilously close to not being able to service our interest payments, let alone retire principal. I've seen this situation in many businesses, and it usually leads to an inevitable death spiral.

Companies cut wherever they can, sell whatever they can, but they usually can't get out of the trap. It's commonly called "burning the furniture," and I'm certain most of our peers thought that's what we would do. This was the world we were entering in 1992.

Our first course of action was to stay solvent. We cut salaries, perks, benefits, and consolidated our staff; an already lean operation got leaner. But that wasn't enough. We had to sell some of our radio stations so we could use the proceeds to pay down our debt. We first put our underperforming stations on the block: Boston, Washington, Minneapolis, Houston, and San Francisco. Each had been ravaged by the downturn, so their cash flows had declined. For example, our Top 40 station in San Francisco was generating less than $1 million a year. Luckily, buyers were still paying high multiples of cash flow, banking on a turnaround. We sold San Francisco for $20 million, which reduced some of our outstanding debt. Unfortunately, selling those five stations didn't lower our leverage ratios enough.

By far, the most painful sale was our all-sports radio station, WFAN-AM, New York. After all, it was my baby, and I was more emotionally attached to that station than anything we had ever owned. But we knew that Infinity Broadcasting's Mel Karmazin coveted the station. He understood that WFAN and Don Imus were revered by investment bankers, traders, and investors; after all, the station's macho image was a perfect fit with the go-go era of Wall Street. Unlike just about everyone else in the industry, Mel saw that the station would be the perfect anchor for his planned initial public offering (IPO). He knew that with Imus and WFAN in his portfolio, the stock he issued to the public would get wide support, making his IPO a smashing success. Little wonder that he wanted WFAN in the worst way. Mel was the legendarily difficult wizard of Infinity, working his way up from management to ironclad control of the company. He and I always had a testy, yet fun relationship, but growing up in poverty in New York had given him a "take no prisoners" personality. My favorite quote about Mel was from network owner Norm Pattiz, who once stated, "Mel would never stab you in the back; he enjoys stabbing you in the chest too much."

Meanwhile, we had finally concluded that to solve our debt problems for good, we either had to sell WFAN or Hot 97 FM, New York. We knew WFAN was growing spectacularly, but we believed that Hot 97, as one of the market's biggest music stations, had more upside. We also were aware that AM radio had already begun its inexorable decline. Moreover, we were sure that Mel would pay a higher price for WFAN than we could get for Hot 97, going that much further in reducing our debt levels. Nevertheless, I really didn't want to sell WFAN, and that made the negotiation with Mel even more fun than usual. He and I went back and forth—I kept holding out for $75 million and he kept countering. At the end of the day, he reached my number, complaining to anyone who would listen that he overpaid by at least $10 million. When we got to the closing, Mel tried to claw it back and pay only $65 million; he couldn't help it, he had to try to beat the other guy at every turn. But I knew I had the upper hand, and after some bluster, he backed down.

At the time, $75 million was the most anyone had ever paid for an AM station. That was of little solace, but down deep I knew that selling WFAN was essential to save Emmis. As my friend Paul Taubman remarked, "Jeff would cut off his arm to save Emmis." Luckily, it didn't come to that; we saved the company and all my body parts were intact.

Now that our survival was assured, we set about improving our operations and were aided by a recovering economy and one very fortunate decision. As I mentioned, our two urban hit stations, Power 106, Los Angeles, and Hot 97, New York, had suffered brutal declines during the downturn, with Power dropping the most. We decided that Doyle would leave Minneapolis to run the Los Angeles station and Rick would join him to fix the programming. Doyle made major changes and the station's performance picked up markedly. Even more importantly, Rick discovered a key problem with the music. Delving into the market, he found that the audience that had formed the original coalition of Power 106 now preferred rap music over urban hits. Realizing that rap would be a radical departure from the music that had built the station, Rick spent countless hours in LA's clubs and poring over sales reports. Afterwards, he promptly began moving rap music onto the station playlist, much to the chagrin of many of our advertisers. Replacing Michael Jackson with Snoop Dog wasn't welcomed in most circles, but it was the right call. The station's ratings improved dramatically, and we created an East Coast version for Hot 97, which ironically led to the infamous West Coast-East Coast hip-hop battles for years to come. With the programming shift, Power 106 and Hot 97 became the world's leading hip-hop stations, a position they have held for most of the last thirty years.

In addition to the improved performance in New York and Los Angeles, we were able to increase profits just about everywhere else in the company. By the end of 1993, we were firing on all cylinders, our near-death experience largely in the rearview mirror. Success took much of the sting away from the Mariners debacle and so many station sales; by 1994, we were ready to embark on the next phase of Emmis's development: becoming a public company. We chose our investment bankers at Morgan Stanley to lead the IPO. By 1994, both Mel Karmazin of Infinity and Lowry Mays of Clear Channel Communications had taken their companies public, both with positive receptions. By the time we did our IPO, radio was once again considered a great business, and Wall Street had largely forgotten about the challenges of the 1991–92 recession. The country was booming again, and with it, the industry's profits. We launched our stock at $15.50 and saw it rise steadily. Such is the joy of being in a growth industry.

At this point, Emmis had survived its first major financial disaster and was on its way again. Now was the time for me to look seriously at what made us tick. To come back from the ashes in any venture, you have to have the passion and perseverance that only comes when you are fully committed. As I've often stated, adversity is the world's greatest teacher, and to understand how Emmis worked through both its first crisis and those that came after, it's important to understand the culture that allowed us to survive. Without having a firm set of individual and corporate values, I don't think it's possible to endure life's inevitable setbacks. Naturally, I bring my personal values to Emmis, but the organization's culture is based on a set of core values we do our best to follow scrupulously. They crystallized over forty years ago, in the early days of the company, when one of my managers asked, "What are the key values of Emmis?" We were at a restaurant at the time, and I took a napkin and started writing down, in a stream of consciousness, the list we now call the Eleven Commandments of Emmis:

1.   Be flexible—keep an open mind.
2.   Be rational—look at all of your options.
3.   Have fun—don't take life too seriously.

4. Never get smug—arrogance kills.
5. Don't underprice yourself or your medium—don't attack your industry, build it up.
6. Believe in yourself—if you think you can make it happen, you will.
7. Never jeopardize your integrity—we win the right way or we don't win at all.
8. Be good to your people—get them into the game and give them a piece of the pie.
9. Be passionate about what you do and compassionate about how you do it.
10. Take care of your audience and your advertisers. Think of them and you will win.

After the Mariners experience, we added an Eleventh Commandment:

11. Admit your mistakes.

I have to confess, I didn't put these commandments in order of importance, because of the whole stream of consciousness on a napkin thing, but the list was distributed company-wide as written.

That being said, maintaining integrity is absolutely our First Commandment—nothing else comes close. As I have discussed with Sammie many times on our school car rides, "If your word to others is good, nothing else really matters in life. And if your word to others is no good, nothing else really matters either." If people trust you, that's just about all you need in your relationships. If you're someone they can't trust, there's really nothing else you can do. It's shockingly simple. Do people believe you when you tell them something? When you give someone your word, do they know you will live up to it? Listen, all of us have had situations in which the circumstances change, and we make agreements we would like to get away from. At Emmis, it's happened on countless occasions. There are times when it would have been a lot more profitable to break a commitment, but I've learned that, to me, it's a lot more important to eat bad agreements than be someone who doesn't live up to his word. As I've said, I have to be able to look at myself in the mirror and like what I see, and that is more important than an occasional bad decision that ends up costing me some money.

Perhaps one of the benefits of spending my life in Indianapolis, a relatively small town, off the beaten path of America's financial centers, is that people seem to be more straightforward than those you encounter sometimes on America's coasts. Many years ago, a friend of mine summed up this outlook: "If you're a bad guy in New York or LA, it might take years to figure it out. In Indianapolis, they're going to learn it very quickly, so I think it makes people think twice about screwing others in a smaller town." I've always thought that if someone in Indianapolis gives you their word, you can take it to the bank. Of course, there are bad actors everywhere, from the smallest towns to the largest; it's just harder to hide in a small place. One lesson I've learned: If your due diligence about someone reveals that their ethics have been questionable in previous deals, don't assume they're going to change when you work with them. A friend of mine notes that "You will never do good business with bad people!" How do you figure people out? I've had a saying for years: "Scouting reports don't lie." In my industry, where most of the players know each other, if you ask ten people about someone's character, you're likely to get at least nine similar answers. Earlier in my career, I sometimes took the risk of doing a deal with a bad actor. Even when I got the deal done, it was an arduous, frustrating process. As I've gotten older, my motto has changed. Now I just say, "Life's too short to deal with bad people."

Integrity is a critical part of my leadership style, because trust is the glue that binds all of us at Emmis together. In addition, I've always believed that people need to know that you will go through more walls for them than you'll ask them to go through for you. A leader needs to be on the front lines every day. I've never believed you can build a corporate culture if you aren't fully engaged. There's an old Cadillac ad that demonstrates this commitment by showing that the boss's car is always the last one in the parking lot every night. People need to know that you're in the trenches with them. There are thousands of times I've thought about that ad when I've left the office and seen my car, alone in the parking lot. I don't know how it's possible to lead when you're out on the golf course every afternoon, or if you're taking multiple vacations. The leader sets the tone for an organization. If you demonstrate your commitment, it's easier for others to be committed as well. Of course, there's the typical Emmis anecdote that backs up what I'm saying. My late assistant, Robin Rene, who passed away several years ago, worked with me for thirty years. She was one of the most wonderful human beings I have ever known and I miss her every day. The joke around the office was, "Do you know how to make Robin the happiest woman in the world? Have her find out that Jeff is going to play golf on Friday afternoon!" It's true, being a workaholic, I'm sure I never left the office enough, and I know it had to drive Robin, and a host of others, crazy that I was always around. But at least they understood that I was leading by example.

Good leaders also value their people highly. I was never a big Woody Hayes fan, but the legendary Ohio State coach had a favorite saying: "You win with people." It's a motto I've always believed in, and therefore I'm always baffled by those who are reluctant to hire great people under them because those new staffers might make them look bad and threaten their position. This is remarkably stupid thinking. If you hire great people, they will do great things, and leadership always looks good when your people do great things. We have a management rule: "Always hire people smarter than yourself." Then, in true Emmis fashion, we added, "When dealing with Emmis management, that means the talent pool is roughly seven billion candidates!" As I've mentioned, I have a related maxim (a Smulyan original): I've never seen a human being come to work every day and try to do a lousy job. Nobody ever gets up in the morning and says, "How can I screw up my job today?" It's the job of the CEO and the rest of the leadership to inspire their employees and to give them the tools and the strategy to succeed.

One way I do that is by asking my people two important management questions. The first is: "What surprised you about this situation positively and negatively?" Surprises are what jump out at you, and to me, they are the best way to gauge any decision. In essence, you analyze the decision by pinpointing potential aberrations in the process that led to that decision. My second question is: "If you had to make a decision now and you couldn't consult with anyone else, what would you decide?" This inquiry forces people to confront the reality of a situation quickly, come to a conclusion, and then take responsibility for that decision. Again, to my earlier point, employees want to succeed; they don't want to screw up their jobs. When you give people decision-making power, they're no longer on the sidelines, just able to pontificate, but instead they have the responsibility to make the call. I've found most do focus and invariably, their judgment is very good. Of course, when you have a culture like ours, sarcastic answers will always pop up. Once I asked our CFO Walter Berger a variation of that second question, "What would you decide to do if you were me?" Without missing a beat, he replied, "Jeff, if I were you, I'd kill myself!" It was a memorable response.

Valuing people is baked into the commandments of Emmis: Be good to your people; give them a piece of the pie. The idea is that your people not only receive stock and other tangible benefits derived from the company's economic performance, but also have a "piece" of the ideas of the company. I describe this as the "twin ownership" concept: employees own both stock and the decisions of the company.

When things are most challenging, that's when leadership really matters. The number one job of a leader is to build a corporate culture that bolsters your company in adversity and ultimately leads to success. To me, that means creating an atmosphere in which people are allowed to do their work free of micromanagement and office politics. Moreover, to be effective as a leader, you need to credit your team with success when something works and take the blame on your own shoulders for failure. We added "admit your mistakes" to our commandments after baseball, but I believe we lived it long before Seattle. Show me an organization in which the CEO points fingers at others when something fails and I'll show you an organization that is doomed. It's empowering to everyone when the CEO says, "I screwed up." It gives every other employee permission to say the same about themselves. Conversely, when a CEO attempts to place the blame on others, everyone else ends up doing it, too. I've seen it happen countless times in organizations. This attitude really does start at the top. If everyone in a company is looking for others to blame, you quickly have a culture where office politics rule. Everyone is trying to climb the ladder over the mistakes of their peers. To position themselves in the best possible light, they usually try to shift blame to others. With the opposite approach, a CEO can usually generate an open, collaborative enterprise.

Not surprisingly, my favorite question for the CEOs of businesses I'm acquiring is: "What did you do when you made a mistake? How did you handle it with your people?" You'd be amazed at the number who don't think they've made any mistakes. Trust me, these people are not very self-aware and certainly can't count very well. We've also encountered what I call the Infallible Boss Syndrome. That occurs when you ask a senior executive in a company how they tell the CEO when he or she is wrong. Stunningly, several times we've gotten an answer that their CEO has never been wrong. Even more stunningly, none of these people worked for the government of North Korea, or for that matter, the Trump Organization.

I'm a lot more comfortable with our approach. When one of our people thinks I'm crazy, they simply walk into my office and tell me that I'm crazy. It gets my attention every time. However, I will tell you a story about such a situation that had a slightly different twist.

Years ago, we had a disc jockey named Star on Hot 97 in New York, and he was part of a morning show called "Star and Buc Wild." The two of them had been a management challenge and, after a difficult contract renewal, we decided to let them go across the street to our competitor's station. Star continued his feud with several of our on-air people, and one day, he decided to attack one of our disc jockeys (and her infant child) on the air. The tirade was vicious and grotesquely offensive as Star talked about sexual acts he wanted to perform not only on our personality, but also on her infant daughter. It was the evening news's leading story and graced the front page of the *New York Post* and the *Daily News*. If there ever was a career-ending event, this was it. The next morning, Rick Cummings and I were discussing the incident. Suddenly, I decided that we should have some fun. I told Rick, "Let's call David Barrett and tell him we want to rehire Star." David, a brilliant young attorney, was only a few doors down the hall, but I knew I couldn't keep a straight face if I brought him into my office, so I conferenced him in with Rick by phone. At the time, David was the newest member of our legal team, and therefore he hadn't dealt with us for too many years.

When I got him on the phone, I said, "David, have you seen the stories about Star this morning?" He replied yes, "It's just despicable conduct." I agreed, but then said, "Look, his conduct was awful, but he's the hottest thing in New York right now. We want to bring him back to Hot 97. The ratings will be sensational!" David, stunned, replied, "Are you kidding, how can we put him back on the air after what he did?" Trying to be as nonchalant as possible, we said, "Oh, there will be some controversy, but everyone will be listening." David tried his best to dissuade us, calmly giving every legal argument against the move. We batted away every one of them. Finally, after a few minutes of this exchange, he said, "Look, I have no seniority here, you guys are my bosses and you can fire me for what I'm about to say, but as your attorney, with all due respect, I feel compelled to say, are you two completely out of your minds? Am I working for two fucking morons?" We then exploded in laughter. David later told me, "I knew about the culture and how open you are, but I hadn't been here that long and I quickly calculated that it was about fifty-fifty that my response could have been a job loser."

That story may be a little extreme, but the point is, telling me the truth can never hurt you. Not telling me can kill the company. And that goes for every enterprise out there. Another way to bring down morale, and thus performance, is for a CEO (or any manager) to think they're the smartest person in the room. By the way, anybody who does, isn't. People who think this way spend most of their existence convincing everyone else that they're the smartest individual around. Lording your intelligence over others is a terrific way to get them to stop listening to you or following you. I don't know where you come from, but I've never known anyone who wants to be bullied, intimidated, or looked down upon. That arrogant behavior is guaranteed to turn people off, and it's always the hallmark of the "Smartest Person in the Room" syndrome.

In contrast, I believe the smartest individual in the room is the one who makes others feel valued, who listens to their ideas, and who considers their opinions. And it's not manipulative, because that rarely leads to a real buy-in of your position. Give your people genuine input into your decision-making, and odds are they will support whatever decision is reached, even if it's not theirs. Another advantage of not coming off as the smartest person in the room is that you may do better in negotiations. I've advised my managers to "try to make people think you're the dumbest in the room. Not only will they treat you more kindly, but they also might underestimate you, which could actually help you strike a better deal."

There you have it; that's how our leadership style has contributed to the highly engaged and collaborative culture of our company. Years ago, I was traveling with one of our younger executives. We were on our corporate jet (yes, at our most flush, we had a Gulfstream that I dubbed "heroin for a workaholic"), and we started to compare the different cultures of Emmis and his previous employer, a major company in the region. He noted that the top-down style of his former company led to a rigidly stratified culture, in which lower-level executives weren't supposed to mix with the senior people. He said it was an unwritten rule that if you were in the executive dining room for a lunch meeting, you needed to finish before the top executives came in. What a contrast to the fluid culture at Emmis! Of course, being the wiseass that I am, I immediately told him: "We have a similar rule at Emmis, if you take the last cheese Danish when you're on the Emmis plane, I will ask you to leave immediately, even if we are at forty thousand feet." That story shot through the company like wildfire, and upon boarding the plane, new riders were always told, "For God's sake, don't take the last cheese Danish."

Now, I know that every corporate culture is different, but I've always believed that the traditional, top-down, autocratic company can't possibly compete effectively in a modern, global economy. People need to be empowered, they need to be entrusted to do their jobs, and they need to be held accountable for their performance. You can't dictate your way to success, and you can't micromanage your way to success. The biggest challenge for new managers is to convince them to let their people do their jobs. When you're promoted, it's human nature to think that you can do your old job better than the person who replaced you, but if you don't empower people to do their job, it's impossible for them to succeed. It's a common trap for new managers to try to do their new job and their old job. It's a recipe for failure, but it is remarkable how often it happens.

No discussion of our culture is complete without noting that underlying everything is our ability to laugh—at ourselves, at our colleagues, at just about anybody. I used to give a speech to managers and to industry groups and I told them: "Have fun, don't take this too seriously; it's just radio, this isn't brain surgery." Then I told them that one day, I met a brain surgeon and I asked him what he said to get ready for surgery. His reply was simple: "Have fun, don't take this too seriously; this is just brain surgery, it isn't radio, we don't have to pick the right records or hire the right morning guy." That line always got a big laugh, but it's important to understand, whatever you do, approach it with joy. Now, if I ever have to have brain surgery, I hope the surgeons won't be cracking jokes as they open me up; however, I do hope they have a positive attitude when they go to work.

To put it another way, have you ever seen someone who carries the weight of the world on their shoulders, who is always depressed and radiates depression and anger to everyone around them? How effective do you think they can be at motivating others? Do you want to follow anyone into battle who has an impending sense of doom and panic? An atmosphere of enjoyment creates a culture in which everyone can relax and be free to produce their best work. We have a saying that autocrats die quickly at Emmis. We want happy, positive employees who can bring out the best in their people, and I've never seen that happen in an atmosphere of doom.

I'm very fortunate to have been raised in a household where humor was everywhere. Perhaps it's an enduring tradition of Judaism, which seems to have produced more humor per capita than just about any group. My late mother and grandmother were natural comediennes. My mother and I definitely inherited the same sense of humor, and until the day she died, we used to amuse each other daily. One of my greatest regrets is that I don't have audio of some of our conversations, because they made me laugh more than just about anything else. We both used to agree that life could throw some pretty hard things at you, and at the end of the day, sometimes all you could do is laugh. In this case, the cliché is true: laughter really is the best antidote for whatever ails you.

Along with having the ability to laugh is the ability to make fun of yourself. At work, my self-deprecation is one of my hallmarks, and I believe it puts other people at ease. Now, do I believe I'm fundamentally inferior? Of course not. I have an innate self-confidence that has served me well, but I've never needed to tell people I'm great. My late mother taught me that. When I got some award that happened to be mentioned in the newspaper, one of her closest friends called to congratulate me and to excoriate my mother for not telling her; she didn't like learning about it in the newspaper. We laughed about it at dinner, but my mother said something that has rung true to this day: "I don't need to brag about you. If you're good, there's no need to tell anyone about it. People will figure it out. If they don't figure it out, maybe you really weren't that good."

The Emmis culture is what has always gotten us through hard times, and it's been founded on getting hard-working, collaborative people and creating an atmosphere of fun and dedication. As for our commandments, they were designed forty years ago with radio in mind, but even with the changing face of our company, I'm incredibly proud that they have endured.

That list of ours has been widely disseminated outside of Emmis, and countless times, I've been asked if others can use them. I always answer in the affirmative, with a caveat. These commandments work for us because we believe in them passionately. Have we violated them over the years? Of course. I'm sure we haven't always lived up to all of them, nor have our people. However, they remain part of our core values, and we live up to them pretty well. We think about what they stand for and why they are important to us. People are always free to use them, but if our commandments don't reflect the core values of the folks who own and run the company, they will be meaningless. If you don't believe in these things, there is no chance your people will believe you. The key is to pick the principles that you believe in; they may be wildly different from mine, but if you believe in them, they will have credibility within your organization.

Top: As a child, my idol in baseball (and life) was Willie Mays. Meeting him at a Spring Training game was a thrill. Here he is pictured (far left) with Ken Griffey Sr., me, and Ken Griffey Jr. *Bottom:* This was our group that bid on the Washington Nationals franchise. Front row (from left to right): Peter Keefe, Art Monk, Jeff Smulyan, and Bob Pincus; middle row (from left to right): Max Berry, David Carmen, Dick Wiley, and Dickie Carter; back row (from left to right): Ernie Jarvis, Calvin Hill, Rodney Hunt, Charles Mann, Bill Jarvis, Eric Holder, and Dwight Bush.

The Siren Call of Sports (Ownership)

When Emmis was back on its feet, I was tempted to get into sports ownership again. We had all that knowledge from the Mariners—organization, marketing wizardry, civic savvy— that I knew we could use to build a fabulous franchise. Unfortunately, the Houston Rockets were no longer available. My pal Jerry Reinsdorf couldn't let it go: "That has to be the single stupidest business decision in recorded history!" Honestly, I think IBM turning its software business over to Microsoft was probably number one, but mine had to be in the top five, considering how the value of the Rockets has skyrocketed, while the businesses I have been involved in have gone south—actually a lot further south than Houston, Texas, now that I think about it. And for years, whenever I saw David Stern, he reminded me how well the Rockets were doing.

While I wanted to prove we could run a successful franchise, I also realized that the economics of sports were changing dramatically, and the opportunity to participate in the remarkable growth was especially enticing.

How did the value of teams grow so impossibly high in the thirty years since we owned the Mariners? When we bought the team in 1992 for $76 million, that was average for a lower-end franchise. Better franchises were valued around $10 million to $15 million more, with the largest franchises worth about $30 million more than midlevel teams. A few years ago, the cheapest Major League Baseball team, the Florida Marlins, sold for $1.2 billion, and that for a franchise that lost staggering amounts of money. Most MLB teams are now worth at least $1.5 billion—a phenomenal increase. The NBA has been on a similar trajectory. The average NBA team in 1989 was worth about $45 million. Today, it is impossible to buy one for less than $1.25 billion.

Of course, the granddaddy of them all is the National Football League (NFL). When we studied values in 1989, we determined that the average price of an NFL team was around $125 million. Today, it would be impossible to buy an NFL team for less than $2.5 billion. Obviously, if you invested your money in sports in those days, your returns would have been spectacular. There are three simple reasons for this remarkable appreciation:

1. Obscenely rich guys
2. Rich guys
3. Television

Since the 1980s, our economy has fundamentally shifted, with income being distributed to those at the top of society at the expense of everyone else. Consequently, we now have hundreds of billionaires—745 to be exact—while in 1987, we only had forty-one. And a greater percentage are worth tens of billions. When that much money chases a limited resource (like sports teams), economic rationality goes out the window. In every era, you have rich people who throw extra dollars at anything they want, and clearly sports franchises are viewed as trophy assets. I called Paul Taubman when he sold Dan Snyder the Washington Redskins (as they were then known) and their stadium in 1999 for the spectacular sum of $750 million, and Paul pointed out that Snyder had actually paid one multiple of cash flow less than I had just paid for a TV station in Orlando (ten times versus eleven times cash flow).

For many years in the sports business, there was a correlation between projected profits and purchase prices. Today, because of the proliferation of bidders, those numbers have gone out the window. Take Steve Ballmer, who paid $2 billion for the NBA's Los Angeles Clippers, a barely profitable team supposedly making less than $20 million a year. On top of that, they played in someone else's arena and were locked into bad TV contracts. Those things can be solved, but Ballmer was paying a hundred times cash flow. Now, he's done a wonderful job with the Clippers, and I'm sure the franchise is in much better shape than when Donald Sterling ran it, but Ballmer could pay whatever he wanted, because when you're worth over $50 billion, you don't have to worry about cash flow multiples. To a lesser extent, other extremely wealthy individuals have bid up the prices of sports franchises over the past twenty years, adding to the run-up in valuations.

The same phenomenon has happened in my hometown: the NBA's Indiana Pacers, valued at $240 million in 2003, are now worth over $1.5 billion. The NFL's Indianapolis Colts went from a valuation of $419 million in 2002 to $2.7 billion today; moreover, Jim Irsay, the Colts' owner, announced recently that he had rejected an offer of $3 billion. Had I bought the Houston Rockets in 1992 for $100 million, I would have a team valued at just under $2.5 billion today. Granted, the increase in sports revenue is part of the reason, but it's the out-of-sight multiples of cash flow that are driving up prices. That's what you get when you have a number of staggeringly rich people swimming in the sports ownership pool.

The second reason for the astronomical increase in franchise value is the number of rich people who attend games. When the O'Malley family owned the Los Angeles Dodgers, they took remarkable pride in holding ticket prices down. Most tickets in Dodger Stadium in that era cost between four and six dollars, and O'Malley didn't raise prices for years. Cheap pricing was the order of the day. When my friend Buzz Shafer and I walked across the USC campus to the Los Angeles Memorial Coliseum on January 15, 1967, for the very first Super Bowl (then called the NFL-AFL World Championship Game), we were thrilled to buy two six-dollar tickets for four dollars apiece on the forty-yard line (my memory may be faulty here, since research indicates the face value was ten dollars, but I am certain we paid only four dollars!). Today, the face value of a Super Bowl ticket is $3,300 and that's before resellers bid up the price!

I believe Jack Kent Cooke, who owned the NBA's Los Angeles Lakers (and later the NFL's Washington Redskins) was the first person in the United

States to apply market-based pricing to sports tickets. He kept testing demand by constantly raising prices, discovering that businesses and rich people would pay ever-increasing premiums, especially for the best seats. Sports owners everywhere followed his lead. As ticket prices kept climbing into the stratosphere (especially for the most desirable seats), middle-income attendance started to decline sharply. How many families of four can afford $200 for the cheapest seats these days? As a result, sports franchises earn most of their revenue from wealthier fans. Moreover, adding suites and higher-priced concourses has exacerbated the situation. All of us have read stories about the average fan being priced out, and it's the result of corporations and the wealthy being able to buy more and more of the tickets.

The third and most important factor in the remarkable growth of franchise values is television. The potential for greater TV revenue was the reason we purchased the Mariners, and in our wildest dreams we never envisioned just how significant TV would become to sports. That came about for a few key reasons. First, sports, not religion, is the American opiate. Millions live (and sometimes die) with the outcome of every game. As mobile sports betting becomes routine, life-and-death matters probably will transition to every single play. Second, as we've turned into a society that time shifts or binge watches our programming, sports is now practically the only category that people must consume when it occurs. I'm aware that some people record games to watch later, but they are a small minority and are viewed as outliers, generally dangerous to a free society. As traditional viewing patterns have shifted, sports has become more valuable to TV networks. It's the only programming, other than news and a very few unscripted shows, that people watch in "real time," as it is known in the TV industry. Over the years, sports has grown in relation to everything else; today, almost every program in the top twenty ratings spots is NFL programming. The runaway hit is NBC's *Sunday Night Football*. Given the number of eyeballs they attract, sports leagues, especially the NFL, have commanded astounding sums for TV rights. In 1990, the league signed a four-year deal for an average of $900 million per year. In 2019, the league divided over $8 billion in annual TV revenues. With its improved ratings, the NFL was able to up that figure to over $13 billion annually in its new contract. Currently, the NFL averages over $6 billion annually from CBS, NBC, and Fox for their prime Sunday packages, as well as $2.7 billion from ESPN for *Monday Night Football*. Add in $1 billion from Amazon for *Thursday Night Football* and $2.5 billion for the new *NFL Sunday Ticket* contract, and you can understand why the NFL stands above everything else in American television programming. And the Super Bowl, with audiences averaging over one hundred million, has at this point become almost a national holiday.

Of course, it's not just television's fervor for the NFL that has propelled sports revenues. The NBA is in the middle of a nine-year national TV deal worth $2.6 billion per year. Major League Baseball gets about $1.5 billion annually from national TV contracts with Fox, ESPN, and WTBS. However, for the MLB, the majority of its income is derived from local rights, coming through regional cable sports networks. This was the pot of gold that we hoped to find in Seattle.

How did these numbers get so high, especially from ESPN and the regional cable sports channels? The answer is: the per-subscriber fee. As cable TV evolved, sports content became its most valued inventory. With ESPN leading the way, cable and satellite companies were forced to pay ever-increasing sums to hold on to the Holy Grail that was sports in America. For years, when addressing the economics of TV, I would tell audiences: "There's an eighty-year-old grandmother in Pasadena who is paying the following figures each month in her cable bill: ten dollars for ESPN; four dollars for the Lakers; six dollars for the Dodgers; four dollars for the Angels; one dollar for the PAC-12; plus a few other sports surcharges. Not only doesn't she watch any of it, she doesn't realize the Dodgers left Brooklyn!" The great bonanza for sports was that every cable subscriber paid for every sport whether they watched or not. In other words, non–sports fans have been subsidizing the most expensive programming in the cable universe and the winners have been everyone in sports. Today's concern is that this subscriber fee bubble will burst. Seven years ago, ESPN had over 105 million subscribers, but it's now down to 76 million; with the pandemic, people in sports believe that decline will accelerate to warp speed. When people abandon cable TV for Netflix or Amazon Prime or any other over-the-top (OTT) streaming services, owners, players, and everyone else in sports weeps a little bit.

However, until now, the economic return for sports has been on a remarkable upward trajectory. For that reason—as well as wanting to prove we could operate a successful franchise—I was intent on owning another team. Our first opportunity came courtesy of Cincinnati Reds' infamous owner, Marge Schott. She was a loose cannon, and when she opened her mouth, you steeled yourself for some racist remark or a mash-up of the facts. Baseball was in mortal terror when Marge took to a microphone on the field at the 1990 World Series during the first Gulf War. Their worst fears were realized when Marge offered a tribute to "our servicemen fighting in the Middle West." I turned to Gary and said, "Boy, if Saddam Hussein has gotten to Cleveland, we're all screwed." A few years later, Marge was suspended for uttering racist remarks. A Cincinnati reporter called Gary because he had heard that Bud Selig or someone high up in Major League Baseball wanted Gary to take charge of the Reds during Marge's suspension. Gary, in his usual dry manner, told the reporter that even if the rumor were true, he wasn't interested in the job: "The town is too small, the team is lousy, and the owner is stark raving crazy. I've already had that job in Seattle." While he admitted he hadn't actually said that, I thought it was one of his better lines.

Ultimately, the MLB couldn't deal with Marge any longer and forced her to sell the Reds. I would have been a contender, but I decided that if I got back into the game, I wasn't going to do it in a small market where revenues always pale beside those of bigger markets. Given the explosion in values to come, it was probably an unwise decision, but then again, hindsight is 20/20.

We had several other opportunities to get back into the game shortly after we sold the Mariners, but those proved fleeting. Then we were offered the makings of something big. It started with a phone call to my friend Bill Schweitzer, then the American League general counsel, who also directed baseball's lobbying efforts in Washington. I had seen in the papers that the NFL's Minnesota Vikings were for sale, with a bidding process set for a few weeks later. I told Bill that baseball's Carl Pohlad (owner of the Minnesota Twins) should buy the Vikings, because it would go a long way toward solving his stadium issues.

Carl Pohlad was a remarkable success story, building an empire in banking, real estate, and just about everything else in the Twin Cities. He stepped in to buy the Twins when the city was faced with losing them to Tampa. It was a wonderful civic venture, because Carl was never enamored with the economics of baseball, especially those in Minneapolis. Carl and I grew close when we became the two leading proponents of revenue sharing, an idea that was embraced by most baseball clubs but made me persona non grata with the largest teams, especially the Yankees and the Dodgers. Initially Yankees owner George Steinbrenner was one of my biggest boosters when we bought the Mariners. In our first month, he put his arm around me and said, "Jeff, we need to get you out of that goddamned Seattle and get you to Tampa." It was my first inkling that baseball's love affair with Seattle was clearly on life support. After I led the revenue sharing charge, George was less than thrilled. In fact, several years after we exited baseball, I went to Bud Selig's sixtieth birthday party in Milwaukee. George was effusive when he saw me, but Jerry Reinsdorf pulled my date aside and said, "See the guy Jeff is talking to, see how happy he is to see Jeff? Well, if he were armed, he would probably shoot Jeff in front of all these people."

My idea for revenue sharing was simple. Roughly eight teams had a much higher value than everyone else: the Yankees, Mets, Red Sox, Cubs, Phillies, Braves, Dodgers, and Angels. By properly valuing each team and paying them for their excess valuation vis-à-vis everyone else, we could equalize every club's value. I thought we could raise the funds to pay out the higher value teams by tapping into Japan's fervor for baseball. At that time, Japan was experiencing an economic renaissance and had more baseball fervor than anyone and money to burn. I envisioned putting on a global World Series, in which the US World Series champion (or an all-star team) would play Japan's greatest players in a best-of-seven series. I sensed that we could fund much of the payout just from the healthy pay-per-view market in Asia; after all, in those days, even Steinbrenner's Yankees were only worth about $350 million, and the values of the seven other teams descended from there. I even had plans for getting the players union on board. The beauty of this idea was that by equalizing the teams' values, we could justify sharing all revenue—from TV, stadium receipts, and regional sports network deals—equally, thus replicating the NFL's wildly successful TV model. In the NFL, Green Bay grosses nearly as much as New York, because each team shares the $13 billion in annual TV revenues equally. That distribution leads to a much more competitive balance, and there's one further benefit. Baseball's weakness is that in labor disputes, its teams are not on the same page. The

Yankees or the Dodgers will settle almost any labor dispute at almost any price because their franchises are very profitable. However, the Kansas City Royals, or the Mariners, or many smaller market teams, know that the deal the big guys are willing to strike will probably guarantee that their franchises will lose money. The players union is fully aware of the split and is adept at getting owners to break ranks, making MLB's union dramatically stronger than the NFL's union.

Several people loved the idea, but naturally, as with many of my "big ideas," it went nowhere. Several years after I was gone, somebody floated a variation of the idea in a baseball meeting and George Steinbrenner thought it was brilliant. When he was discussing it with Reinsdorf, Jerry pointed out: "When Jeff introduced that idea a few years ago, you wanted to kill him." Baseball ultimately achieved a limited form of revenue sharing a few years later, when it became obvious that otherwise many small teams would go out of business.

When Carl Pohlad and I first discussed the revenue sharing idea, we joked: "The Yankees get $50 million a year for their TV rights. We get almost nothing. How about when they come to Minneapolis or Seattle, we just turn off their cameras!" It didn't happen during my tenure, but finally the small teams got their due by threatening similar actions.

Carl Pohlad's problem in Minneapolis was familiar to me. The city, like Seattle, had a long, proud tradition of Scandinavian populism, which in many respects had expanded to the Pacific Northwest. The public and their elected officials had a genuine mistrust of big business and always resisted any attempts to pursue a public-private partnership with sports franchises. Unfortunately, public financing is critical in smaller metropolitan areas. Now, I've been on the other side of this debate for many years because I'm active in Indianapolis civic affairs; I understand and fully appreciate the argument that something is wrong if the average taxpayer has to subsidize (usually through stadium construction) wealthy team owners. If you don't understand the reluctance, you haven't seen the quality of urban school districts or decaying urban infrastructure. Nevertheless, if one community doesn't support major league sports, another one always will, and therein lies the dilemma. While I respect the vigorous debates about the economic impact of sports franchises, the loss of a team, especially in a smaller community, can be devastating, not only for economic development, but also for the city's psyche.

Carl, who had led the Twins to their only world championships in 1987 and 1991 (with a bit of help from Kirby Puckett, Scott Erickson, Jack Morris, Kent Hrbek, and others), was vilified for claiming he was losing money on the Twins, and thus he was considering selling the team, most likely to out-of-state buyers. Carl didn't want the team to leave, but it was clear that no one in Minneapolis-St. Paul would step up to buy the Twins, so everyone assumed—as was the case with me in Seattle—that the team was headed out of town.

My idea was that if Carl owned both the Vikings and the Twins, he would have enough negotiating leverage with the city and the state to solve the stadium problem in Minneapolis. Both the Vikings and the Twins played in the Metrodome, a domed stadium similar to Seattle's Kingdome, but dramatically better because at least it had a translucent fiber roof, which let light in. Still, the Metrodome was an awful place to play baseball, and it wasn't much better for football. Clearly, both teams would have to upgrade or build a new stadium if they were to remain competitive. Of course, with football and baseball's differing economics, the Vikings were more likely to succeed than the Twins. I explained to Bill Schweitzer that if Carl owned the Vikings as well as the Twins, he could bring city and state leaders together to craft a plan to sort out the Metrodome's problems. I thought there was a strong likelihood they would find a long-term solution.

Bill loved the idea and called Bud Selig, who by then was baseball's commissioner. Bud called Carl, and an hour later, Carl called me and said, "Jeff, if you will do this, take charge of it, I'll do it. I don't care how much of it you want to own, but you'll have to put it together." Like David Stern's proposal on the Rockets, the offer was incredibly gracious, but this time was different from 1992, when Emmis was struggling. This was 1998, and the company was once again hitting on all cylinders. I loved the idea and I called Gary, and we immediately dug into the process of preparing a bid. Then, after a few days of working on it, we realized that the bids were due two weeks later, when both of us were taking our families on long-planned vacations. I was taking my kids and my sister and her family to Israel, Hungary, and London. The trip to Israel was special, because my family was seeing the country for the first time, and the Israeli government was rolling out the red carpet (I'll discuss why later). Gary had his own family vacation scheduled as well, and after we contemplated all that we had to do to put in a rational, yet winning, bid, we decided we should just pass on buying the Vikings. Carl had said he wouldn't pursue the purchase if we weren't going to put it together. Ultimately, both Gary and I picked our families over business. That's a sign of maturity, right?

In retrospect, that was the biggest mistake of my career. With Carl, we would have put together a terrific bid, and, because we saw the value of increased leverage in stadium negotiations, we probably would have out-distanced the other bidders who did not share that incentive. Certainly, there's no guarantee we would have won: Red McCombs of Clear Channel Communications was always a formidable bidder (he ultimately prevailed), and Glen Taylor, the Timberwolves owner, was also well qualified to run the team. Still, we should have moved our vacations and vigorously entered the bidding process. The main reason I regret losing the Vikings, despite my lifelong love for baseball, is that I missed out on the superlative economics of the NFL. I may be a gigantic sports fan, and live and die with my Trojans, Colts, and Pacers, but when it comes to business, I try to focus strictly on the numbers. And that is painful, because, while nothing is certain in this life except death and taxes, I would add to the list the ever-increasing amounts of money you earn by owning an NFL team. Unlike other sports, which have to worry about the significant consequences of cord-cutting and the rise of OTT TV services, the NFL is largely immune. Most of football's TV revenues come from the broadcast networks, which will almost certainly be distributed to everyone, either through cable or home antennas. Because the NFL has significant value compared to any other programming, its rights fees will likely increase in almost any environment. As an example of how life has changed in the past thirty years, back in the early 1990s, the NFL would never air *Monday Night Football* against the World Series, because baseball would have dominated the ratings. Today, any old regular-season NFL game, competing head-to-head with a World Series game, will attract several million more viewers than baseball's premiere event. Simply stated, it's the NFL's world, and we're all living in it.

When I started my career, in a world of three or four local channels, I used to joke that a CBS-TV affiliate was the best business to own. "All you have to do is remember to turn on the network feed and you'll make ridiculous amounts of money." Later, when we were struggling in Seattle, I bemoaned our fate compared to the Dodgers. "If Peter O'Malley can just remember to turn the lights on at Dodger Stadium most nights, his franchise will make a fortune!" It was reminiscent of what Buzzy Bavasi, a former Dodgers executive, noted when he was running the San Diego Padres. When asked about the comparative challenges of running the Dodgers as opposed to the Padres, Bavasi said, "There are enough people in Los Angeles who accidentally get off the freeway at Dodger Stadium for the Dodgers to make a profit." However, these days, a CBS affiliate isn't the gold mine it used to be (I know, I've owned a lot of them) and neither are the Dodgers. Today the NFL is America's gold mine.

I've always said, if you can have even a little leverage in a negotiation, it's a nice spot to be in. The NFL has leverage in EVERY negotiation—with the TV networks, the advertisers, the local communities, and even the federal government. And when it comes to the players union, believe me, the league has leverage there, too. One example is my favorite. I was part of the bid committee when Indianapolis was selected to host the Super Bowl in 2012. As usual, the city did a remarkable job; our organization and volunteers blew the league away. As with our hosting of college basketball's NCAA Final Four, visitors came away marveling at the experience that Indianapolis provides. It's one of the things I'm most proud of about my hometown. To this day, the Indianapolis Super Bowl is considered the gold standard of the event. Even though most people assumed a small northern city was only going to get one Super Bowl (the unwritten league policy was that if you build a new stadium, you're likely to get a Super Bowl), Indianapolis's performance was so stellar, league officials encouraged us to bid again.

So, there we were, bidding on the 2018 Super Bowl in 2014, a mere two years after our successful 2012 event. Competing against New Orleans, a perennial Super Bowl host, and Minneapolis, which had its own magnificent new stadium coming on line for the 2017 season, we knew we were a decided long shot. (By 2014, both the Twins and the Vikings had solved their stadium problems that we discussed in 1998.) However, given the rave reviews of our game, we dug into the work. One of the most interesting features of the bid package is that you have to guarantee all of the city's hotel rooms not only for the game weekend, but also for the next two weekends after that, in case of a problem with the game. As you can imagine, this is a challenge for hotels, because if your city is selected, they can't book any rooms until the game is played on the target date. Minneapolis complained about the process after learning that NBC, which would air the game, was also broadcasting the 2018 Winter Olympics, scheduled to start on February 5, the day after the Super Bowl, and end on February 18. NBC had told the NFL that the Super Bowl could not be played on February 11 or February 18 because of Olympic conflicts; therefore, holding those dates open as a contingency was meaningless. When the Minneapolis group went back to the NFL expecting to be able to free up the hotel rooms on the eleventh and the eighteenth, the NFL said no, you must still hold open those dates. Now that is the hubris and chutzpah that comes from unlimited leverage. The NFL wanted hotel rooms blocked for contingency dates, but NBC said those dates were absolutely not available to the NFL. The NFL replied: We don't care, hold the rooms anyway. Folks, this is why the NFL is your best economic bet. I know people are concerned about concussions. I'm also aware that some believe that the next generation will write off all professional sports in favor of e-sports. Regardless, if you're betting on anything for the next ten years, bet on the success of the NFL. It's why I regret not postponing my vacation, and it's why, in a lifetime of few regrets, this one sticks out.

It wasn't until 2003 that we found another intriguing opportunity: Rupert Murdoch's News Corp had decided to sell the Los Angeles Dodgers. Obviously, when you have seen baseball from its basement, the prospects of seeing the game from the penthouse is attractive. News Corp had owned the team for six years, and the experience had been an artistic and financial disappointment. News Corp, adept at just about everything, was a remote and unsuccessful owner and by the time they put the team up for sale, everyone in the organization was ready to get out of baseball. We had the advantage of good relationships with just about everyone in senior management. Rupert Murdoch had a great fondness for Greg Nathanson, who had run Fox's entertainment group and its TV stations group. Peter Chernin, then chief operating officer of the company, had actually worked for Nathanson at Showtime, and they were good friends. Mitch Stern, president of the Fox

Television Stations, viewed Greg as his mentor. Tony Vinciquerra, then second in command to Chernin, had started his career years ago with Randy Bongarten in Albany, New York, and they had remained close friends. In addition, we had purchased our first TV stations from the ill-fated SF Broadcasting LLC, the partnership between Murdoch and Barry Diller. During the negotiations, I had gotten to know Murdoch's right hand, Chase Carey, very well. In addition, as I was working on our wireless TV initiative and other industry issues, I had spent a lot of time with Tony, Peter, and Mitch.

We had something else going for us as well. Although it had been over a decade since we sold the Mariners, many friends in the game were interested in our return, and a number of baseball executives strongly suggested we take a serious look at the Dodgers. We were appealing because we always believed strongly in the game as a whole, not just in our own interests. While this approach sometimes cost me money over the years, I'm convinced that if you care about your industry, you'll ultimately help yourself (Emmis's Fifth Commandment). Bud Selig also believed you had to care about the "good of the game." It was the reason his tenure as commissioner was so successful, despite the dark clouds that always come up in baseball. All the other owners trusted Bud, knowing that he cared about everyone's well-being. Bud and I talked at length about this; he revered John Fetzer, the late owner of the Tigers, because "John always cared about the game, and he sometimes put it above his own immediate interests." I told Bud that those values were ingrained in many of the great broadcasters I had known. While Fetzer was already getting out of broadcasting when I was starting, I knew that he had an unyielding passion for the communities he served, like so many of the pioneers of the industry that I have known. Well earned or not, most felt that we possessed those characteristics, in spite of our challenged tenure in Seattle. In addition, by 2003, our successful track record in business was extremely well known—and several of our friends thought we would be ideal stewards for a marquee team like the Dodgers. It was all very flattering, and it certainly gave us an advantage in any bidding process. Baseball doesn't have to take the highest bidder, and sometimes, the league even sets prices at a certain level that they know most bidders will meet. In that case, MLB can pick someone they want to own the team. This was the situation with Fox's sale of the Dodgers. The price was set at $350 million.

Looking at the financials, we could see that the Dodgers were definitely a fixer-upper. Hard to believe, but the team was losing almost $50 million a year. I remember commenting, "Anyone who can lose that much money running the Dodgers has to win the Nobel Prize in economics, because they have clearly invented a new economic theory." The losses were daunting, but we were certain we could turn the franchise around in short order. Poring over the books, we found areas we could change to improve both the experience on the field and, as important, the economic performance of the team.

Peter Chernin oversaw the Dodgers, and although it was way down on the list of businesses he was responsible for, the team was the one that gave him the most headaches. In one meeting he said to me, "I absolutely despise being involved in this thing. I wake up in the morning and see that I'm being called a moron in the sports pages every day. I hate it." Recalling my last six months in Seattle, I offered only a bit of comfort: "Peter, it could be worse. In Seattle they used to call me a moron every day on the FRONT PAGE."

We were eager to take on the project but decided that, as a public company, buying a baseball team losing $50 million a year would absolutely tank our stock. Just the news that we were looking at the team caused several analysts to question our sanity. Ultimately, we came up with an elegant solution. If we packaged the Dodgers with seven of Fox's smaller TV stations, it would provide cover for the Dodger deal and excite the markets with our renewed growth in television, since Emmis was becoming a major TV operator. News Corp would be selling their non-core assets, or television stations in markets below the top fifteen: in our case, markets like Memphis, Birmingham, Kansas City, St. Louis, Greensboro, Salt Lake, and Cleveland.

The joint acquisition would be slightly over $1 billion, and we determined that it would be easy to fit within our capital structure. We also thought that while it wouldn't necessarily help our stock, it wouldn't greatly harm it either. Knowing that we were likely to eliminate most, if not all, of the baseball losses meant that our aggregate cash flow would be enhanced quickly if we did the deal. We loved the Fox TV stations, and based on our experience with the SF Broadcasting LLC, we felt that with some care and feeding they could be improved as well. Because they were at the bottom of the Fox food chain, these stations would never get the attention that Fox stations in New York, Los Angeles, or Chicago commanded; however, they would be our top priority.

We floated the plan by the senior leadership at News Corp and everyone liked the idea. The Fox executives were also aware that several of the potential bidders did not have the enthusiastic support of Major League Baseball, and they were comfortable that wasn't an issue with us. But, just as the process was moving forward, it hit a major snag. Mitch Stern and Lachlan Murdoch (Rupert's elder son) voiced strong opposition to the deal. I was stunned. Mitch and I had discussed the deal a number of times, but something had given him cold feet. It was clear to us that without the stations, it was impossible for us to buy the Dodgers. I attempted repeatedly to convince Mitch that the stations were unimportant to Fox—a point he had agreed with earlier. It was to no avail. Toward the end of the process, I learned that Lachlan had decided that he didn't want to part with any of his fiefdom. Ironically, I understood that many people at News Corp, apparently even Rupert Murdoch, were in favor of selling the TV stations as part of the package. Tremendously disappointed, we dropped out of the bidding.

Right before the contract to sell the Dodgers to Frank McCourt was announced, Tony Vinciquerra called me and asked if I would reconsider. Knowing that News Corp was on the verge of announcing the McCourt deal, I asked Tony why he was asking, since he already had a buyer. He explained that they didn't love the terms of the McCourt purchase. When I learned what they were, I understood why. McCourt basically pledged his ownership of valuable land in South Boston that was supposedly worth $400 million in exchange for ownership of the Dodgers. I'm pretty certain that he put little, if any, money into the deal. Years later, News Corp sold the land in South Boston for considerably less than the $400 million. McCourt's ownership of the Dodgers became a disaster. Although he turned the finances around, his messy divorce and lavish spending contributed to bankrupting the franchise, and Major League Baseball became embroiled in multiple lawsuits with McCourt. Nevertheless, he was able to sell the franchise for $2.1 billion and still keep ownership of half of Dodger Stadium's massive parking lots. It was a significant win for McCourt and a loss for everyone else involved.

A few years later, I learned why Rupert Murdoch did not overrule Lachlan and Mitch Stern. Supposedly, our deal was happening at the same time that he changed his will to include his youngest children with his third wife, Wendi, and the provision caused a major rift with Murdoch's older children, especially Lachlan. I was told that Rupert decided that angering Lachlan at that time was the last thing he wanted to do. As usual, our timing was impeccably awful: Lachlan left the company a short time later to return to Australia, and a few years after that, News Corp sold those seven TV stations. Such is life.

Eighteen months after pursuing the Dodgers, we started thinking about baseball again. The MLB was about to auction off the Washington Nationals, baseball's reincarnation of the Montreal Expos, and as I studied the market, I concluded that, despite baseball's sad history in DC, owning the Nationals would be a terrific idea. In the decades since the Washington Senators had left town, the character of the nation's capital had changed dramatically. The population of the metropolitan area exploded, and with it, remarkable economic growth in diverse fields. In addition, the rise of the lobbying industry meant that just about every major American corporation needed a presence in DC. Given that, we knew that the ability to entertain political figures and regulators at a night at the ballpark would be a significant opportunity for the Nationals' new owners. Unfortunately, it didn't look like that would be us, because at the time (the summer of 2005), we were bidding for the ABC radio station group. Its owner, the Walt Disney Company, had reached the conclusion that continuing to own radio made no sense. They had seen the spectacular run up in asset values in the late 1990s and had also watched the industry slowly decline after 2001. I'm certain that their financial wizards had discovered the elusive metrics that somehow indicated that radio had seen its last significant growth spurt. Besides, radio was a very small part of the Disney empire.

Within the radio industry, however, the ABC assets were a significant prize. Comprised of stations in every major market, the sale attracted every significant radio company still standing, with the exception of CBS and Clear Channel, who were precluded because they both already owned the maximum number of stations in the largest cities. For everyone left, it was a feeding frenzy; the winner would become radio's third largest company.

In spite of our skepticism about the high valuation of the stations, we, too, entered the fray. Jill Greenthal and Credit Suisse couldn't represent us, so Drew Marcus of Deutsche Bank and Stan Shuman of Allen & Co. were our investment bankers. As usual, the bidding was spirited and, as usual, our early bids were underwhelming to Disney; we exited the process at an early stage. Citadel Broadcasting, led by Farid Suleman, won the bidding war in a drawn-out battle with Entercom and emerged as radio's third largest company. That victory must have been bittersweet when Citadel filed for bankruptcy in 2009 as the economy slid into recession. After the company emerged from bankruptcy, it was acquired by Lew Dickey's Cumulus Media. A scant six years later, the pattern repeated itself: Cumulus filed for bankruptcy. In 2020, at the height of the pandemic, Cumulus, having emerged from bankruptcy, was trying to avoid the same fate for a second time. Hopefully it doesn't happen, but if it does, the same Disney assets will have been the key component of three bankruptcies!

When we exited the ABC bidding process, we immediately informed our friends in baseball that we were ready to pursue the Nationals seriously. We were greeted with a very warm response, and it was clear that we were the early favorites to win. As with the Dodgers' sale, baseball was going to set a fixed price for the team and then would pick the winner from those who met the price. I learned later from a close friend in the game that MLB had even delayed the auction until we let them know we were going to be involved. It was an incredibly gratifying feeling, and one that gave us confidence that we could put together a winning bid.

As one friend in baseball told me: "We think you will be the perfect antithesis of Dan Snyder [the owner of the then Washington Redskins], and that's exactly what we need." Now as you read this book, you'll probably conclude that statement was correct. Snyder is smart and rich; I'm dumb and poor; we are indeed polar opposites. Nevertheless, Snyder's tenure has been marked by controversy since the day he bought the team (now known as the Washington Commanders). His mercurial personality has been a lightning rod for criticism throughout the region. One newspaper headline summarized the situation: "You think your team owner is bad. Dan Snyder is worse." The Snyder years in DC have been marked by bad performance on the field, controversies everywhere, and fans who now come to the game with signs that say "Sell the team." Clearly, people thought our style would be a great contrast to Snyder, and I certainly agreed.

Baseball saw an opportunity to capture the hearts and minds of our nation's capital, a place that had been held for generations by the once-revered NFL team. In the pre-Snyder era, the joke was that you had to be the most beloved heir in the family to get Redskins tickets in your parents' will. In the era when Jack Kent Cooke owned the team, they clearly owned the town. Their popularity grew even greater throughout the region when the Colts left Baltimore for Indianapolis in 1984. (By the way, as a matter of historical perspective, most reports say that the Colts stole away from Baltimore in the middle of the night. Even today, you see pictures of the team sneaking away through the snow in Mayflower moving vans. That may be the view in the rest of the country, but here in Indiana, we insist that the Colts were liberated from Baltimore!) The opportunity for the Redskins to be the only NFL team for both DC and Baltimore ended in 1996 when Art Modell moved his Cleveland Browns to town and they became the Baltimore Ravens.

While investigating the Nationals further for a bid, I got a call from Steve Goldsmith, a close friend and a former mayor of Indianapolis who had also served with me on the Finish Line board. I had worked with him in 1998 when we built our downtown headquarters on Monument Circle, and besides spending countless hours together on Finish Line matters, he and I had evaluated the economics involving both the Colts and the Pacers. Steve, who later became Michael Bloomberg's deputy mayor in New York, has also held an endowed chair at Harvard Kennedy School of Government for many years. He has become known as America's leading expert on municipal finance and efficiency, and he has always been considered one of the Republican Party's thought leaders. Once, when we shared a dais at an event at our synagogue, he joked, "Jeff and I have been friends for many years, yet he has never once donated to any of my political campaigns, and I'll bet he's never even voted for me!" As a lifelong Democrat, I can confirm his first statement and refuse to answer the second.

One of Steve's great strengths, which could also be considered a weakness, is that he can never turn down a request to help a friend. The Democratic mayor of DC, Tony Williams, had asked Steve to evaluate the new stadium district and give him advice on how it should be developed. Steve called one day and said, "I just read in the paper that you're interested in the Nationals. I'm helping the mayor figure out what to do with the area around the stadium. We should talk." We spent several months discussing the project when I finally asked, "Steve, you're really putting in a lot of time on this, how much is DC paying you?" He answered, "Nothing, I'm just trying to help Tony." In all of my life, I've never known anyone who did more pro bono work than I have, but unlike me, Steve gives advice that usually leads to great results. As we studied the Anacostia Waterfront Initiative, I realized that the area around the new stadium could become one of the great urban renewal efforts in the United States. It was slightly more than a mile from Capitol Hill and was bounded by the Anacostia River. The more Steve and I discussed the site, the more excited I became about the atmosphere that we could create in the area around the ballpark.

In fact, everything about the Nationals' purchase seemed to create a great opportunity for us as we analyzed every part of the franchise. Unfortunately, our major competition was headed by Fred Malek and Jeff Zients, who had assembled a blue-ribbon group that included Vernon Jordan, Colin Powell, prominent DC attorney Steve Porter, former Clinton appointee Frank Raines, and cofounder of AOL Jim Kimsey. They had been endorsed by Mayor Williams and seemed comfortable in the knowledge that they were likely to own the team. Malek had been an investor in George W. Bush's Texas Rangers and was a long-term leader in the Republican Party as well. Zients later became Barack Obama's chief economic adviser and made a fortune in a number of other ventures. With Powell and Jordan, they had two of America's most successful Black leaders, so it was understandable why everyone thought they were the frontrunners.

However, it apparently came as a big surprise to them that they weren't the front-runners in MLB's eyes. A friend in baseball gave me a heads-up: "The Malek group thought they were a lock to win the team, and then they got word that, in fact, baseball wants Smulyan, and he's the lock to own the Nationals. They've decided that to win, they're going to have to disqualify you, so get ready for an onslaught." I soon learned that the group had close ties to Thomas Boswell, the well-respected sports columnist who was a leading authority on baseball. Another call informed me that Boswell was about to launch the campaign with a hatchet job on me, and a mutual friend set up a call with him to see if I could allay the damage. Tom Boswell and I had a very enjoyable conversation, touching on what I knew would be the two main arguments against me: (1) I was a carpetbagger, living in Indianapolis, and (2) I hadn't exactly succeeded in Seattle. I thought I had mitigated the damage and told two friends in baseball that it might turn out better than expected. Because of my legendary perception, I was dead wrong. Boswell wrote that I was indeed a carpetbagger and a lousy former owner at that. It was a stinging indictment by someone who was certainly beloved in DC and who was widely read in the *Washington Post*. Several friends consoled me and noted that the column had probably been written well before our conversation. In retrospect, I hope that was the case; if not, I certainly didn't acquit myself well in our conversation.

From there, the big guns were arrayed against me. I went to George Michael's studio at WRC, Channel 4, to be interviewed for his nightly sports segment. I had known George and his weekend segment, *The George Michael Sports Machine*—it had even aired on several of our TV stations. The interview went well, and I turned on the news that night to see how it came out. After the interview, George turned back to Jim Vance, the longtime anchorman for Channel 4, and I was stunned to hear Vance announce, "That guy's a carpetbagger, we don't need him owning our baseball team!" Michael sheepishly smiled and Vance was on to other news. Now, I've certainly been panned in newspapers and have endured some tough interviews, but to see the anchorman attack you on the eleven o'clock news was a painful rarity.

The next day, I called George Michael, who apologized profusely for the incident, but it was clear that the carpetbagger label was going to stick unless I surrounded myself with some strong local partners. My friend Art Kellar, who had sold EZ Communications a few years earlier, had called me when he first heard I was interested in the Nationals and offered to invest whatever I wanted. We quickly went to work to bring in others and assembled our own all-star, all-Washington, local group. Others we added were: close friend Alfred Liggins, CEO of Radio One, the nation's largest Black media company; my attorney, Dick Wiley, founder of a leading DC law firm and a former FCC Chairman; Max Berry, a prominent investor and attorney; Calvin Hill, the former Dallas Cowboy and his wife, Janet; former Washington

Redskins player, Art Monk; and Eric Holder, another prominent attorney and former judge.

It was clear that we had to go immediately on the offensive. For two months, we talked to anyone in DC who would meet with us: city council members, the mayor, members of Congress; we also did countless media interviews. I developed a close relationship with Tom Heath, who was covering the Nationals story for the *Washington Post*, and we would discuss endlessly the various nuances of the bidding process. Max, Alfred, Eric, and I had a long meeting with the entire *Washington Post* editorial board, and I had a separate meeting with publisher Don Graham. Our goal was to demonstrate that we would be great stewards of Washington's baseball team. We unveiled a creative idea to engage the children in the Anacostia district, adjacent to the new stadium, with a plan to tie free tickets to each game with academic success in the economically challenged area.

Our group developed a remarkable camaraderie as we pursued our mission to make the Nationals more than just a winning baseball team, but an organization that was going to make a difference in the community. We came up with an entire plan that would bridge the gap between the inner-city neighborhood and the gentrification that was about to develop on the other side of the stadium. Eric and Max became more and more involved, and as they did, I began to appreciate the skills each brought to the table. All of us were becoming partners in this mission, not only to win the Nationals but to make a corner of DC something unique. Gary Kaseff, who had told me at the outset that he wouldn't move across the country to run the team, was surprised several months later when I told him I had found the perfect team president, Eric Holder. I realized that we could put the operational plan together quickly, and that Eric would be the ideal guy to implement it. Eric was brilliant, likable, and had an engaging way with everyone he met, and it would be fun to work with him every day. We didn't have the same chemistry that Gary and I had developed over thirty-five years, but it was clearly going to be a terrific partnership. I relied on Max Berry's innate ability to assess DC politics, and the three of us spent countless hours together working on our plans.

After a few months, we had repaired much of the damage of the original campaign against us, and we all thought we had reversed the notion that I was a carpetbagger who should be disqualified. Our sources in baseball let us know that they were impressed with the work we had done, and Steve Goldsmith relayed a message from the mayor that even though he was backing the Malek/Zients group, he thought we had a terrific plan for the Nationals and DC. In addition, something happened to buoy our spirits. It became well known in baseball that the Malek/Zients group was suspected of being behind the attacks on not only me, but other groups as well. To this day, I have no idea if they really were, but certainly the attack on me was well thought out and effectively organized. Several sources let me know that Bud Selig was convinced that the Malek/Zients group had launched the negative campaigns and he was furious. I've never discussed the incident with Bud, but my guess is that their behavior encouraged him to disqualify them. If they were innocent, they were about to be executed for the crime anyway.

As we got closer to the selection, I was encouraged by reports that we had regained our status as frontrunners. While a number of other groups were contenders, most were considered long shots. Bud summoned Max, Eric, Alfred Liggins, and me to meet with him in Milwaukee. We had a very productive meeting with Bud, discussing every element of the project. Afterward, we all felt really good—except for Max. "Jeff," Max stated, "I don't think we're going to get this team." The rest of us were stunned but he continued, "Look, it's obvious Bud has tremendous affection for you, and it's clear that he was very interested in getting you into this. But I noticed something. He never looked you in the eye all night. Not once, and that told me all I needed to know. When you think you're going to hurt a friend, you can't bear to look at them. That's what I saw tonight."

Max Berry is a very wise man, and he had understood Bud better than anyone else, including Bud's best friends in baseball. Bud had decided not to pick the Malek/Zients group, but selecting me was still going to leave the carpetbagger issue alive. He had another alternative. Ted Lerner, the multimillionaire real estate magnate, had met with Bud several times; unbeknownst to anyone else, he had convinced Selig that he was the safest choice. Ted didn't need any partners, he was from DC, and he promised Bud that he would bring in someone of Bud's choosing to run the team. While most sports leagues have had challenges with owners from the real estate industry, Lerner was able to convince Bud that he was the ideal candidate. I suspected that Bud had one more reason for disqualifying us. He had been very open about his interest in getting us back into the game, and since there were always going to be other opportunities, I'm sure he just figured that he would send the next franchise opportunity in our direction.

A few weeks after our meeting in Milwaukee, one of my closest friends in the game was still confident that, at the end of the day, Bud would select our group. Since Max's observation was the outlier at the time, I was hopeful that we would prevail. Those hopes were dashed when, shortly before the decision was to be announced, that same friend called and said, "I can't believe it, Bud's really going to pick Ted Lerner, I just can't believe it."

So, Ted Lerner and his family won the Nationals, and they brought in Stan Kasten to run the team. We were deeply disappointed, but the Lerners have been good stewards of the franchise and it has been a terrific success in the community. Do I believe we would have been more innovative and had more impact on the lives of kids in DC? You bet I do, but sometimes that's the way things work out. Besides, Eric Holder, who was not running the Washington Nationals, was free to become an excellent attorney general of the United States.

Top: Meeting with Bill Clinton after being appointed a US Ambassador.
Bottom: Shaking hands with the Israeli and Palestinian ambassadors after we had reached an agreement.

7

The Inquisitive Ambassador

Back in August 1991, I was knee-deep in Mariners business when a friend asked me to meet with Bill Clinton, who was in Seattle for the National Governors Association. I knew that Clinton was planning to run for president and looking for early supporters, but at the time he was largely unknown—the definition of a long shot. Nevertheless, I was delighted by the opportunity. I've been a Democrat my entire life and come from a long line of Democrats. I still remember my grandfather telling me: "When I was a young man, I had to become a Democrat, because in Indiana in the 1920s, the Ku Klux Klan controlled the Republican Party." I'm also an outspoken Democrat. Once, during an interview about the success of Emmis, I was asked, "Why are you still a Democrat? With the money you've made, you should be a Republican." Instantly, I responded, "I'm not, because I'd rather teach economics to Democrats than compassion to Republicans." Another time, during a speech, I was asked about the rising number of Jewish Republicans. I answered off the cuff: "A Jewish Republican is someone who will trade six thousand years of values for a saving of 4 percent on his taxes." Neither comment endeared me to my state's Republican Party, or to some Jewish Republican friends.

Clinton's people scheduled a breakfast at his downtown hotel and what was supposed to be a one-hour meeting stretched to nearly three. We talked about baseball, economics, politics, international affairs, and probably everything else under the sun. What you discover rather quickly about Bill is that he has a virtually unmatched intellectual curiosity and the ability to connect with anyone. To me, those two are the most important characteristics of any political leader. At one point I referenced President George H. W. Bush's spectacularly high approval rating and asked: "Why do you want to do this? President Bush looks unbeatable." His reply was simple: "Jeff, in politics you just never know." It turned out to be a remarkably prescient observation! While I was up to my ears in Mariners and Emmis problems, I promised I would become actively involved in his campaign.

The following February, I held a fundraiser for Clinton in Indianapolis. Both of our lives had changed dramatically since our first meeting. He had become the darling of the Democratic field, only to be battered by the Gennifer Flowers allegations before the Iowa caucuses. Meanwhile, I had been enmeshed in all of the Seattle controversy in the intervening six months. As we sat down to dinner, we bonded over how difficult it was to be in a firestorm, comparing notes about how much "fun" we were having embroiled in controversy.

We both survived. I sold the Mariners six months later, and Clinton went on to get elected the forty-second president of the United States that fall. While I was called an FOB (friend of Bill), I was never that close to him. That being said, I liked him a lot and greatly respected his intellect and political skills. I saw him on several campaign visits to Indiana, and I was a delegate to the Democratic National Convention that year. After his election, his staff asked me what I would like to do in his administration. I told them that my major goal was rebuilding Emmis, so I had no interest in a full-time job. However, if there was something I could do on a part-time basis to serve, I would be happy to do it.

Early in 1993, the White House called and asked if I would like to be the US ambassador to the ITU Plenipotentiary Conference in 1994. The ITU is the International Telecommunications Union, which is part of the

United Nations. It is the international governing body for all telecommunications rules, and it meets every four years. The 1994 session was to be held in Kyoto, Japan. An ambassador only serves for a fixed term, which expires at the end of the conference. For that reason, you don't have to undergo Senate confirmation. However, because you receive top-secret security clearance, you have to go through all of the standard FBI checks and other vetting. In Kyoto, I used to receive top-secret cables all the time, and it seemed like most days I could get much of the same information from the *New York Times*. I always wondered whether some ambassadors got "double" top-secret cables.

The job requires meeting with the rest of your delegation on a regular basis and making a number of bilateral meetings around the world in the months leading up to the conference. By early 1993, Emmis was getting back on firm footing, and after discussions with my then teenaged children, we agreed that it wouldn't be that much time away from home, and it would be a great opportunity to serve. I was also aware that the position could serve me as well. As I've noted, I admire intellectual curiosity, and I'm always asking probing questions of my friends, managers, and basically anyone I meet with. The chance to learn the international landscape from seasoned professionals was going to be an added bonus.

I accepted the position, went through the vetting, and was sworn in as a US ambassador. While technically, you never lose the title, once I finished in Kyoto, I never used it again. That didn't stop me from joking with my assistant, Robin, that she needed to refer to me as "Ambassador Smulyan." She countered, "Well, we thought instead of referring to you as 'Mr. Dickhead,' we would just call you 'Ambassador Dickhead.'"

My first bilateral meeting, in Beijing, was memorable from the beginning. Upon checking into the hotel, my State Department attaché informed me, "From the minute you walk into your room, assume that every word you say will be heard by the Chinese government, because I guarantee you that it will." Then, the next morning, I broke off a cap of a front tooth by attempting to open shampoo with my teeth. Not a wise move, but it allowed the government to hear both my swearing as I was picking up the tooth from the floor, and my plaintive call to my friend and dentist, Harold Smith, who calmly responded to my plea for help with: "Jeff, it's ten o'clock at night here, and I'm ten thousand miles away, what exactly do you think I can do?" Obviously, my call to him proved that the US government didn't require IQ tests for every ambassador. I finally made my way to a hospital where I found a nice dentist who had actually been educated at UCLA, and he repaired the tooth.

At a meeting held early in my Beijing trip, I gained some fascinating insights. I was sitting with an American telephone executive and his German counterpart as they bemoaned their joint venture to develop a phone system with Russia (after the fall of the Soviet Union). Both agreed they should have partnered with China instead, and their rationale has always stayed with me. They noted that the Soviet Communist system had smothered innovation in Russia for over seventy-five years, and the population had become used to bureaucracy over the decades. The result was a stifling environment where it was almost impossible to get anything done. These executives talked about how the nature of the workforce in Russia was always tilted toward inaction and indifference. They contrasted Russia with China and asserted that, in spite of Communist control since 1949, the Chinese people had remained entrepreneurial and industrious. By 1978, Deng Xiaoping and Chen Yun had begun to unlock that entrepreneurial spirit to allow China to compete more effectively on the global stage. I've always believed the Chinese economy works a lot like bookmaking. The government, controlled by the Communist Party, allows a relatively free economy to take place under its control. Like a bookmaker who takes ten percent off the top (the vigorish), the Communists allow free enterprise to flourish; they just take their cut off the top. This arrangement has enabled China's economy to explode over the last forty years. The industriousness of the Chinese people has lifted millions of people out of poverty and created a thriving middle and upper class. Meanwhile, the Communist Party has enriched itself while controlling the country with an iron fist. Of course, this shift from communist to capitalist economics goes against the beloved teachings of Chairman Mao, whose communism was unquestioned and whose words were viewed as gospel. To resolve this conflict, Mao's successors decided to modify Mao's teachings to endorse capitalism. And with Mao long gone, he wasn't around to challenge the new ideology.

My only other bilateral meeting of note was with the German telecommunications officials in Munich, and that was a function of my accommodations. I was housed in an elaborate lodge outside of town that had been one of Hitler's favorite hotels. It's hard to describe the experience of walking through the halls thinking that Hitler had stayed many nights in the same place, fifty years earlier. Eerie doesn't begin to describe it.

Despite a few hiccups, I enjoyed my months of preparation leading up to the conference; I was given a spartan office in the State Department and had regular meetings with the delegation in Washington. I've always loved fish-out-of-water scenarios, and leading our delegation was the ultimate for me. Almost every person in our delegation of fifty had years of technical expertise with phone companies, satellite companies, government agencies, and other parts of telecommunication infrastructure. I, on the other hand, knew as little as was humanly possible about every issue. Saying that I was a "telecommunications expert" compared to my delegation was like saying that a Little League baseball player was comparable to Babe Ruth! While I was out of my depth, I freely admitted that to everyone in our group. However, my job was to set policy and push goals based on the expertise of our assembled group. At Emmis, we've always been proud to admit when we don't know something. Or as I've said it, we're smart enough to know what we don't know, and if we don't know something, we're smart enough to listen to people who do. You would be astounded at the number of organizations that can't get that right; they veer into areas they don't understand without seeking help. That is a recipe for disaster.

As our group prepared for Kyoto, I was encouraged by how well everyone was working together. Most had known each other in various capacities around Washington, and they complemented each other nicely. When we finally headed to Kyoto in September 1994, I was comfortable with everyone and believed we had set a reasonable agenda for the meetings. I loved the conference. Getting to know the ambassadors and delegates from around the world was an unforgettable experience. Microsoft played a large role in our delegation, and they helped organize a spectacular welcoming party that the US hosted. It was policy to exclude a few countries, notably Cuba and Iran. Naturally, I let the word out to both delegations that they were free to come to the event anyway, which they gladly did.

Overall, the conference changed my perspective on the US and its place in the world; I realized we weren't fully prepared for the post-Soviet period. No longer was the globe divided between the American sphere of influence and the Soviet sphere of influence. No longer did the countries aligned with one or the other take marching orders from their protectors. After the Soviet Union collapsed, so did its allies behind the Iron Curtain. In places like Poland and the Czech Republic, democracy flourished and standards of living improved, while in Yugoslavia, the absence of Soviet rule allowed ancient hatreds to resurface and ignite into a civil war that lasted for years. With repression comes order, while freedom occasionally leads to chaos. Meanwhile, the countries aligned with the United States realized that they didn't need to hide under our skirts anymore while we protected them from the Soviet threat. That dependence had covered up a myriad of differences, especially with the French, who had resented going along with the "culturally inept American buffoons." Of course, when the culturally inept buffoons were keeping the Communists away from their borders, we were much more tolerable. Now, our former allies were relishing their new-found independence as democracy and free enterprise became the coin of the realm.

My observation upon getting to Kyoto was that just about everybody in the world had figured out the above, except for our State Department. They expected everyone to play by the old rules and heel and fetch whenever we barked a command, but the dogs weren't as obedient in this new era. Over drinks one night, the Canadian ambassador was remarkably candid: "Your government hasn't figured this out yet, but without the Soviets to worry about, a lot of these countries (always led by the French) don't have to do what you want them to do. They are now your competitors in the global marketplace and they absolutely relish that they don't have to rely on you anymore." I quickly learned during a leadership vote that our reliance on the old order was a flawed strategy. It was fascinating to observe, but we were slow to adapt to the new realities of the world order.

A prime example of this archaic State Department thinking emerged during an incredibly mundane event. The British had come to us to secure our support for some membership rule they wanted to get passed at the conference. We agreed with them and sent our formal request to Washington for approval. On the day of the vote, the British ambassador came over to me in the delegate hall and said, "We're dropping our support of the resolution because we can't get enough votes." I nodded and said, "No problem, we'll drop our support, too." As I turned away, one of my State Department attorneys said, "You can't do that, Washington has already approved our position." I replied, "Well, we can't support a resolution that the British are dropping, we'll look like idiots. Just call Washington and tell them we're changing our position." She said, "I can't do that, it's the middle of the night back there, no one will be around." Now a bit exasperated, I responded, "How about waking someone up?" She admitted she couldn't do that, and I'm certain that she would never awaken anyone who had seniority. I said, "I've got a great idea. Why don't you leave them a voice mail, they'll get it in the morning, and I'm sure everything will be fine." She told me she was not allowed to do that.

By that point, I didn't know whether to laugh or cry. So, I plowed ahead: "Well, I'm not going to embarrass my country by supporting a resolution that is being withdrawn. We'll look ridiculously stupid." She responded that I had to follow State Department rules. I told her, "Look, I'm not going to be doing this job in a few weeks, but while I'm the ambassador in charge of this delegation, I'm not going to take any action that isn't in the best interests of the United States. If the State Department wants to fire me for that, they can be my guest."

She asked, "Is that your final answer?" (Now I thought I had landed on a game show.) I was adamant: "Yes, I'm withdrawing our support." Then she said something that I will never forget if I live to be a thousand: "Jeff, you made the right decision." I nearly fell out of my chair. She couldn't buck the official rules, even though they clearly led to nonsensical results. Instead, she had to reinforce the company line vigorously, so she wouldn't be reprimanded. As long as she did that, she was covering her ass.

A few weeks later, the White House sent an official delegation to visit us. One of the members asked me: "Has the State Department driven you crazy yet?" I replied, "No, I love all of them, but I have to admit, they have come close a few times."

On the other hand, the State Department staffers assigned to us were open and casual, at least relatively speaking. I had one of my favorite evenings around the bar, when one of our diplomats was conversing with a Russian delegate. After the Russian left, my State Department friend alerted me: "That's Ivan, I've known him for years; he used to be KGB in the old days. We've been friends forever." My friend, who had probably been in the CIA, talked openly about the Cold War. Again, I was all ears, hoping to learn something valuable. My maybe-CIA friend explained that "everybody knew the Soviet Union was falling apart, we knew it for years. It was just a matter of time." He talked about visits to Moscow during the end of the Soviet era when the government was near collapse. The ultimate novice, I was astounded: "If everyone knew about this, why didn't anyone say anything?" His response was simple: "First, you didn't want to be the guy to deliver that news and be six months or a year early. That would pretty much destroy your career. Besides, the last few years of the Soviet Union were good for business. No one viewed them as much of a threat at the end, and our defense business was thriving. Look at what's happened just to California's defense industry since the Soviets disintegrated!" It was a fascinating look at the end of the Soviet era.

My most memorable experience happened a bit later in the conference. I awoke one morning to the news that Saddam Hussein was amassing troops on the border with Kuwait. Three years earlier, he had invaded, and President George H.W. Bush organized a multinational effort to drive him from Kuwait. Many Americans wanted him to chase Saddam back to Baghdad and eliminate the Iraqi ruler once and for all, but Bush decided not to because he believed it would violate the agreement he had with other nations. As a result, in 1994, Saddam was once again lining up troops on the Kuwaiti border. Watching CNN that morning, I saw a briefing by President Clinton promising that the United States would stand with Kuwait and would not allow Iraq to invade.

As I walked into the delegate hall, the Kuwaiti ambassador was looking for me. She intoned, "Mr. Ambassador, my country is in danger of being invaded again. My family is in Kuwait. I need to know that the United States will stand by us." Having just seen CNN, I told her, "Madame Ambassador, President Clinton has given assurances that the United States will defend you. We will not let Saddam invade your country." She was utterly jubilant and thanked me profusely as she walked away. I'm certain that she believed I had been on the phone all night, conferring with the president on the proper course of action. As I walked away, one of my friends in the delegation who had witnessed the event said, "Thank God you were watching CNN this morning instead of Cartoon Network like you usually do!" Not true, but still a good line.

My most enduring experience occurred several weeks into the conference, when we got word that the Arab bloc was interested in supporting the Palestinian Liberation Organization (PLO) in obtaining critical telecommunications infrastructure for its emerging new government. In exchange, the Arab bloc would support the recognition of Israel, which would be a first in the United Nations ecosystem. Today, after all the years of strife between Israel and the PLO, it's hard to imagine what the region was like in 1994. The Oslo Accords had been signed earlier in the year, and it seemed as though Israel and Palestine were on an unalterable course for peace and a fully functioning two-state solution. We thought of the request as a way station along the road to a full peace, and we viewed our potential agreement as an important step. As ambassador, I was thrust into the middle of the negotiations (a fish out of water, again), but this time, the meetings involved various parties. Some Arab states wouldn't meet with others. Some wouldn't meet with the PLO, so we engaged in multiparty negotiations with the various parties to the agreement.

Making the entire experience even more bizarre was that I was obviously an amateur when it came to these matters, and Jewish, at that. I assumed that the Arab side knew, while it was clear Israel did from the first moment. I've read accounts that, as a Jew, Henry Kissinger always felt the need to bend over backward when dealing with Arab states to prove that he could be trusted as a neutral party. I found myself doing the same thing, subconsciously. I believed that it would be impossible to reach an agreement if both sides didn't trust me or believe that I could be an honest broker. It's been many years now, but I still remember feeling genuinely moved by the plight of the Palestinian ambassador as he recounted the feelings he had for the land of his ancestors. We developed a sound working relationship, and I don't believe I ever could have fully understood all of the dynamics in the region without our discussions. It was always difficult to comprehend the relationships among the various Arab states; while all held a long-standing antipathy toward Israel, each had a different attitude toward the Palestinians and a different level of commitment to their cause. It was easier for me to understand the Israeli position because of my knowledge and fundamental belief in the Jewish state, but I quickly came to realize that if I couldn't represent the interests of the Palestinians fully, I would never be able to find a solution. After several weeks, we reached an agreement—a very gratifying moment. We received remarkably kind statements from numerous other delegations about our leadership of the negotiations. Our leadership succeeded because we adhered to the most important Emmis Commandment: If your word is good, nothing else matters, and if your word is bad, nothing else matters either. I wince when I think back to how close we were to an enduring peace in those days. The next year, I was invited to join President Clinton's delegation at the signing of the peace agreements between Israel and Jordan. It was a time when solutions seemed possible; today, they seem light years away.

My four-month tenure as an ambassador gave me perspectives I had never considered, especially when it came to Israelis and Palestinians. I returned a little humbled by all the high-stakes negotiations (although no one at Emmis ever commented on that humility). I also had a much clearer idea of how the Russian, Chinese, and Eastern European economies worked. The business intelligence I had gathered would not go to waste.

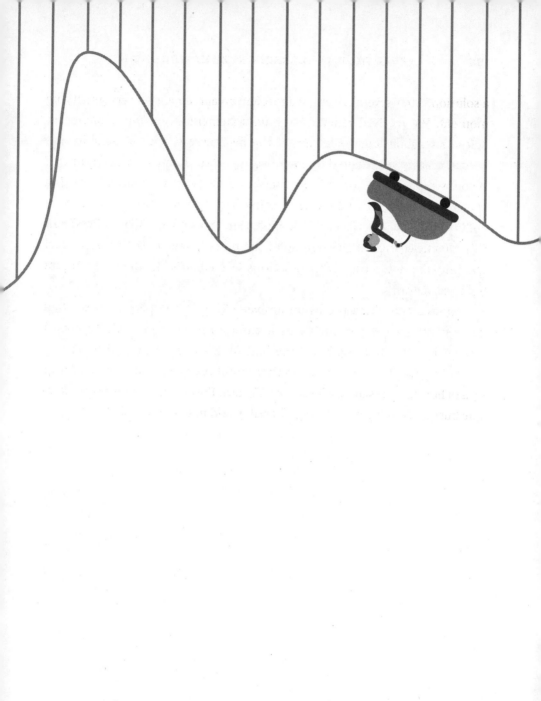

Belgium and Hungarian Bumeráng teams photo taken at the Tucson Emmis Managers Meeting. From left to right: Barbara Brill, Lajos Boros, Deb Smulyan, Jan d'Haese, and Gábor Bochkor, with Luc Sterckx and Paul Fiddick standing. Bochkor and Boros were hosts of the wildly popular Bumeráng Morning Show at Sláger.

Best of Times,
Worst of Times

My time as an ambassador convinced me that the democracy that had flourished in the former Soviet client states of Eastern Europe would soon lead to the privatization of their media. In Kyoto, I had numerous discussions with Eastern European delegates who wanted to know about American media. During this time, governments from many countries were descending upon our Federal Communications Commission, looking for assistance in setting up their own systems, invariably designed to mimic what had developed with great success in the United States. Everyone loved American enterprise and democracy in the early post-Soviet era, and the newly liberated states of Eastern Europe wanted to emulate all things American.

Even before my stint as an ambassador, Emmis had explored a few opportunities outside of the United States. In 1993, we briefly had been partners in an ill-fated launch of TalkRadio in the UK; we had been brought in to be the operating partners of Great Britain's first national talk station. It was an exciting idea, and we partnered with British investment bank Hambros, Canadian broadcaster Canwest, and British Television producer MTM. As the project got closer to launch, MTM decided that they really didn't want us or anyone else dictating programming to a British audience. In one memorable meeting, one of the MTM partners admitted, "Look, we know you are trying to give us ideas that will give us good ratings and program it in a way that will get the most economic success, but this is more important than that. This is about putting the proper product before the British people. We have different values that we want to impart." (Later I learned that what he really meant was, "We want programming that will curry favor with the people we want to do business with.") His presentation left the other partners around the table stunned. I replied, "Look this is just business to us. We want to create a network that attracts a lot of people and allows us to make a profit off of our audience. That's the only way we know how to operate. This sounds more like a religious mission for you. We appreciate it and we respect it, but that's not what we do. If that's what you want, we'll be happy to leave the venture." It was definitely one of the most bizarre meetings I've ever had. Of course, my comments became famous in our company, and for years after my remarks in London I was called upon to give the "it's just business, this isn't religion" speech whenever one of our managers thought that our creative types were going overboard with ideas.

The launch was a disaster, and despite fervent requests from the other partners that Emmis take over the operation, MTM held firm. We agreed that they would buy out the three of us so they could continue with their plan. Afterward, I wrote in a shareholder letter: "I think on my tombstone they'll say he didn't accomplish much, but at least he got out of TalkRadio UK at eighty-five cents on the dollar." When the venture quickly went bankrupt, I was rather proud of getting as much as 85 percent of our money back—so it just might end up on my tombstone.

Because of the business insights I had gained in Kyoto, by 1995 we were seriously considering investments in various countries in Eastern Europe. The most interesting prospect was Hungary, which was getting ready to auction off two new national licenses. Each license would broadcast throughout the country to ten million people on a series of state-owned towers that the winners would rent. While there had been a few successful local stations in Budapest and other cities, clearly the new national licenses were a great opportunity. We put a terrific team together led by Maggie Dugan, Deb Smulyan, and Marty Greenberg. Marty and Maggie had been friends from the American radio business, and Deb and I met when she was working for an Indiana congressman. She was from Pennsylvania and came into my office and said, "With a last name like Smulyan, we have to be related." In fact, we were distant cousins, and my dad vaguely knew her father. Deb would go on to help run the Democratic Leadership Council, whose first chairman was Bill Clinton. A few years after his election, she left the DLC and joined us to help scout international opportunities.

When we launched our bid in Hungary, we were competing against a number of other broadcasters, mostly from around Europe, for one of the two radio licenses. We were the only American bidder for radio and, initially, thought that gave us an advantage. However, as luck would have it, a bidder for one of the two TV licenses turned out to be an American group headed by Ronald Lauder, heir to the Estée Lauder fortune. He had won a new TV license in the Czech Republic, and for some reason, his bid angered the Hungarian government. During the process, we were worried that the taint of Lauder's bid might lead to repercussions against us, even though we had no ties to his group. In fact, Lauder lost the TV bid and promptly filed suit against the government. Fortunately, that wasn't held against us, and we won one of the radio network licenses. A British firm won the other, and both of us scurried to build our respective networks. Hungarian media law, like most of the other regulations in the emerging Eastern European countries, was largely patterned after US media policies, with close attention paid to how the FCC regulated us in America. That was important because you don't want to invest capital and build a business unless you know there is regulatory certainty. America has been a repository for capital from all over the world because of the transparency of our government agencies and the adherence to the rule of law in our judicial system. In America, you must comply with FCC rules, but if you do, you have virtual certainty that your license will be renewed. In reviewing Hungarian media law, we were encouraged that we would receive similar treatment.

Of course, a new regulatory system always has glitches. We were granted a license and then given four months to get on the air. That might seem like a reasonable time, but almost everything we needed to broadcast had to come from out of the country and getting it shipped to Budapest at times was a challenge. To meet our deadline, Deb and Maggie pulled out all the stops. I'm fairly certain that Deb was doing everything humanly possible to get equipment into the country. We pushed contractors, suppliers, and everyone else to get the newly named Sláger (or Hit Radio) on the air, but we made our deadline.

One of my favorite memories of the experience was picking the format. While we had to meet Hungarian guidelines to be a "popular music station," there was wide latitude to decide what exactly was popular. When we researched the market, the results were astounding. By far, the most desired music were hits from the 1960s and 1970s. Preferred artists were the Beatles, Rolling Stones, the Beach Boys, and many from Motown. Yet, this was 1996, a long way from that era. My first response was, "How can they want this music, wasn't it banned in Hungary during all of those years?"

We insisted on another round of research and it gave us our answers. The music was desired precisely because it had been banned. Hungary may have been behind the Iron Curtain, but recordings were smuggled in, and people could also listen to a few stations outside of the country. To Hungarians, the music represented freedom, creative expression, and a way of life that they could only dream about. The Beatles came from a world that represented the perfect counterpoint to the drab, soulless existence of Soviet-style communism in Hungary during that period.

After we had been operating in Hungary for a few years, I asked one of our local employees how he was adapting to the new freedoms of the West. His answer surprised me. He told me that while living under communism, they imagined life in the West to be perfect. People not only had unlimited freedom and economic success, but it led to a flawless life. He believed that in the West, the streets were "paved with gold" and "people didn't get sick"; their lives were sort of a heaven on earth.

The fall of communism had jolted him. "Yes," he told me, "our lives were dramatically improved and we understood the opportunities created by democracy and free enterprise. But that could never match the fantasies we had. People still got sick and died, the market economy led to winners and losers, life still had many of the same challenges it would have in any politi-cal system. Our lives got better, but nothing could match the dreams we had of the nirvana we had imagined."

So, this was the mindset in Hungary when we launched Sláger Rádió in 1997. We did a terrific TV campaign, highlighting the music we were play-ing as well as the personalities who would entertain the country every day. Everything clicked. The station quickly became a national institution. Our morning team, Boros and Bochkor, became two of the most revered celeb-rities in the country, with their morning show named Bumeráng. Sláger's ratings dwarfed our other national competitor, and we siphoned audience away from almost every local station in the country. Our business grew geo-metrically, along with our ratings; at its peak, the network reached nearly five million people a week in a country with a population of 9.8 million. Upon meeting with me while on a trip to Washington, the country's prime minister shook my hand and then started a discussion about how he woke up every morning listening to Sláger and then described his affection for Boros and Bochkor.

Once again, Emmis was hitting on all cylinders, but that set off alarm bells, given our history. I remembered what Woody Woodward, our general manager with the Mariners, always used to say: "You're never as good as you think you are on your best days, and you're never as bad as you think you are on your worst days." In other words, minimize the highs and elevate the lows. That dovetails with the advice found in my favorite poem, "If—" by Rudyard Kipling: "If you can meet with Triumph and Disaster / And treat those two imposters just the same." Well, if we started off with triumph, you knew that disaster was out there, lurking in the shadows.

Dealing with the Hungarian regulatory commission was sometimes challenging, because bringing American-style radio to a new democracy sometimes shocked their sensibilities. Sláger wasn't doing Howard Stern–type radio, but morning-show pranks, silly promotions, and unusual con-tests sometimes made the regulators go crazy. This was standard for a country wrestling with the freedoms inherent in a new form of commu-nication. Occasionally, we would get called on the carpet and had to pay a few fines for "going over a line" that usually had never been drawn, but that was to be expected in a system that didn't have the sixty years of regulatory infrastructure we had in the United States. Still, by every measure, Sláger was a critical component of the cultural landscape in a new Hungary. But none of that would matter if we didn't have a regulatory framework we could rely on. Our license was for twelve years, with a nominal renewal after seven years, which was granted without issue. Vital to our existence was an "expectation of renewal" at the end of our license period, so long as we met all of the criteria as a licensee. This "expectation" was patterned after US regulations that guaranteed that political games couldn't be played if you met the government's standards. Anyone investing capital in a foreign country needs to have assurances that the government will always play by these rules. While we had a few skirmishes along the way, our relationship with the Hungarian regulatory body was good, and everyone agreed that Sláger demonstrated how the Hungarians hoped this new system would work out.

As we approached the end of our twelve years, we had no inkling that the climate was about to change. Two years before our expected renewal, I met with Viktor Orbán, a former prime minister, who was leading the opposition to the ruling Socialist Party. Orbán's previous term as prime minister had been widely considered a disaster, and I was told that part of that problem was his awful relationship with the United States. My sources also said that if he ever became prime minister again, he would have to mend fences with the US. With Sláger being one of the leading American entities in Hungary, Orbán would be wise to develop a great relationship with us. When he and I met, all of that was in the back of my mind, and it was a cordial meeting. I never dreamed what the name Viktor Orbán would soon mean to me (or to the rest of the world, for that matter).

Earlier, I said, "Scouting reports never lie." Until they do. I'm not sure if the report on Orbán was as bad as the scouting reports Neville Chamberlain got about the Nazis' intentions in 1938, but they had to be close.

In the summer of 2009, six months before our license renewal, Barbara Brill, our manager in Hungary, called Paul Fiddick, president of Emmis International, to recount a strange meeting with a member of the ruling Socialist Party. He had told her that "to get your renewal, you're going to have to give up editorial control of your news, and you're going to have to give up half of your business to us." He was a lower-level party functionary and Barbara assumed he was merely joking around with her. When we made further inquiries, we got incoherent answers that led us to believe that nothing serious was afoot.

One of the reasons we were unperturbed was that the Socialist Party was falling apart. A Watergate-type scandal had erupted after a tape was released showing that the economic minister had deliberately lied about economic data he had released to the country. That tape was a deathblow to the already struggling Socialists, and their prime minister, Gordon Bajnai, was clearly a lame duck until the elections the following March. It was widely assumed that Viktor Orbán was going to be prime minister, but we thought that he would be relatively passive, especially since he wanted to get on the US's good side. Again, bad scouting reports were about to lead to bad results.

By the middle of the summer, Orbán dispatched his emissaries to the other national licensee, Juventus (sold earlier by the British to an Austrian firm). While also a national network, Juventus was a much smaller player than Sláger. Months later, we learned that the message from Orbán was similar, but the tone was frighteningly different from the one we received from the inept Socialists: "If you want to stay in business, you will give us complete editorial control and half of your company." Very simple, very direct. Our Austrian competitors, incensed, dismissed the request, unwisely believing, as we did, that Hungarian law would protect them, since they had met the tests for renewal that had been written to shield companies from just such an activity. I'm not sure what the Austrian equivalent to "pound sand" is—I think it's "piss up a rope"—but that was their position.

A month later, the Socialists revisited us with a slightly more coherent, if still unconvincing request. I think they said, "We're serious, you really have to do these things or you're not going to get renewed." With the Socialist Party in complete disarray, the Keystone Kops nature of their request didn't completely hit home with us.

Unfortunately, a month after that, we started to receive the message loud and clear. Although not yet elected, Orbán was striking quickly. He carried out a coup within the Hungarian regulatory body, forcing the resignation of key members and replacing them with allies who would clearly do his bidding. Around the same time, we learned that Orbán was deliberately avoiding a confrontation with us so as not to provoke the US. Cleverly, he had approached the Socialists months earlier with an offer: When he took over Hungary, they would be out in the cold, but, in the interim, they could take one gem for themselves—control of Sláger. Orbán wasn't going to go after us, but they could. That would give him plausible deniability when the American license was revoked. Being inept and in disarray, the Socialists reluctantly went along with him. By the time we entered what should have been an automatic license renewal, the rules had completely changed. Some of the most competent Socialist regulators had been booted from the regulatory body, and the ones who remained had been neutered and acceded to Orbán's plan.

All the media rules were rewritten, so instead of a straightforward renewal, both national licensees would receive no renewal at all. Howls of protest went up throughout Hungary, and numerous newspaper articles decried the takeover of the regulatory regime. The process attracted attention throughout the European Union, and numerous legislators and civic leaders complained, but the die was cast.

Bill Kennard, a friend and a former FCC chairman, was the newly installed US ambassador to the European Union. As our nightmare scenario was unfolding, I placed a frantic call to him at his office in Brussels. "Bill," I intoned, "we're being nationalized in Hungary." "Jeff," he responded dismissively, "you're not being nationalized. They can't do that; they're a member of the European Union. They just can't do things like that."

"Bill, I'm telling you, we're being nationalized," I responded, definitely in a more desperate tone.

"Jeff, I'm telling you that it just can't happen; they can't nationalize you," Bill replied, probably thinking that I had completely lost my mind.

In a depressing, yet somehow vindicating call with Bill a week later, he admitted, "Damn it, Jeff, they really are nationalizing you!"

I'm not sure of my exact response, but I believe it was, "No shit, Bill."

I flew to Budapest to meet with Prime Minister Bajnai to state our case. At the time, Sláger was one of the most successful enterprises of Emmis, producing more than $12 million in cash flow a year. Given the storm clouds of economic uncertainty gathering in the United States, Sláger was likely to be critical to our ability to weather any downturns in the future.

The prime minister was a genuinely decent man. We met alone in his office. I told him that what was happening to us was absolutely a crime in my country and was clearly against the media rules in Hungary. He responded, "Look it's a crime in THIS COUNTRY. I know that. But there's nothing I can do." He was honest, and his statement revealed the current and future prospects for Hungary. Even before he was stripped of his office by a constitutional election several months later, he had already succumbed to a coup. He was powerless to stop the Orbán train from arriving at the station, even though it was there months ahead of schedule. Orbán had seized power, and it was an excellent precursor of what was to come, given how brazen he was before the election.

I have the distinction of being the first victim of the Orbán regime in Hungary, which continues to this day. Volumes have since been written about his total destruction of any democratic norms in Hungary, his modification of the media, the courts, and the economy, and of course the free election process. It was all to come later, but it started, even before his election, with the two national radio networks.

When our license was finally taken away, a firestorm ensued. Protests roiled Hungary. A documentary, *The Taking of Sláger*, achieved great critical acclaim. Ten embassies, led by the United States and Austrian ambassadors, issued a formal protest. The European Union weighed in and we went to work back home. Led by the Indiana congressional delegation, a resolution condemning Hungary was passed by the House with over 380 votes. Mike Pence, then a congressman, had worked for Emmis when he hosted a statewide radio show in Indiana, and he led the effort on our behalf. In Mike's office, he and five other Indiana congressmen met with the Hungarian ambassador to the United States. While they peppered him with questions, it was really a pathetic meeting. He didn't disagree with anything they were saying but merely responded that he was powerless to do anything. Like his boss, the prime minister, he was representing a government that by every measure had ceased to exist.

Even with all the support, the case was futile. We received an endorsement from the newly elected Obama administration, and Vice President

Biden delivered a sharp rebuke to Orbán on a visit to Hungary later in 2009, but to no avail. Orbán wasn't going to reverse himself, and we weren't going back on the air. We tried to press our case in the Hungarian courts and even won two lower court decisions, but it was clear that even if we won at their supreme court level, the government wasn't going to give us our license back.

We then began the arduous process of appealing to the International Centre for the Settlement of Investment Disputes. Several years later, we were stunned to learn the case was dismissed on a procedural technicality. We ended up with no compensation, and we became a mere footnote to Hungarian history.

I learned a few things after we were gone. When the Socialists first took over Sláger (Orbán's Fidesz Party took over the Austrian network), they kept the profit from the network, as Orbán had promised. However, once Orbán became prime minister, he steered all the radio advertising dollars to his new Fidesz network and promptly bankrupted Sláger. I've always said, don't ever do the expedient thing, do the right thing. The Socialists opted for expediency, and it didn't help them one bit.

Years later, when reading *Red Notice*, Bill Browder's remarkable book about the rise of Putin and the Russian economic model, I learned something I should have realized years before. Viktor Orbán was Putin's very first client. Since the Orbán takeover of Hungary, Putin has orchestrated chaos all over the western world, but his first lab experiment was Viktor Orbán. The prime minister has followed the Putin playbook brilliantly. In fact, during the takeover of Sláger, long before I knew of their relationship, I called Orbán "Putin without oil." Little did I realize how accurate that assessment was. Even the business model was right out of the Putin playbook. As I've mentioned, the Chinese model is that the Communist Party gets ten percent off the top, and generally entrepreneurs are free to run their businesses as long as the government gets its cut. It has led to a thriving economy, because there are significant incentives to create value. Russia, on the other hand, has developed a different system. A few powerful oligarchs control everything. They are protected by the government and are insulated from serious competition, leading to a bloated and inefficient economy. The Putin deal is simpler than the Chinese model. He gets half off the top and obvious control. In the media business, that means strict editorial control. Until I began to understand the Putin model (which most believe has made him the richest person in the world), I never realized that Orbán's offer was patterned exactly after Putin's system.

Looking back, I can say we would never have agreed to give away editorial control and half the company; it goes against everything Emmis stands for, to this day. Still, it would have been nice to understand what Orbán was doing before it was too late.

You haven't really lived until you've been nationalized.

Top: With Paul Taubman, celebrating the purchase of several radio stations. *Bottom:* Daughter Cari and me, both proud USC Alums, enjoying a Trojan football game.

9

The Golden Age of Exuberance

The meltdown from the 1991–1992 recession had left the radio industry battered. While we had survived our crisis, many others went bankrupt. Even before the economy started to rebound, the FCC decided to give the radio industry a boost: In 1992, they permitted companies to own a second radio station in their markets. The idea was that, through joint operations, radio companies could achieve cost synergies by cutting redundant jobs. In addition, they would be able to garner more revenue by selling the combined audience to advertisers. Comedians even did bits about disc jockeys switching back and forth from Top 40 to easy listening by going across the hall to a different studio. These duopolies definitely made the industry more attractive, as did a rebounding economy. By 1993, radio was growing nicely again and outside capital was coming back. But the business was not going to return to the realistic pricing of the 1980s. Instead, we were in for a wild ride!

The drivers of this golden age were Wall Street exuberance and acquisition fever. In contrast, over the decades spanning from the 1950s (the dawn of the modern radio era) to the 1980s, the industry had undergone steady, if unspectacular growth. Most years, revenues grew from 4 percent to 7 percent, and with the fixed-cost nature of the business, that growth could usually provide double-digit increases in cash flow. Asset values also remained steady, with purchase multiples for good stations always hovering at about ten to eleven times cash flow (that meant the purchase prices equaled ten to eleven years' worth of cash generated by the station). So, when Lowry Mays took his small radio company, Clear Channel, public in 1984, his stock limped along, making few waves in the market. The same thing happened when Infinity Broadcasting went public in 1986: Its stock performance was so underwhelming, the company bought up all its shares and thus "went private" two years later. Only when the 1992 duopoly rule took effect and the US economy started coming back strong in 1993–94 did radio's bottom line start to take off.

With its cash flow generating power back on Wall Street's radar, radio was once more an industry darling. In 1992, fueled by the purchase of WFAN, Mel Karmazin took Infinity public again. The stock grew steadily, pleasing investors. Clear Channel's stock finally rose out of the doldrums, as well. By the time we went public in 1994, our stock was also poised for the run-up that we enjoyed through the rest of the 1990s. Entercom, Chancellor Broadcasting, and Evergreen Media joined us in the public markets, and at industry conventions you could feel the renewed optimism for the radio business. Station acquisitions accelerated, but nothing crazy, yet.

At Emmis, we took the proceeds from our IPO and, along with paying down debt, purchased our original major competitors in Indianapolis, WIBC-AM and WNAP-FM. My career had come full circle, from owning a small daytime station to owning the market's two dominant stations. Well, at least one was dominant. You may recall that back in 1981, when Emmis owned WENS, Indianapolis, we effectively destroyed the ratings of our competitor, WNAP, with better programming and successful ad campaigns. Now Rick and I joked that we had to live with the consequences of our past success: WNAP had never regained its market dominance. After operating the station for a year, with no significant rise in ratings, I ruefully commented that we had managed to kill this station fourteen years ago, and I'd be damned if I knew how to bring it back to life in 1995!

Taking advantage of the duopoly rule, Emmis also bought WRKS, a large urban-targeted station in New York. We modified the programming to focus on urban oldies and started a major rebranding campaign. Our team created a very effective TV spot with Barry White pitching the glories of our rhythmic oldies, and then we installed Isaac Hayes as our morning man. Both the commercial and the host were well received, and our ratings and revenues grew at a rapid pace. Meanwhile, WRKS's sister station, Hot 97, parlayed the immense popularity of hip-hop to the top spot in the market, and thus we had two stations firmly ensconced in the very upper tier of New York radio. In fact, in 1995, Hot 97 and Power 106 both became number one in their markets. It was the first time in history that one company had owned both top-rated stations in New York and Los Angeles. It certainly seemed as though we were benefiting from this "Golden Age of Radio."

Then in 1996, our world changed dramatically. Wall Street and the newly minted public companies in the broadcasting industry lobbied Congress to relax the ownership rules in the Telecommunications Act of 1996 even further. The Clinton administration, eager to show its bona fides to the business community, worked with a Republican Congress on the bill to deregulate much of media and make it more responsive to market forces. Along with just about everyone else in the industry, I lobbied fervently for the new rules. I can still remember Tom Milewski, who ran Greater Media, one of the largest private radio companies, at one of our meetings solemnly warning, "You'll be sorry." Tom was essentially a lone voice in the wilderness, drowned out by the rest of us clamoring for regulatory relief that would lead to more access to capital. Now, twenty-five years later, long after Tom has passed away, I can admit that for the most part, he was right.

The call for deregulation also meant that radio companies would be able to acquire more and more stations. Lowry Mays at Clear Channel was the most ardent proponent; even before the Telecom Act of 1996 bill was passed, Lowry's company was the first to reach the statutory limit of thirty-six stations. As he acquired and acquired, he noticed that his stock trended upward, or, in the parlance of the day, each station he bought was accretive to his valuation. If "accretive" wasn't the favorite word of every broadcaster in those days, I don't know what was. What Lowry realized was that if his stock was trading at twelve times cash flow, and then he purchased stations for eleven times cash flow (no matter what the actual price), Wall Street would label the deal accretive, and Clear Channel's stock price would rise. This accretive method of acquisition was about to cause a remarkable run-up of market value in the industry.

The proposed easing of the rules would bump up the number of stations you could own in a single market to eight, with a total limit of ninety-six stations. All of us were thrilled about the possibility of owning five FMs (along with three AMs) in the best markets, and no one worried about the overall cap because we thought it would take years to get there. Lowry, on the other hand, had a grander vision. Understanding the "accretion" strategy better than anyone, Lowry supposedly went to Eddie Fritts, the NAB's longtime president, just as the debate over the 1996 bill was ending. Apparently, Lowry proposed eliminating all caps on ownership, meaning that a company could theoretically own thousands of radio stations. Eddie and Senate Majority Leader Trent Lott had been best friends from their days at the University of Mississippi, and at Lowry's behest, Eddie supposedly convinced Lott to add the provision at the last minute, and it went through without much debate, virtually unnoticed.

When the bill came out, with the unlimited ownership provision added, the rest of the industry asked in unison, "Who in the world would want to own a thousand radio stations?" After all, running a thousand radio stations isn't like operating a thousand hamburger stands. Album rock in Toledo, Ohio, may bear little resemblance to album rock in Portland, Oregon, and standardizing your stations is a very difficult task. As I used to tell my investors, "Radio isn't like hamburger shops; you can't cook the fries the same way in a thousand different locations." History, and many years of chaos, have proven me largely correct, but at the time, the Telecom Act of 1996 set off a feeding frenzy, with Lowry leading the way. I'm not certain how long it took Lowry to acquire a thousand stations, but it was within five years. And Clear Channel's stock price was amply rewarded by Wall Street's appetite for companies with boundless radio.

As with Michael Milken's junk bond era, nothing kills a good idea like excess, and radio in the second half of the 1990s was ground zero for irrational exuberance. Accretive acquisitions were one reason the concept of unlimited ownership led to disaster. The other reason was that, unlike the rest of us owners, Lowry and Mel Karmazin had the brilliant insight that radio valuations depended not on how well you operated your stations but solely on the opinions of Wall Street. Make Wall Street happy and capital poured through your doors. Lowry, a Harvard MBA, had a background in finance and only entered radio by accident. In contrast, Mel was a lifelong radio operator, but he grew up in the shadow of Wall Street and was a genius about how the financial markets worked. My friend Peter Lund, former president of CBS Television (who was forced out by Mel when he later ran CBS), noted that, "Lowry and Mel were playing a different game than the rest of us. We spent lifetimes in the industry, thinking about audiences, advertisers, and community service. They understood that, but their total focus was on Wall Street. They both understood and delivered what Wall Street wanted and it gave them the ability to take over much of the industry." I heard stories that Mel even threatened his board of directors at Westinghouse, CBS, and Viacom, respectively, that if they didn't allow him to do as he pleased, he would tank their stock. Perhaps that's apocryphal, but at any rate, Mel regularly prevailed over his boards.

Both Lowry and Mel mastered the accretion game spectacularly. After the passage of the 1996 Telecom Act, Clear Channel and Infinity Broadcasting's stock prices rose steadily, and as their valuations went up, they were able to offer higher and higher amounts to prospective sellers. This cycle continued for several years, and before the music stopped, both companies were trading at over twenty times cash flow. That meant they could buy radio assets at nineteen times cash flow and still watch their stock prices appreciate. The problem was that the industry's true annual growth of 4 percent to 7 percent was never going to come close to sustaining those multiples over the long run.

From the seller's standpoint, this future growth problem didn't make much difference. People who had been in the industry for decades were receiving offers for their holdings that sometimes doubled their previous expectations. Fresh with funds from Wall Street, a multitude of buyers were eagerly searching for acquisitions. A number of people I knew in the business sold their assets and exited the radio industry. You can see many of their names on university buildings all across the US.

At Emmis, we weren't one of those sellers; we were in the business for the long haul. And we were as ready to play the acquisition game as Lowry, Mel, and a host of others. In early 1997, we got our first big chance. Viacom's Sumner Redstone, long before he took over CBS, decided to sell his radio group to pare down some of his $10 billion of debt. Bids were due on the Friday of Valentine's Day weekend, and I happened to be at the Ritz-Carlton hotel in Laguna Niguel, California, but I was completely focused on the bid. The Viacom assets were an absolute top target for us, with FM stations in New York; Los Angeles; Chicago; Washington, DC; and Detroit. It was a perfect opportunity to dramatically expand our holdings in top markets. We worked diligently on our offer, lined up all of our financing, and were optimistic about our chances. At this point, no one in radio really understood how quickly the "accretion game" had ratcheted up prices, and a CNN story indicated that we were a likely contender, along with Infinity and Scott Ginsburg's Evergreen Media.

As we submitted our bid, I eagerly awaited a call from our investment banker, Credit Suisse's Kristin Allen. Kristin had worked with us for years and we had a great working relationship. When I called her, right after the 5 PM deadline in New York, I asked, "How did we do?" I was stunned when she told me that we were "hopelessly out of it." She indicated that we might be able to get the Chicago FM, but even that was a long shot. Since I believe we bid around fourteen to fifteen times cash flow—a dramatic stretch for us—I was incredulous that our bid was blown out of the water. Usually, we do very well in "beauty contests" when our culture and our history enable us to win bids if we're almost at the level of other bidders. I've always been gratified that most people would rather do deals with us. Nevertheless, I know from experience that if you're more than one cash flow multiple behind someone else, your charm and culture have absolutely no effect. Given Kristin's comments, I realized that there was no way Emmis would be willing, or able, to raise our bid high enough to prevail.

At the end of the weekend, Hicks, Muse, Tate & Furst (Hicks, Muse), a private equity fund with a voracious appetite, announced that it had merged with Scott Ginsburg's Evergreen Media and that the combined company had purchased all of Viacom radio. While most analysts had expected the Viacom stations to fetch $825–850 million, the sale price was $1.075 billion, a multiple of eighteen times cash flow. The deal easily eclipsed the multiple that the merged Westinghouse Broadcasting/CBS Radio had paid for Infinity right after the Telecom Act passed in 1996 (supposedly fifteen times cash flow). Shortly after that agreement, Mel Karmazin went from running the radio group to quickly ousting Westinghouse Broadcasting CEO Michael H. Jordan and taking over the entire company.

The Viacom sale was our first clear signal that the feeding frenzy for radio was on. To us, the purchase of radio stations at these multiples made little sense. While we entered a few auctions, we resolved never to pay prices that we thought were unsustainable. Meaning, we struck out on new radio acquisitions.

I can best illustrate our mindset during this time by relating a conversation I had with my friend, Marty Pompadur, former president of ABC Television. He called to ask my advice (which I've said for many years is always free, and at free, it's still overpriced). Marty owned a few stations in Cleveland and had decided to package them with additional stations in the Cleveland area that were owned by two other small groups. That way, he would create a full cluster of eight stations for sale, and he asked the best way to go about it. My flippant response was, "Call Mel Karmazin, pay him $5 million to announce publicly that he wants to buy your stations. That will immediately induce Scott Ginsburg to enter the bidding. Scott wants to beat Mel any way he can, and he'll buy your stations at a higher price than Mel will pay." Marty laughed uncontrollably. I continued, "Of course, Emmis will bid, probably around thirteen times cash flow because they are good stations, but I guarantee you, Mel or Scott will get you closer to seventeen times cash flow." Our motto in those days was: "Let's hang around the hoop and see if something bounces our way, but we're not going to pay these prices." In other words, we had become resigned to being rational in a world of irrational exuberance.

Marty didn't pay Mel anything, but he did conduct a mini-auction. By the time he took bids, Scott's Evergreen Media had merged with Hicks, Muse, and Scott had taken the money and run. However, as I had predicted, Hicks, Muse continued Scott's bidding style and outbid Mel for the Cleveland assets. As the deal was about to close, Marty called to inform me that the cash flow of the stations had dropped in the three months since the deal had been announced and that Hicks, Muse was coming in the next day to finalize the sale. I told him not to worry: Hicks, Muse would probably drop their purchase price, but it should still be more than Mel had bid and thus Marty would still come out ahead.

A few days later, Marty called to tell me about the sale agreement he had reached: "After the cash flow dropped by a few million dollars, what do you think they did?" I guessed they had dropped the offer, but only a bit. He replied, a little awestruck: "They actually raised the price! I can't believe it, Jeffrey, your industry is the biggest house of cards I've ever seen!"

It was the Wild West out in broadcasting land, as my next story shows. In 1998, Bob Sillerman, founder of SFX Broadcasting and SFX Entertainment, decided he was ready to exit the radio business. SFX's entertainment division was the first concert aggregator and ultimately became the behemoth that is today's Live Nation. Paul Taubman and I joined Bob for dinner at his favorite restaurant at the Sherry-Netherland hotel in Manhattan. A legendary character, Bob had an intriguing proposal for us: He wanted to merge Emmis and SFX. He would keep the concert business and Emmis would run the combined radio group. Bob's radio assets supposedly had $1 billion of debt and $95 million of cash flow. After the meeting, Paul asked what I thought. I told him I had two problems. First, most of Bob's radio stations were in smaller markets, with Indianapolis and Pittsburgh being his largest clusters, so they weren't nearly as attractive as ours. Second, knowing Bob, I was nervous that he was exaggerating his cash flow and its growth prospects for the future. After kicking some numbers around, we decided to pass on the deal. A few months later, Bob sold his radio assets to Hicks, Muse for an astounding $2.1 billion, retaining his concert business. When the deal was announced, the stations had a reported cash flow of $160 million. I called Bob's investment banker in disbelief: "How can his cash flow increase from $95 million to $160 million in just a few months, it's impossible!" The banker

replied, "They just put lots of synergies into the projected cash flow at closing." Meaning the buyer assumed a lot of cost cutting and joint advertising
power (greater revenue) going forward. But why was the current cash flow
so high? Because of pro forma accounting, which allowed the buyer to show
current cash flow as though the radio stations were already part of one big
company, and already benefitting from synergies.

Ah, pro forma accounting—the solution to any pesky math problem.
Here's how it worked in connection with Wall Street's exuberance. Let's say
your stations have $10 million of cash flow and I buy them for $180 million.
Because my company can do wonders just by operating more efficiently, I can
project that your cash flow will grow to $15 million when I integrate your sta-
tions. I can declare to my bankers and shareholders that those increases will
occur by the time the deal closes. Now, I've brought my purchase multiple
down from eighteen times to twelve times; that makes the deal more accretive, exciting both Wall Street and my shareholders as my stock price spikes.
You're probably saying, "It seems like a ridiculous leap of faith to assume the
synergies will add that much cash flow," and you would be right. However,
in those days, capital flowed freely, because of a loose Federal Reserve policy,
dot-com exuberance, and banks taking on riskier and riskier loans. No one
paid much attention to the results until later, when the music stopped.

We used to refer to this cycle as the "Pro Forma Olympic Relay." Companies would make acquisitions and finance them on the basis of unreach-
able projections. In the above example, I would be able to borrow say, eleven
times projected cash flow, or $165 million (that's almost the whole purchase
price!). At prevailing rates, I would owe nearly $15 million in interest each
year. If my cash flow ended up less than that, I wouldn't be able to cover my
interest payments, let alone reduce principal during the early years of the
loan. Unsurprisingly (at least to us), the pro forma projections that allowed
companies to get loans started to create problems when actual performance
began to diverge widely from the projections. By the third year, there always
seemed to be an "oh, shit" moment, when the acquiring company realized
the math wasn't working. As I've said for years, "All of the world is a math
problem," and if you tell somebody you will have $25 million of cash flow in
your third year and you only have $16 million, you have a *big* math problem.
However, with so much capital sloshing around in the system, someone else

always seemed ready to buy your assets and take the baton from you, thus continuing the Pro Forma Olympic Relay.

The irrational exuberance wasn't limited to the broadcasting industry: The dot-com boom was also in full swing. Every entrepreneur was tapping the capital markets to fund their latest internet ventures. Early on, some founder concluded that marketing was critical to raising awareness, and thus capital; meanwhile, radio was touted as the ideal place to reach young, internet-savvy consumers. For two years, dollars flowed into radio from every conceivable start-up idea and massively inflated radio revenues. In 1999, the industry's best year, growth was over 13 percent. Given its fixed capital structure, radio enjoyed booming cash flows that set a new benchmark for the industry. The heightened performance played into the "radio renaissance theory," and with it came more capital and ever higher valuations. Clearly, the dot-com boom fueled excessive radio station valuations and enabled the pro forma shenanigans to continue longer than they should have.

During this period, we were reluctant players, at best. Because Emmis was smaller and hadn't purchased as many assets, we always had a lower valuation than our high-flying peers. Don't get me wrong; the valuation was still hefty. As an example of everything being relative, I can still remember being on vacation with my family, cruising on a yacht in the Caribbean, when our stock reached its all-time high of $124 per share, a mere six years after our IPO price of $15.50. Despite this ridiculously heady number, I remember thinking that it paled in comparison to the valuations of my radio competitors who had purchased hundreds of stations and had gained accretive valuations, seemingly every month.

Even when the frothy atmosphere benefited us, we remained skeptical and started openly questioning the situation. At investor presentations, we stated our belief that the radio industry was solid, but we worried that it was being viewed as something it was not. After the dot-com boom crashed, radio revenues fell back to earth, to around 5 percent annual growth. On a conference call, an analyst asked me, "When do you think radio revenues will get back to normal?" I asked what he thought normal growth would be. He responded, "Somewhere between 12 percent and 14 percent per year." I told him: "Never would be a good time frame." Unfortunately, his reasoning was baked into Wall Street expectations for radio—expectations that became problematic a few years later.

My friend Greg Nathanson, who was on our board, watched my performance at an investor conference and summed up our less than stellar standing among most of the large media investors very succinctly. Greg said, "Look, there's no doubt in my mind that you are completely accurate about this business. It's a train wreck waiting to happen. The numbers are unsustainable and yet investors haven't figured it out. Here's your problem: Most of these investors have made a fortune with the radio consolidators. They have invested in them and the returns have been great. Their inclination is that the big guys are right and you aren't, so they are just going to buy shares in the largest companies and ignore you. Even if they believe you, you're still screwed, because then they'll conclude that the whole thing is a house of cards and they'll just get out of radio." As usual, Greg was absolutely correct. And that's exactly what happened a few years later.

Ironically, the deal that signaled the end of radio's wild ride involved Bob Sillerman's SFX concert business; Hicks, Muse; and Lowry Mays. Hicks, Muse had continued its acquisition binge through two companies it controlled, Capstar Broadcasting and Chancellor Broadcasting. In 1998, these two merged to form radio giant AMFM, and in the following year, Mays's Clear Channel bought them in a reported $17 billion deal. Meanwhile, with the cachet he had gained by selling his radio assets to Hicks, Muse, Bob Sillerman took his concert business public and went on a wild buying spree of concert venues, usually paying ridiculously inflated prices. Two years later, he sold the concert business to Lowry Mays's Clear Channel for $4.4 billion. The question was: How could these assets be worth that much that quickly? The initial marketing pitch proclaimed that the combination of 1,200 radio stations and concert venues all over the country would create magical synergies. For the first time in years, the public markets were skeptical, and the deal was roundly criticized. It was the first time since the 1996 deregulation that Wall Street took a dim view of radio consolidation, which triggered a downgrade in the entire sector. The bloom was off radio's rose, never to return.

So, if we understood what a house of cards this "golden age" was, why didn't we sell and get rich? Let me tell you my Sam Zell story.

Sam Zell, a legendary entrepreneur, has amassed fortunes in real estate, media, and just about everything else. In 1992, he purchased a small, Cincinnati-based radio company named Jacor that had gone bankrupt during the downturn of 1991–92. With Randy Michaels, Sam began his radio consolidation plan. Randy and I have been friends for many years, and he is one of the most creative executives I have ever known. I've always marveled at his brilliance, although I sometimes cringe when his stunts cross the line and cause challenging consequences for him and his company.

It was 1998 and Sam had studied Emmis and had concluded that the combination with Jacor would be a perfect match. When Sam makes up his mind, he becomes an unstoppable force of nature. He courted me for a number of weeks, and we met several times in his Chicago offices. When we convened for our final lunch, Jerry Reinsdorf and my banker Paul Taubman joined me. Sam and Jerry had done several business deals together and were old friends. In addition, I would have never considered a sale or merger without Paul's input. Sam's sales pitch was simple: If we put our two companies together, the resulting entity would become a significant player in radio, practically overnight. He obviously had whatever capital we needed to grow the business and told me, "You're the only guy in the industry that Randy will work for." Sam gave me assurances that I would control the company, and Jerry noted that when Sam gave you his word, you could take it to the bank. We discussed the merger and finally I said, "Sam, if I wanted to make the most money, I would do this in a heartbeat. You'll know when this industry has hit its peak and you will want to sell at the right time. My problem is that I love my company and I love this industry. I know its current growth is unsustainable, but at the end of the day, radio will still be a good business and I don't see any threats on the horizon."

With that, I turned Sam down, and he and Randy continued their buying streak. A few years later, when Sam determined that valuations had peaked, he sold Jacor to Lowry Mays at Clear Channel for a multibillion-dollar price. He even got Lowry to name Randy president of Clear Channel as part of the deal. Years later, Sam and Randy were reunited when Sam purchased the Tribune Company and he brought Randy in to run it. Unfortunately, it was at the start of the 2008–2009 downturn, and the deal ended in disaster for both of them: Tribune went into bankruptcy during their second year of ownership.

For years, whenever I would see Sam, he would remind me that I should have gone into business with him. Just about anyone else would have taken his offer, and from an economic standpoint, I was insane to turn it down. Especially when I knew the industry was wildly overvalued. But in this situation, my intellect collided with my emotions. I've distinguished the two in literally thousands of meetings. Intellectually, you know the right answer, but your emotions lead you in a different direction. For me, though, as always, keeping Emmis intact and under my control was the most important objective. Would most other people make the same choice? Of course not! Looking back, over twenty years later, my decision to turn down Sam and stay in the radio business appears even more insane, because the decline has been more precipitous than I could have imagined. Still, running this company has always been my passion. Even when we hit rock bottom, ten years after turning down Sam, I was always comfortable with my decision not to merge. Of course, by any measurable standard, it was still a remarkably stupid decision!

So, what did I learn from this period of irrational exuberance? Mainly, watch out when your industry becomes a Wall Street darling. Investment banks and their research analysts converted radio into a speculative trading business, with stations changing hands at a rapid pace. Too many Wall Street players (especially private equity firms) entered the game. With the money spigot open, too many dollars chased a finite number of stations, pushing prices into the stratosphere. Valuations of radio companies soared, but they bore no relation to the underlying fundamentals of the business. To navigate this Wall Street–fueled exuberance—which can happen in any industry—an entrepreneur needs to stick to the fundamentals: what the economics are and what the industry's prospects for growth really are. Most important, decide what business you want to be in. If you want to be a speculative company, then join the fray and cash out; timing the market will be your main obsession. But if you want to be an operating company—just as Emmis was a radio company—treat valuations with skepticism so when the exuberance deflates, you're still standing. How do you choose? I go back to what I said earlier: Do what you love.

Top: At an Emmis Managers' Meeting after we had just purchased more TV stations (from left to right): Gary Kaseff, Rick Cummings, CFO Walter Berger, me, Robin Rene, radio president Doyle Rose, and TV president, Randy Bongarten. *Bottom:* Gary Kaseff, Greg Nathanson, and me. Greg was the original head of our TV group and has been a member of our board for nearly thirty years.

10

How to Fix Television (Or Not)

With radio valuations at unsustainable heights, we knew we had to find other sources of major growth. While we had expanded our magazine holdings and had ventured into international radio, neither would be able to provide that engine. Television was a logical extension, and I started exploring the idea with Greg Nathanson, an early investor and a member of the Emmis board. He had run TV stations for the Tribune Company, served as president of Showtime, and now was president of Fox Television Stations and Fox Entertainment.

Greg's knowledge of the TV industry was off the charts. Back in 1990, I was seated at a dinner next to the former president of NBC Entertainment, Brandon Tartikoff. Considered one of the greatest geniuses in TV programming, Brandon had this to say about Greg: "I've become an incredibly well-known executive, getting credit for anything that happens on my watch, and I've got public relations people to make me look good every day. I can guarantee you that Greg Nathanson knows more about TV than I will ever know, and he's had more great ideas than anyone, but he doesn't care about credit, he doesn't care about glory or money, so it's a very well-kept secret."

Tartikoff was right on all counts. If you saw Greg on the street, your first inclination would be to hand him a dollar to get something to eat . . . and Greg assuredly would take it. When he was running Channel 5 in Los Angeles, his secretary was late to work. She had been in an accident that totaled her car. Greg knew replacing it would be beyond her means, so he gave her *his* car. No questions asked. He would give you the shirt off his back, but his shirts were so ugly, few would take them. Greg so didn't care about money, he didn't realize when it might be good to spend it; while heading Emmis TV, he once took an executive we were recruiting for lunch at Costco, where they dined on free samples! He could get away with that because he was brilliant. When he left Fox to run Emmis TV, Sallie Hoffmeister of the *Los Angeles Times* did a profile, noting that when Fox's Rupert Murdoch wanted his daughter to learn TV operations, he wanted only Greg to teach her. Greg was also the only one who could manage his boss Barry Diller's legendary temper. In one meeting, Diller reportedly threw a phone at Greg, who instantly threw it back. As Diller admitted, "Only Greg could do that, we both knew that he couldn't care less if I fired him!"

It was 1998, and Greg and I both understood the major flaw in the industry: TV stations still had only one source of revenue, advertising, while cable also had subscriber fees. Cable wasn't much of a competitor when it started in 1948 in Western Pennsylvania—it was a solution. Because TV signals (like FM) travel on a line of sight, if you lived in a town on the other side of a mountain from the closest TV stations, the mountain blocked your reception. The answer was simple: just string wires to homes to pick up the signal. Soon, cable was able to offer a better picture and a few new channels in urban areas. For a slight monthly fee, you could remove the antenna from your roof and take advantage of these benefits. The key to this proposition was that once you took your antenna down, you were a captive of the cable company. Even broadcast networks and stations became captives of the cable companies because Congress, in an effort to help the fledgling cable industry, had passed laws in the 1960s forbidding broadcasters from getting paid for their signals; in return, the cable companies had been required to carry their signals. This was the "retransmission consent, must-carry" system, and it was wonderful for (1) cable companies, who were able to hit consumers with an ever-increasing monthly bill, and (2) the early cable networks that received a small fee per cable subscriber. In many cases, the cable companies even owned these cable networks. The problem was, the channels getting the lion's share of viewing on cable—the local network affiliates—were barred by law from charging anything at all for their signals.

As a protected industry, cable flourished. By the early 1990s, John Malone, head of the country's largest cable company, TCI, was using his clout and ingenuity to extract ownership stakes from cable networks that needed access to his systems and from small cable companies that needed to obtain his favorable rates on content. Most remarkably, whatever Malone decided to do, the rest of the industry followed without question. I once asked Greg's brother, Marc Nathanson, who owned Falcon Cable, "Why do you guys follow John Malone so religiously?" Marc noted: "Simply because when we follow John, we all make money. You guys in the broadcast industry are always at war with each other. We're always better off than you." As time went on, Malone's behavior became more egregious. My favorite Malone line is from the end of the Reagan administration. When asked whether he was worried about antitrust enforcement from the Justice Department, Malone calmly replied, "I'll worry about the Justice Department when there is one."

As cable's monopolistic behavior became more pronounced, pressure to regulate the industry increased. Broadcasters led the charge, along with a myriad of consumer advocates, and Congress passed the Cable Act of 1992, which included a retransmission consent provision, finally allowing broadcasters to be paid for their signals by the cable industry.

You would think that now it would be simple for broadcasters to get paid for their signals, giving them that critical second revenue stream—and you would be wrong. Just because they had the right to get paid didn't mean John Malone was going to pay them—the amounts would certainly total billions of dollars over the next decade. In another example of his brilliance, Malone concluded that if he could split the networks apart from each other and their affiliates, he could still control the landscape. Here's how: While all the broadcast networks own their stations in New York, Chicago, Los Angeles, and other major markets (about sixty stations in all), they own almost none of the nearly nine-hundred stations outside of the top twenty cities. Malone played on the fact that networks and their numerous affiliates have always had a love/hate relationship.

Malone started with Rupert Murdoch, making him essentially the following offer: "Look, I have only thirty channels in my cable system, but I can add another one and give it to you. You create whatever cable network you want, I'll pay you twenty-five cents per month per subscriber, and those subscribers are in every household and in every market. Of course, I'm not going to pay you anything for the Fox network; I'll still get that for free. But if I paid you for your main network, 80 percent of your distribution is controlled by your affiliates, so they would get that money, not you. This way, you get every cent." After Murdoch took the deal, Malone went to ABC and NBC and essentially offered the same thing: he would create additional cable channels for them, and they ended up launching ESPN 2 and the fore-runner of MSNBC, respectively.

Malone could give cable channels away to the networks because he understood that cable programming capacity was about to become virtu-ally unlimited (in effect, the five-hundred-channel universe). The broadcast-ers didn't. As someone said later, "It wasn't a fair fight; it was John Malone against every other television executive!"

So, this was the world Greg and I were looking at six years after the 1992 retransmission act. Cable had started offering advertising, and it was a small, but growing, second source of revenue. Meanwhile, broadcasters had still not been able to obtain a second revenue stream, partly because trying to fight cable operators to get paid risked your carriage on their system. If they decided to drop your station, you would lose as much as 70 percent of your audience overnight. Granted, viewers could still receive your signal over the air, but most people had taken down their antennas long ago and wouldn't know the difference between "rabbit ears" and Bugs Bunny. No, going up against cable operators was tantamount to Armageddon. Still, Greg and I were sure that broadcasters would eventually band together to fight cable. We were buoyed by the news in July of 1998 that John Malone had exited his cable systems by selling TCI to AT&T for $48 billion. Clearly, not having to deal with Malone had improved the industry's hopes.

Our strategy for buying TV was rather simple. Most TV station owners had not been as entrepreneurial as radio operators, who cut their teeth
having to scrape out a living in markets of twenty to thirty competitors. In
contrast, the TV industry was growing by leaps and bounds and its markets usually consisted of only three or four stations. Most importantly,
unlike radio, which was not wildly valued by advertisers, TV was a primary
medium, attracting almost every advertiser and every ad agency that wanted
to create more expensive and thus more profitable commercials. We thought
that by bringing a more aggressive management style to local TV stations,
Emmis could move the sales and ratings needles. Greg was as good as anyone
at tinkering with news and other programming, and Emmis had developed
significant expertise in sales, marketing, and ratings analysis. And of course,
the Holy Grail—the second revenue stream—would be a revenue bonanza
for broadcast television; we thought it had to be coming soon. Another area
of growth was political advertising. With the rise of Newt Gingrich and his
"take no prisoners" approach to campaigning, both Democrats and Republicans began ramping up their spending in almost every local market. Long
before the Citizens United Supreme Court case in 2010 showered TV with
hundreds of extra millions of dollars, the floodgates were already opening,
and local TV was the biggest beneficiary.

After I told Greg that I wouldn't get into TV unless he would run the
new group, he left Fox and joined our new venture. We made our first two
acquisitions simultaneously. The first consisted of the four stations of SF
Broadcasting LLC, a partnership between Barry Diller and Rupert Murdoch.
Diller had served as Fox Television's first president, and while he had led
the successful launch of America's fourth network, his relationship with
Murdoch frayed over time. Their stations were all VHF (essentially stronger signals), and the four had been purchased to switch affiliations to Fox.
Prior to that, Mobile, Honolulu, and Green Bay had all been dominant NBC
affiliates, while WVUE, New Orleans, had been a less successful ABC station. None of the transitions to Fox had been particularly successful; most
employees (and many viewers) missed their previous, more prominent networks, and the strong local news franchises had suffered. In addition, having two owners who were sometimes on separate pages had taken its toll

on operations. In essence, the group was a fixer-upper, precisely the type of challenge we loved to tackle.

The second acquisition was the Hulman family stations, which included WTHI-TV, Terre Haute, the long-dominant CBS affiliate, and WFTX, Fort Myers, a Fox affiliate in what was to become one of America's fastest-growing markets. As part of the deal, we also bought Terre Haute radio stations WTHI-AM, WTHI-FM and WRVR-FM. All three dominated Terre Haute radio as much as their sister station dominated Terre Haute TV. As a result, these Hulman stations always took the lion's share of revenues. Nevertheless, we had no illusions about Terre Haute, which always had a challenging economy and wasn't expected to improve markedly. The prospects of operating in Fort Myers, however, had all of us excited.

Shortly after these first two deals closed, both Nick Trigony, president of Cox Television, and Dennis FitzSimons, chairman of Tribune Broadcasting, called to invite me to join the Television Operators Caucus (TOC). Surprised, I asked, "Why do you guys want me? We own just six stations." They assured me their interest was genuine and that they very much wanted me to be a member.

The TOC had been formed in 1985 to represent the major non-network companies that owned most of the largest network affiliates in America. It was viewed as a somewhat exclusive group, made up of, among others, Cox, Tribune, Post-Newsweek, Belo, Media General, and Scripps. The TOC's purpose was to act as a counterweight to the power of networks NBC, CBS, and ABC shortly before Fox came into the picture. It was also tasked with providing industry leadership through seats on the NAB board. Representing a new company with stations in relatively small markets, I wasn't sure why I was the newest member when I attended my first meeting. Four hours later, I had my answer. When Trigony asked for my thoughts, I replied, "Nick, I had no idea why I was here before the meeting, but I've watched you guys spend three hours figuring out how to get one more thirty-second promotional spot from ABC on Tuesday nights, and the last hour figuring out who will be on the TOC slate for the next NAB elections. As an entrepreneur, I would have spent all four hours trying to figure out how to get a second revenue stream. Everything else is irrelevant." Nick confessed that was exactly the reason I was asked to join the group; I was an entrepreneur, and those were in short supply in the upper echelons of the TV industry. Almost every group owner in the room was a division of a major newspaper company, and in every case, newspapers were the company cash cow. In fact, the joke in the industry was that in the early days of broadcasting, the newspaper giants who owned fledgling broadcast stations placed the family "ne'er-do-wells" and black sheep in charge of the newer, largely unprofitable enterprises. In the ensuing decades, the TV industry had grown dramatically, and although the parent companies still looked primarily to their newspapers for the largest portion of their profits, the broadcasting side had recruited or developed seasoned, talented executives. However, none of those executives were entrepreneurs or even had ultimate control of their businesses.

I later learned that the only other prominent entrepreneurs in the industry, David Smith of Sinclair Broadcasting and Harry Pappas of Pappas Telecasting, were considered undesirable candidates for the TOC. Smith had a well-deserved reputation as a brilliant but difficult operator, and that continues to this day. Pappas was also viewed as someone who didn't fit in with the others. At a dinner a few months later, when it was clear that I had been chosen to fill the "entrepreneur's seat," I joked, "I'm not very attractive, but I guess you think you can at least dress me up and take me out to dinner." It was a very low bar, but I had just cleared it.

In one of my early meetings with the group, I inquired why the TOC didn't lead the charge to get a second revenue stream. With three of the networks effectively neutered, and the NAB usually deferring to the wishes of the TOC on TV matters, it seemed that the group was the ideal choice to lead the effort. Someone answered with a statement that almost knocked me out of my chair: "The cable guys aren't gentlemen; they are impossible to deal with, and it's not a fight any of us feel like having." My response was, "They may not be gentlemen, and they may be impossible, but you're in a gunfight, and if you don't bring some guns, you're going to die." Talking further, I realized that all my cohorts understood the stakes and knew that their industry was going to suffer, but none were the decision-makers for their companies, and therefore none wanted to risk a stable corporate career fighting what might be a losing battle. One friend, Andy Fisher, who replaced Trigony at Cox, said, "Jeff, my boss likes to play golf and hunt. Do you think I want to get him off the golf course and tell him that his multibillion-dollar television business is jeopardized by this issue? I don't think I'm willing to do that!" That was the crux of the issue. None of the corporate executives relished the fight, especially with a strong, well-organized cable industry, even though their market power ultimately gave them the leverage to win the war. Think about it: In those days, even with the steady growth of cable channels, the major networks—represented in almost every city by their affiliates—controlled well over half the viewing on those cable systems. What was really holding up this fight?

It turned out that these executives thought of the war over retransmission payments as a multiyear, difficult challenge. I was convinced that many of them believed that by the time this thing was over, they would be retired and have expended a lot of energy for something that didn't matter to them. This outlook became the basis for what I termed "the Boca problem." As in, "If there's a good chance that by the time this thing is over, I'll be retired and living in Boca, why should I start this fight in the first place?" The phrase earned me a lot of notoriety around the industry, so much so that a few years later, when I received the Broadcasters Foundation Golden Mike Award, a hilarious video roast—featuring just about every prominent industry executive, as well as Bill Clinton—essentially blamed me for the demise of American broadcasting. Blatantly displayed on screen, throughout, was the temperature in Indianapolis as well as in Boca. It was a not-so-subtle jab at the problems the industry was facing.

The TOC experience highlighted something I had sensed intuitively for decades. A manager rarely has the same passion for an idea as an owner/ entrepreneur. An owner views an issue like the second revenue stream as a matter of life and death. If he gets it, his success is assured, while if he fails, his company is endangered; he has no choice but to engage in the fight. A manager usually says, "Hey, this isn't my problem; if this doesn't work out, I can still keep my job, and if it does succeed, I may be gone before the benefits accrue to me." Put another way, the owner of a business is far more concerned about the long-term success of the venture; he's there until he sells the business or they carry him out. That's why it took two entrepreneurs, the aforementioned David Smith and Perry Sook of Nexstar, to win the battle for the second revenue stream years later. They fought the cable industry with everything they had, because failure wasn't an option.

Our foray into owning television stations was basically rewarding. Emmis was able to buy assets at more reasonable prices than radio stations, and operational efficiencies increased our cash flow. Turning around a television station is trickier than radio, because your results are mostly dictated by the quality of your network's programming. In addition, a local news franchise is usually difficult to improve because the viewers are generally older and more resistant to change, and a station's news image is cemented in a community's mind over many years. For all those reasons, you rarely see the "worst to first" turnarounds that were common for us in radio. Still, by creating a more entrepreneurial atmosphere, we were able, as time went on, to become very adept at the business of television.

We also struck a blow for getting paid a decent price for our signals by negotiating with satellite companies (DirecTV, Dish). Unlike cable systems, they had few subscribers and thus, less leverage. When we owned KOIN-TV, I had my first skirmish with DirecTV. They were offering the munificent sum of eight cents per subscriber and we were demanding twenty cents. My argument was simple: "You pay ESPN $3.50 for every household in Portland, Oregon. KOIN is the CBS affiliate and it averages five times the audience of ESPN. What's wrong with this picture!" We ended up playing hardball, pulling our signal from DirecTV until they paid us closer to our ask. It was a big victory at the time.

Despite our relative success in television, my efforts to obtain a second revenue stream went nowhere. I used my positions at both the TOC and the NAB to recommend that the TV industry push for an antitrust exemption so it could negotiate as one entity with the cable industry, or at least a limited exemption so competing stations in each market could band together. That idea died on the vine. I also suggested that each broadcasting company reach an agreement with their networks, so that ABC, CBS, FOX, and NBC could use their viewing power to strike a national deal with the various cable providers. Even though the networks owned various cable channels, they were attracted to the idea of getting paid for their cash cow—their core network. This proposal gained traction at various times, but at the end of the day, the relationships between the networks and their affiliates were so strained that many affiliates didn't trust their networks to negotiate their rights in good faith.

l even got the TOC to commission a study by Joe Kraemer, a well-respected economist, who did a brilliant job of articulating all of the reasons why failing to obtain a second revenue stream would send American television into a slow, inevitable decline. But after his presentation to our group, he confided in me that "your group is hopeless. As l was presenting my report, l looked around the room and everyone but you had his head down. They actively didn't want to know the conclusions. Jeff, they understand this stuff, but they don't want to confront it, it's just too difficult an issue for them to tackle." Their attitudes were a perfect example of the Boca problem, and it drove me stark raving crazy.

When Greg's brother Marc sold Falcon Cable to Paul Allen for $3.6 billion in the summer of 1999, it became clear that Greg, Falcon's second largest shareholder, was not going to run our TV group for much longer. And while l would have a better chance of getting nuclear launch codes than of finding out how much Greg made on the deal, it was clear that it was going to be tough to keep him flying to Green Bay, Terre Haute, and Mobile after he cashed Paul Allen's check. Not long thereafter, Greg did retire, largely to stay home and watch White Sox baseball games and old movies. To this day, more than twenty years later, he is still retired and I've thought it's been a monumental waste of talent that Greg has stayed home all those years, especially since for most of that time, the White Sox have been unwatchable!

Randy Bongarten, who had been running our international radio business, was more than willing to take over for Greg. As noted in chapter three, Randy had been president of radio at General Electric (GE) when newly installed CEO Jack Welch announced that GE was exiting the radio business, and Randy was tasked with selling the division and ending his job. He then landed at NBC Radio, but shortly after he became president, Jack Welch's GE purchased NBC, and once again Randy was told to sell the division. I'm not sure what the odds are of liquidating the same business for the same man twice in the same decade, but Randy won that daily double. When we bought the NBC Stations, l was thrilled that Randy was interested in joining Emmis. He's a remarkably talented executive and has become a close friend. Randy stayed with Emmis until 1992, when he was recruited by Sam Heyman of GAF to run his single FM station in New York and to create a major radio company. Unfortunately, when Heyman was offered $90 million for that station, his plan to have Randy build a major radio company evaporated. We, however, were thrilled that he was available again.

Randy was a terrific steward of both our international stations and, after Greg retired, our television group. As Emmis continued to grow, reaching sixteen stations with the purchase of Lee Enterprises, Randy and his lieutenant, Ray Schonbak, did a great job of leading the stations. My greatest management challenge with Randy was that he really was the smartest guy in the room, but his style infuriated some of our managers. As I've said before, if you act like the smartest guy in the room, you aren't, because if you're really smart, you don't drive people away by lording your intelligence over them. During budgeting, I learned that Randy was belittling our station managers when they presented their budgets. Now, managers want to understate their projections and overstate their costs so that bonuses are easier to achieve. This maneuver is affectionately known as sandbagging, and most managers have perfected it to an art form. Corporate executives are born to sniff out sandbagging and an animated give-and-take always occurs. If done right, it can be a fun exercise; if done wrong, it can be a bloodbath. In Randy and Ray's first year on the job, it was definitely a disaster. Afterward, I discussed the importance of style with Randy. Intuitively, he knew he should have kept his emotions in check, but they had gotten the better of him during a difficult process. I never heard of him belittling his managers again, which wasn't surprising. Randy is one of the quickest studies I've ever known. Of course, in true Emmis fashion, at our annual manager's meeting later that year, we presented Randy and Ray with a special award. It was for the corporate activity that most resembled Hitler's march through Poland in 1939: the Randy and Ray Television Budget Tour of 2000!

For as long as we owned TV stations, I continued the quest for the elusive second revenue stream. When it became clear that the industry was not going to unite to press for retransmission payments, I came up with a substitute that I consider one of my best ideas: wireless TV. During the transition to high-definition TV in the late 1980s, broadcasters were granted additional spectrum. My idea was that they could use this excess spectrum (which wasn't being used) to add leading cable channels and, by aggregating with other stations in their markets, broadcasters could provide a low-cost alternative to cable. Since every channel would be transmitted over the air, we could provide an antenna to receive everything without an expensive cable hookup. As you know, the cable industry grew dramatically by providing an ever-expanding lineup of channels at an ever-expanding price, but surveys indicated that the average American watched only ten to twelve channels a month, and four of those were network affiliates. We knew that we could provide at least thirty channels for under twenty dollars a month; most of these fees would be split among local broadcasters who, for the first time, would be paid for their signals. To me, the best part of this package was that local stations could use unsold airtime to market the benefits of this wireless TV system.

By driving home the notion that most people were fed up with paying fifty dollars a month for channels they weren't watching, we could accomplish three important goals. First, we thought selling low-cost "cable" was a viable business that would deliver proceeds to broadcasters starved for revenue. Second, these same broadcasters would have an ownership stake in the system. Third, by using our airwaves to alert consumers that they were paying too much, we believed we would gain critical negotiating leverage against the cable industry. At the time, US cable companies were the most reviled of all service providers in the country, and if broadcasters could use the most watched signals on each cable system to make that point, we thought that it could help bring them to the negotiating table. We also speculated that if we could demonstrate to our brethren that they could get paid for their stations, they would find the courage to battle on.

Make no mistake—this venture was another of my "moon shots." I had no illusions about how difficult it would be to pull off, but I've always believed that attempting things that most people find impossible has made my life more fun and interesting. Better that than to attempt mundane things that never change the landscape. Not surprisingly, I've been labeled Don Quixote a few times in my life and it's never bothered me.

To analyze wireless TV, I went to Monitor, a boutique consulting business that specialized in game-changing projects. From the outset, we realized that the key to the entire enterprise was convincing the station groups to pool their signals so that we could have enough spectrum in each market to provide a robust offering of channels. As importantly, we needed the support of ABC, CBS, Fox, and NBC; otherwise, it would be impossible to license network content on their affiliates or to have access to the cable channels they owned.

Monitor assigned Jonathan Goodman, head of their Toronto office, and his associates, Greg Loewen and Steve Goldbach, to lead the team. Monitor's ace in the hole was Bhaskar Chakravorti, a former Harvard professor who was advertised as "the world's greatest game theorist." Our sense was that, to get these entities to work together, we had to master game theory. In retrospect, we just needed expertise in aberrational psychology. We started discussions with various groups of broadcasters, and generally the idea was very well received. Intuitively, everyone understood that our excess spectrum, which was providing no value, could be deployed in a way that would change the media landscape. In addition, we soon realized that with compression techniques, we would be able to utilize more and more spectrum as time went by.

While several broadcasters decided that they could improve their negotiating leverage by holding out—professing that they would "do their own thing"—most realized that a collective effort was the only way to find a solution. We always knew that network leadership was critical, because they had the content and the financial ability to put wireless TV over the top. We would make our case by showing them the economic gain of such a system. At the time, all of the networks owned cable channels and therefore were beneficiaries of the status quo. However, we could show that they were leaving hundreds of millions of dollars on the table by foregoing compensation for their broadcast signals. For example, Viacom/CBS was receiving fees for MTV, Comedy Central, BET, and VH1, but the per-channel payments were small (usually less than fifteen cents per subscriber per channel). The CBS network, on the other hand, had audiences at least ten times greater than its co-owned cable networks; if CBS were compensated at the same rate, it would bring in at least $1 per month per subscriber. With 105 million cable homes, this fee represented a huge amount of money for the broadcast networks, even if it would have to be shared with their affiliates.

The math was compelling for everyone except Disney/ABC, because ABC's ESPN broke every rule of TV compensation. When the Rasmussen family launched ESPN in 1979, the network was the province of offbeat sports and constant sports news updates. For several years, ESPN subsisted on the early rounds of the NCAA basketball tournament and the then-unloved NFL draft. Rasmussen got an early infusion of cash from Getty Oil to keep it afloat, and in 1984 ABC purchased 80 percent of the network, with Hearst buying the remaining 20 percent.

With ABC's clout, ESPN headed into the big leagues, picking up rights to college football, basketball, Major League Baseball and, in 1987, its first deal with the NFL for *Sunday Night Football*. Affiliate fees grew steadily, along with America's passion for sports. Supposedly, in the mid-1980s, John Malone looked at ESPN's outsized fees and sent a letter informing the company that if they didn't reduce their fees by 35 percent immediately, he would take them off every cable system he ran. ESPN had to agree, because it couldn't afford the loss of TCI's vast coverage. Apparently, after the network acquired the rights to the NFL and other major sports, it turned the tables on Malone. A few years later, they sent their own note to TCI, demanding double their fees or they would cut off TCI just prior to the New Year's bowl games. Disney/ABC realized that ESPN—the cable industry's most valuable product—had more leverage than Malone. When Malone blinked, ESPN was off to the races, gaining higher and higher subscriber fees every year. Today, even with declining numbers of cable subscribers (down to 76 million households from a peak of 105 million), ESPN earns around ten dollars per subscriber per month. That means that ESPN is receiving more than $9 billion per year before it ever sells commercial time and before the revenues from ESPN 2, ESPNU, ESPNews, the SEC Network, the ACC Network, and the Longhorn Network are factored in. That's the reason ESPN is the top bidder for just about all sports, which has made it the gem of ABC's parent, the Walt Disney Company, for many, many years, despite its losing revenue from thirty million cord-cutters at ten dollars per month.

It was easy to make a case for CBS, Fox, and NBC that, by using their clout to get paid for their flagship networks, they would reap a bonanza. It was a harder sell for Disney/ABC. The Disney executives rightly feared that the cross-subsidy inherent in the existing arrangement might be threatened if everyone else got close to their actual economic value, to the detriment of ESPN.

What was becoming clear was that if the industry could unite, it would reap billions of dollars that it had been denied; unfortunately, getting everyone on the same page was nearly impossible. Besides the ABC dilemma, which Bob Iger clearly articulated, the other networks were not dying to work with each other, let alone their affiliates. Almost everyone agreed the idea had great merit, but getting them over the finish line proved impossible. One of my most depressing meetings was with Peter Chernin and Tony Vinciquerra at Fox. Both had become good friends and both had indicated support for the project. But when it came time to commit, they decided that they had too many issues with many of the participants to lead the charge. By the end of 2004, we realized that the wireless TV idea was not going to happen.

I learned a lot from the experience. Today, many years later, I'm convinced wireless TV was a great idea. From a technical standpoint, it took advantage of excess spectrum that the industry wasn't deploying and that with compression could grow and be efficiently distributed to consumers. Most importantly, it allowed the participants to use unsold inventory to market a venture that all of them owned a stake in. Besides getting paid for their signals, they could use that marketing clout to force their nemesis, the cable industry, to the negotiating table and build a viable enterprise in the process. However, I was naïve when it came to understanding the dynamics and competing interests of the players, which in retrospect was probably inexcusable, because I had labored for years in the same industry with all of them.

Greg Nathanson, as usual, was succinct in his assessment: "You're asking people to come together to act in their self-interest for their future. Most people can't think about tomorrow; they're only concerned about today. Besides that, they have to cooperate with people that they sometimes don't trust. Worse, in many cases, the thought of seeing their competitors make money from the idea troubles them more than the notion that they will be making money, too."

Unlike my experience in Seattle, I had no illusions about wireless TV. Making the decision to buy the Mariners was a mistake from the outset, because given the nature of the community's relationship to professional sports, we never had the financial resources to overcome those challenges. I should have understood that before we started the venture, but, as I mentioned earlier, I missed the course on community dynamics. In television, we went into the project with our eyes wide open. In spite of our inability to get a second revenue stream, we were successful in TV, and we knew that wireless TV was a "moon shot." Given the dollars at stake for us and everyone else, it was certainly worth it, and my personality made me the one dumb enough to try it.

As I've said before, I love to do what people say can't be done; the prospect of failure doesn't make me flee, it emboldens me. Have I wasted time and money on projects that require collective action that I'm not likely to achieve? Certainly, but even in failure, I can look back and appreciate what I learned from the experience. That in itself is remarkably rewarding.

After the wireless TV project, we concluded that the industry was years away from a second revenue stream. As 2005 began, we met for a senior managers' retreat to discuss our prospects. The radio industry had declined from the heady days at the end of the previous decade and had slipped to 1–2 percent annual growth. Between slowing momentum and the recognition that the consolidation frenzy had led to less than stellar results, radio stocks had declined precipitously. When the music stopped, radio was still a profitable industry, but with none of the spectacular growth that the financial markets had assumed a few years earlier.

Our TV business was running well and growing nicely, and Emmis, with a significant magazine portfolio, good international radio stations, and a strong core radio business, was in good financial shape. However, we had nearly $1.6 billion in debt and our leverage ratio was nearly nine to one, meaning we had around $180 million of cash flow and a market cap of over $3 billion. Now, if you are leveraged at nine times today, you're probably reading this somewhere in debtor's prison, but in those days, that multiple was actually normal. In fact, even after the air went out of the radio balloon in the early 2000s, banks were still lending to broadcasters at up to ten times cash flow. To give you an idea of how much has changed in the last fifteen years, if you can find a bank today that will lend to a broadcaster, it will probably cap the loan at three times cash flow.

Now, I would like to tell you that, when we met in the spring of 2005, I was prescient and told our managers, "I think there will be a financial collapse in a few years, and we should get rid of most of our debt right now." But I wasn't, and I didn't. None of us knew what lay ahead—certainly not me. However, all of us thought we had too much debt and we should retire a lot of it. We sat for a full day debating what to do next and concluded that we should sell TV and scale back the company. I have to admit that my frustration with wireless TV and the entire second revenue stream battle had something to do with my decision to jettison TV, but with the natural exception of Randy Bongarten, everyone agreed that TV, not radio, should be sold.

The consensus of our group was that we should scale back our debt to more manageable levels and that our TV assets would be worth over a billion dollars, which would greatly reduce that debt. More importantly, all of us believed that our radio assets, located in America's largest and best markets, would provide us with the security of having more valuable, saleable assets if we needed, in the future, to deleverage further. Our sixteen television stations were in smaller, less attractive markets, with only two stations in the top twenty-five: WKCF in Orlando, a WB affiliate, and KOIN in Portland, a CBS station. On the other hand, our radio assets were in the most desirable markets, including New York, Los Angeles, and Chicago. I had learned at various stages of my career that when smaller market stations were difficult or impossible to sell, there always seemed to be buyers who coveted being in the largest cities. For years we joked that everybody who is in Kokomo wants to be in New York, but no one in New York is anxious to go to Kokomo.

Another issue was central to our thinking. Not only did we control better assets in radio, but we believed there were fewer threats to radio than to TV. At the time, with no second revenue stream on the horizon, we worried about the steady decline of TV viewing as the multichannel universe expanded. All of these new channels were getting subscriber fees, and they would have the ability to bid for more and more content. Of course, 2005 was well before the birth of OTT (over the top networks such as Netflix and Amazon Prime) that would further erode the audience for local television.

For years, we had discussed the benefits and liabilities of television versus radio. As I mentioned, TV is a primary medium, greatly valued by advertisers that spend the bulk of their budgets on TV. This status enabled TV to continue to charge ever-increasing prices for ever-decreasing audiences. If you look at the top-rated TV show in 1975, *All in the Family*, it had a 30.1 rating, meaning that 30.1 percent of all TV households in the country were watching that program. By 2005, the top-rated program was *American Idol*, with a 17.6 rating, representing a 42 percent decline. This number has continued to decrease precipitously over the past sixteen years. Yet even with these declines, TV broadcasters continue to charge more for commercials every year, even though they reach fewer viewers. Again, this disconnect stems from TV being America's preferred medium, but we worried that, eventually, advertisers would reach a tipping point, and would refuse to pay more for fewer eyeballs.

We believed that these two threats, the increased competition from cable channels and the disconnect between pricing and audience, combined with no significant threats to the radio ecosystem and our higher quality assets, made our decision rather easy. Randy, running our TV group, vehemently disagreed, but he was the lone dissenter. Sadly, for the fourth time in his career, his business was being sold out from under him.

We exited television with proceeds of $1.25 billion, representing a profit of well over $100 million. It would have been much higher, but we were selling WVUE, New Orleans, during Hurricane Katrina. It took several years and a number of markdowns, but we finally sold the station two years later, albeit at a steep discount.

Over the years, Randy has always teased me that I had made a mistake in picking radio over television. For years, I joked that leaving TV and staying in radio was like "jumping from the *Hindenburg* and landing on the *Titanic*." Neither business was particularly stellar in the immediate aftermath of our decision. Years later, after the radio industry went through the carnage of the 2008–2009 recession and TV managed to secure its second revenue stream, I finally admitted to Randy that he had been right, keeping our television group would have been the right decision, but it took many years to prove that point!

Today TV is buoyed by the second revenue stream as well as post–Citizens United political dollars, but decreasing audiences have wreaked havoc on its core advertising revenues. The impact of the OTT networks has hastened that decline. One thing is certain—if TV didn't ultimately win the battle with cable, the industry would have certainly gone into free-fall. As someone who will always believe in the critical service that local broadcasters provide, I'm ecstatic that the war was won, even though it didn't happen on our watch.

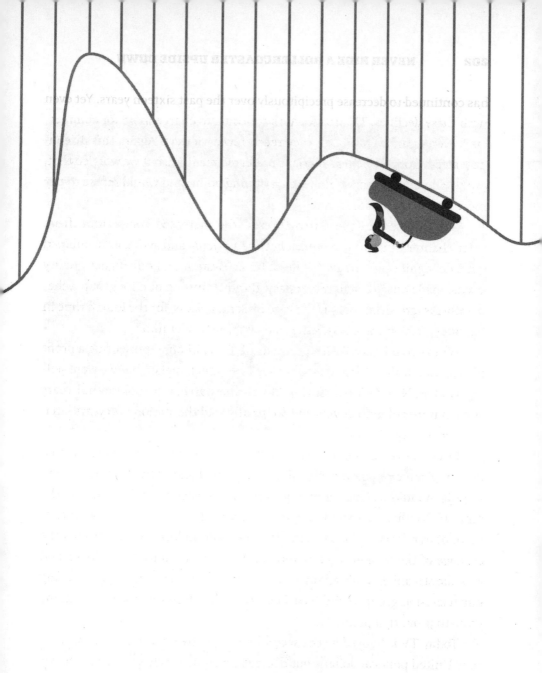

Top: Being inducted into the Central Indiana Business Hall of Fame. *At left:* Our investment banker, Jill Greenthal, who orchestrated our attempt to go private and many other more successful ventures.

Not for the Faint of Heart

B ecause we had launched our IPO at the beginning of the "golden age of exuberance," we rode a run-up that taught us that when your sector is hot, all benefits accrue to you. With a rising share price, you can use your stock for acquisitions, you can more easily obtain financing, and most importantly, you have a windfall that makes a significant difference to you and your employees. When Emmis's stock was going up, one of my greatest joys was visiting our stations and hearing employees tell me how they had benefitted from their stock options. Nothing could match knowing that the company I created was making a difference in the lives of so many people who had chosen to work for us. Once, at a Christmas party in St. Louis, Patty McMahon, our office manager, pulled me aside to tell me that the appreciation of her stock options had allowed her and her husband to pay off their kids' college loans *and* their mortgage. Others told me that their Emmis stock had allowed them to take care of their elderly parents. Years after he retired, Jim Riggs, who had headed our research department for several decades, told me that his Emmis stock had changed his family's life, paying for his home, his kids' education, and even helping them start their careers. It's hard to describe how these comments changed my life as well, and when the stock languished, how frustrating it was.

When we first went public, I learned a valuable lesson about the public markets. Speaking at an investor conference, I was droning on about my long-term vision for Emmis. After I was done, an investor from one of the large investment funds pulled me aside and imparted wisdom that I never forgot: "Jeff, I listened to you speak about the vision for the company, and it was actually very compelling, but let me explain a little bit about your audience. The people who buy your stock want to know what you are going to do in the next quarter. They get paid their bonuses based on the quarterly performance of your stock, so their goal is to buy your stock, hope you improve your earnings over a short period of time, and sell so they can rack up their bonuses. Said another way, if you can make money in the next three months, they don't care if the way you do it causes the world to explode after they're gone. They don't care. This is short-term thinking, and no one has any interest in anything beyond the next three months."

While there are certainly long-term holders of stock—people who do believe in a much longer time frame—they are the exception, not the rule. If you run a public company, you need to understand that your performance is judged by your last quarter, and it's a fact of life that makes most public companies much more focused on the short-term than on the long-term interests of their enterprises. That, I believe, leads to the long-term detriment of almost every company.

I have to admit, I filed that investor's advice away because our sector was booming. Wall Street was hiring analysts who specialized in media, and every bank brought investment banking teams to the table. The best analysts were rock stars, led by Drew Marcus, first at Alex Brown, and then at Deutsche Bank when his firm was sold. The biggest mistake we made when we went public was not being part of Drew's "stable." When Morgan Stanley put together our offering, Drew was on vacation in Europe and didn't respond to our request that he join our IPO team. In retrospect, we should have sent a plane to get him. We've laughed about it over the years, but radio heavyweights Lowry Mays and Mel Karmazin were charter members of Drew's group, and his ability to guide people to their stock made them both millions and millions of dollars. At the industry's peak, it was almost impossible to enter the public markets without Drew and Deutsche Bank on your side. Since everyone needed Drew, Deutsche Bank's investment bankers came along, and the system produced massive fees for the firm. During this time, Drew became the highest-paid media analyst on Wall Street. As a friend of mine said, "I don't know how much they pay him per word, but it has to be a world record."

Even though we were never valued at the same multiples as Drew's largest clients, everyone in the industry followed in their wake. Although I was a well-known skeptic about radio's math, we were still a beneficiary for a number of years. After going public at $15.50 per share, our stock climbed pretty steadily and peaked at $124 per share in January 2000.

And then the music stopped.

As I've noted, after the dot-com era and after the 2000 Clear Channel/SFX Live Nation deal, revenues settled down and the industry's cachet was gone. Radio stocks began a long-term, inexorable decline. Firms disbanded their radio investment banking teams, most of the analysts scattered to the winds, and the stocks receded, never again to come close to their previous lofty levels. At its peak, Emmis had over a dozen analysts following the company. By 2006, we were down to two, and those stopped covering us a few years later.

After we sold our TV group and paid off much of our debt, we were hopeful that our improved balance sheet and streamlined company would be more attractive to Wall Street, but Emmis's share price, like those of all the radio stocks, still languished. At that point, being public was a very unattractive proposition. We were stuck with the expense of interminable Securities and Exchange Commission (SEC) filings. Moreover, the financial reporting requirements of the federal Sarbanes-Oxley Act were a constant burden. But the worst part of the experience was the daily ordeal of watching our stock go nowhere while our financial condition dramatically improved.

It was 2006, and, abandoned by Wall Street, we realized our share price was not likely to increase much at all. Yet, frustratingly, we knew that Emmis was still a valuable enterprise—its industry just had a lot less cachet than it had had earlier in the decade. We understood we were left with a company that, based on our estimation of asset values, was significantly undervalued by the market. That's the curse of being in slow-growing industries that lack appeal on Wall Street. The answer that was staring us in the face was that we didn't have to be public anymore. All we had to do was buy out all our shareholders and we would be a private company again.

That's not a simple operation, and, as I learned, it's not for the faint of heart. For example, you have to offer investors a premium to the current share price, but one that you can afford. What makes that complicated is not all your investors have the same agenda. The process requires the deft touch of a seasoned investment banker. We had switched from Paul Taubman and Morgan Stanley to Jill Greenthal at Credit Suisse because by the early 2000s, Paul had become such a superstar at Morgan Stanley that I began to believe he viewed me as almost a pro bono account. In the past twenty years, Paul has been involved in almost every significant media or telecommunications deal. When he left Morgan Stanley in late 2012, he secured free office space in a law firm while he decided on his next venture. Paul's talents were in such demand, however, that before he hired a single person, he provided enough financial advice to be named one of the ten largest investment banks of 2013!

Jill was (and is!) brilliant, incredibly funny, and unflappable. For those reasons, and more, she became one of the first women on Wall Street to rise to the top of the investment banking field. Early on in our relationship, someone asked if it bothered me to have a woman as my investment banker. Without missing a beat, I replied, "What would bother me is having an incompetent as my investment banker!" For years, my relationship with Jill has been based on nonstop snarkiness. Once, on a road show, I swallowed a piece of gum that I thought was lodged in my throat. I couldn't cough it up but wasn't certain I could swallow it. In short, I was panicked. Jill offered little comfort: "Look, if you're still breathing, it's not going to kill you, so let's go on to our next meeting." One of her assistants added, "It's almost certain to be in your digestive system by now." When I asked how long it would stay there, Jill calmly responded, "I think it takes gum about fifty years to go through your digestive system." Seeing my depressed expression, Jill sweetly needled, "The good news is by the time you die, it will be almost out of your system."

At the beginning of the process to go private, Jill and I met with a banker who provided me with advice that became the cornerstone of my thinking about being private and about nearly everything else I've encountered in the years since. "Jeff," he noted, "when you are raising capital for something like taking your company private, just remember this, 'the hundred-year flood occurs every three years.'" In other words, prepare for the worst scenario— it's not a "once in a lifetime" occurrence. It was simple, yet compelling, advice and it became my North Star for everything that would come after.

After lengthy discussions with Jill and her team, we decided to offer $15.50 per share for the stock of the company, which was a 20 percent premium over its average trading price (oh, how the mighty had fallen!). Through Credit Suisse, we had lined up the debt financing to do the transaction. We made our offer to the Emmis board, and the board set up a special committee to evaluate our bid. The special committee was made up of Frank Sica, who had been our merchant banker at Morgan Stanley and had gone on to an illustrious career at Soros Fund Management and then at the successful private equity firm Tailwind Capital, where he partnered with Tailwind's founder Larry Sorrel, who was also on the committee. The third member of the committee was Peter Lund, who joined our board after leaving his position as president of the CBS television network. The special committee then hired its own outside advisors, Morgan Stanley and Lazard, so the group could evaluate our company's finances independently to determine whether the bid was fair and accurate.

The fun didn't stop there. The minute we made our bid, at least ten law firms, representing shareholders, filed lawsuits within that first day. These lawyers are the ambulance chasers of the corporate world. The lawsuits were usually accompanied by at least three articles in major newspapers claiming that the bid was the greatest robbery since the Brink's heist of 1981. Because I had lived through all those attacks during the last six months that I owned the Mariners, being called the "most outrageous corporate reprobate ever" didn't faze me as much as it would anyone else. Since I've been through this experience more than once, I can tell you it is standard operating procedure. It doesn't matter what price you offer, one dollar or $1 billion per share, your bid is not only inadequate, it is outrageous. I learned quickly not to take offense at those articles; it's all part of an elaborate Kabuki dance that takes place whenever a going-private process is initiated.

The reason the law firms race to be the first to file is that lawsuits always get consolidated, and usually the first firm becomes the lead negotiator.

This firm gets the lion's share of fees when the deal is completed. Obviously, spearheading these shareholder lawsuits is a lucrative cottage industry, as is advising the special committee. The adverse press coverage is designed to put pressure on the advisors and the special committee to make certain that they don't "give away the company." There are few certainties in life, but one of them is that the advisors will convince the special committee that the offering price is too low, and we understood the system very well. Our process was made more challenging because of the nature of the Emmis board and our stock.

Emmis went public at a time when the FCC preferred a "control person" as licensee, so they could hold that individual accountable for regulatory purposes. In effect, when the proverbial "shit hit the fan" at your stations, the FCC wanted to know exactly whom to look for. To achieve this kind of control, companies going public during this era usually had two classes of stock; in our case, yours truly held stock that had ten votes per share, while everyone else owned stock with one vote per share. This arrangement gave me voting control of the company. Obviously, shareholders don't love this system, but it is something that no one willingly gives up once they have it. Because everyone knew I controlled Emmis, the board was viewed as less independent than a normal board would be. While this observation was unquestionably true, the nature of our company meant that our board was incredibly vocal and had never, ever been shy about voicing their opinions. Having said that, it didn't take much due diligence to look at the makeup of our board and see that the overwhelming majority of them had long-term ties to me: Gary Kaseff was my general counsel; Greg Nathanson was my retired TV president and a long-time, original shareholder of Emmis; as mentioned, Frank and Larry had been my bankers at Morgan Stanley. And Susan Bayh, lawyer and former first lady of Indiana, was a close personal friend. The only true outsider was the recently appointed Peter Lund. So, five of the six directors (excluding me) appeared to be people who would generally defer to my wishes. Interestingly, during all of the years we have been public, I can never remember a time when I "lost a vote" on my board, which would seem to lend credence to the idea that I controlled them. However, these were all fiercely independent people who took their responsibilities very seriously. There were innumerable times when something I wanted to do met with resistance from various board members. We always worked it out, usually reaching a compromise that resolved the issue before a vote was called. While some would observe that my board has never overruled me, I can honestly state that it has been as collaborative a process as the one practiced by my management team, with just as much fun and needling.

As the negotiations continued, the special committee wanted eighteen dollars per share, based on the recommendations of the advisors, Morgan Stanley and Lazard. We raised our bid to $16.25, but we communicated that it was going to be impossible to finance our offer at much more. The discussions continued for several weeks. Finally, we raised our bid to $16.80 and said that was as far as we could go. We had determined that any higher price would cause our financing to break down.

As head of the special committee, Frank was adamant that the bid had to be raised to eighteen dollars per share. During one memorable call on a Friday afternoon, Frank said, "If you can't get to eighteen dollars, forget it." He was so unyielding I figured he spoke for the whole committee, and I quickly sat down with Jill. We wracked our brains, consulted with the potential lenders, but came to the conclusion that $16.80 per share was as high as we could go. The next day, I told Frank that we were pulling the bid, and the deal to go private died without fanfare or fireworks. I learned shortly thereafter that Frank had lived up to his reputation as a tough and sometimes strong-willed leader, and he had never consulted with Larry and Peter. When we rescinded the offer, their first response was, "Why did you drop the bid?" I've been involved in giant miscommunications before, but this was one of the worst. I was frustrated, but still certain that doing the deal at eighteen dollars per share, or even close to it, would have blown up the financing.

In retrospect, we possibly could have resurrected the offer, but at the time it seemed best to move on. I'm convinced that the greatest problem we had with this process was that the special committee, especially Frank, believed that they had to be tougher on us, given the nature of my control and the long-term friendships between all of us on the committee. Just as I had been willing to go overboard to see the PLO's side in my negotiations with Israel in Kyoto, I think Frank was determined to be doubly tough with me. Shortly after the deal collapsed, Frank left our board, but we managed

to repair our rift soon afterwards and to this day maintain a cordial relationship. That's probably more a reflection of my personality: I don't hold
grudges, and I'm happy to move on from them.

The other enduring legacy of the process was that the instant it was
over, several shareholders, including those who had called the bid a disgrace,
phoned to tell us that the deal should have happened and they would have
been happy with $16.80. Three years later, when the stock dropped to under
one dollar, I'm certain they regretted the outcome as much as me.

I've had countless people come to me over the years and tell me how
lucky I was that I didn't pay $16.80 or anything near that, because a few years
later, the stock—as well as the industry—collapsed. I've always smiled, but
they happen to be wrong. Back in 2006, if the shareholders had accepted
our bid, I would have sold a number of stations to make sure that our deal
was paid for and that our leverage came way down. The admonition about
the hundred-year flood was always in the back of my mind, and I intended
to move quickly if we went private. By that time, I was certain I didn't want
too much debt, and I knew what my assets were worth and who would buy
them. If the deal had gone through, my company's financial health would
have been greatly enhanced because, in 2006, buyers were willing to pay
much higher prices than they would in 2009. The effort to go private was a
disaster for everybody—the shareholders, all of our employees, and me, not
to mention the special committee—but I never held a grudge and I got over
my frustrations quickly. Through this experience, I learned that anger and
resentment are just wasted emotions. Sometimes things just don't work out.

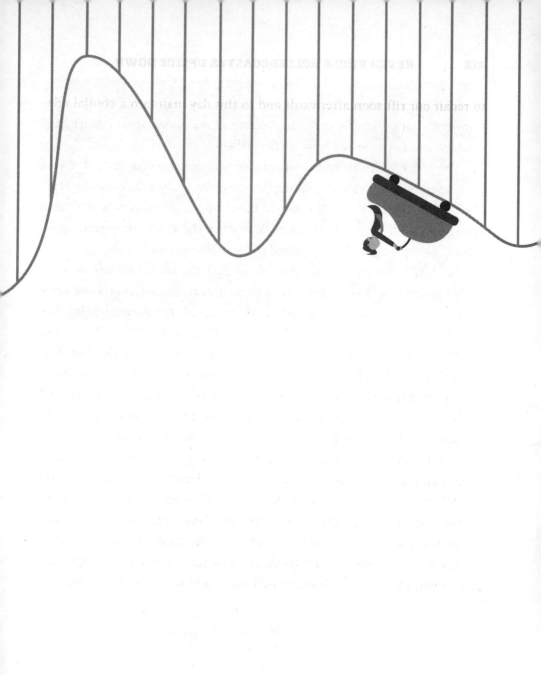

Top: The Emmis Team that allowed us to survive the Hundred-Year Flood. Standing (from left to right): General Counsel, Scott Enright; IT Director, David Blunt; VP of Finance, Chris Rickenbach; Founder, Jeff Smulyan; President/COO, Pat Walsh; Chief Strategic Officer, Greg Loewen; and CFO, Ryan Hornaday. Sitting (from left to right): VP & Associate General Counsel, Elizabeth Ellis; Director of Internal Audit, Julie Shedd; SVP Human Resources, Traci Thomson; and Executive Assistant, Wendy Jackson. (*Photo credit: Tony Valainis, Indianapolis Monthly Photographer) Bottom:* Laughing through the crisis with the Emmis Moose at a Managers' Meeting.

12

The Hundred-Year Flood

fter the going-private debacle, we knew we had to reassess. Our radio stations and print publications were doing well but did not have significant growth prospects. We were hoping to find new areas to kick-start our growth rate. With that in mind, we brought Greg Loewen into Emmis in 2007 as head of strategy. In retrospect, it was like bringing him into Germany in 1944 as head of postwar planning, but we didn't know a financial crisis was in our future.

A Harvard MBA, Greg had been on the Monitor team that had built the plan for wireless TV, and his engaging manner fit well with Emmis. Several years later, Greg left Monitor to head strategy for a newspaper holding company in his native Toronto. We stayed in touch, and at one point I asked if he would consider coming to Emmis. Fortunately, our prospects looked more appealing than those of the newspaper business, and we struck a deal for Greg to come to Indianapolis.

One of his first assignments was to stress test all of our businesses. He looked at the recent history of our assets, with a focus on radio, and built a matrix of possible future outcomes. One of his models showed radio revenues declining 15 percent over a two-year period. As I've noted, dropping 15 percent when you have a largely fixed-cost business is disastrous. When Greg presented the dire projections to me, I dismissed them out of hand. I usually don't display too much emotion in presentations, but I remember chastising him rather vociferously. I told him that I'd been in radio during several downturns, and I'd never seen numbers like his. I wanted different scenarios, but not ones that were completely outside the realm of possibility. This discussion concluded with Greg quietly leaving the meeting, probably feeling that Toronto looked a lot better in the rearview mirror. However, Greg survived that day, and many others. In fact, as of this writing, he's still at Emmis, running two separate businesses. I can also tell you that after 2008–2009, he has reminded me of his presentation many, many times.

Shortly before the financial crisis began, I was serving on the board of Finish Line, an athletic footwear and apparel retailer that had gone public in 1992. Founded by longtime friends Alan Cohen, David Klapper, Larry Sablosky, and David Fagin, the firm had decided my background in sports would be valuable to them. The company had grown consistently over many years and was the second-largest athletic footwear company in America (after Foot Locker). In 2007, Alan, Finish Line's chairman and CEO, decided to acquire Genesco, a large footwear and apparel company, for $1.5 billion. The acquisition would catapult Finish Line into the major leagues of retailing. Unfortunately, the deal hit a snag at the outset. First, questions arose about Genesco's operations. Second, Finish Line shareholders, unaccustomed to Alan having debt, raised major concerns about the agreement. The deal started giving the normally unflappable Cohen significant stress.

At one point, Alan turned to me and Steve Goldsmith, the former mayor of Indianapolis and a Finish Line board member, and asked us to meet with UBS, the investment bank underwriting the deal. They were getting cold feet; although it would be one year until the economy collapsed, storm clouds were already forming, and the bank was reevaluating all its large deals. We brought in Ken Moelis, who had run UBS Investment Bank in New York prior to leaving to start his own successful boutique firm. Ken knew UBS as well as anyone, and he was an ideal partner to help us navigate difficult waters. Steve, Ken, and I flew to New York to meet one of the firm's bankers who had flown in from Zurich.

After pleasantries were exchanged, the banker went through a litany of reasons why UBS was hesitating to follow through on its commitment to fund the acquisition. Finally, I noted, "UBS is one of the leading financial institutions in the world. It just doesn't look good for you to welch on an $850 million commitment." His response will go down as one of the all-time great banking statements: "Well, Jeff, in the last year, I've welched on over $13 billion of commitments for our bank, so what's another $850 million?" Ken Moelis, sitting next to me, whispered, "Touché." As we left the meeting, I sarcastically asked Ken and Steve, "How firm does that UBS funding look right now?"

By the end of the summer, Alan wanted out of the deal and, for good measure, out of his company, as well. He came to my house one Sunday morning to meet with Steve and me, bringing along lifelong friends Sablosky and Klapper to demonstrate his determination. Both had been semiretired for years but had stayed on the board and knew Alan better than anyone. Alan explained with great conviction that he wanted to terminate the Genesco deal and retire from Finish Line. He was worn out physically and mentally. I told him, "Alan, I understand it, but you just can't quit now. We'll figure out how to get you out of this, but until this process ends, you can't leave your company. Right now, you have to be El Cid [the Spanish general who was so inspiring that when he was killed in battle, his generals propped him up on his horse, tied his outstretched sword to his arm, and sent the dead soldier into battle to lead his troops]." I implored Alan to consider that his people needed to see him leading Finish Line during this difficult time. Once it was over, he could ride off into the sunset, but for now he had to be there for his troops even though he felt as dead as El Cid.

Alan stayed, the deal ended (after litigation and a costly settlement), and Alan left his company shortly thereafter. But he knew his path wouldn't be mine, and when we met that Sunday, he made an eerily prophetic pronouncement: "Jeff, if this happened to you, you would never, ever quit. I know you too well."

A year later, Alan's words rang true.

Throughout 2008, radio stocks traded down and signs of trouble in the economy were becoming more pronounced. In March, Bear Stearns collapsed and Lehman Brothers was in dire straits. Our cash flows were steady, but not growing, and during 2008, our leverage was slightly under

six times—not a lot of debt for the radio industry at the time—but still trou-
bling in a challenged industry. In fact, even though the market crashed in
the fall of 2008, we were able to pay off enough debt to bring our leverage
down to under 5.5 times by the end of our fiscal year in February 2009. It
didn't matter—the hundred-year flood was about to drown us. Radio stocks
collapsed by December 2008, and our stock dropped to just over $1 per share.
Wall Street had figured out quickly that once the financial markets failed,
the advertising markets wouldn't be far behind. In 2009, radio advertising
dropped by 30 percent, and in a largely fixed-cost business, you can't cut
fast enough to avoid a catastrophe. Our cash flows dropped by 65 percent in
the ensuing two years. By the middle of 2009, our leverage climbed all the
way up to 11.5 times; add in our expensive preferred stock and our leverage
was over sixteen times. At our peak in 2010, our leverage reached 13.2 times,
or nineteen times, including our preferred stock. Now, the preferred didn't
require current payments, but unpaid dividends kept adding up.

In short, we were a zombie company, dead to the world.

A rational person would have thrown in the towel, and I had a number
of friends who did, and others who were taken over by lenders. At Emmis,
we still believed we had underlying value that exceeded our debt, but clearly
in the maelstrom of 2009–2010, that was hard for people to understand.
During this time, most of my friends advised me to declare bankruptcy,
make a deal with the lenders to retain some equity, and emerge with a manageable balance sheet and significant ownership. But I wasn't going to go
there, not while the company was still breathing.

My father's words kept running through my head during this period:
The hardest thing ever is for someone who is rich to suddenly become poor.
You become used to a standard of living that suddenly disappears. For me,
my net worth (which reached several hundred million dollars at its height
in the late 1990s) was just a way of keeping score. I never really focused on
making piles of money, and at my peak worth, my lifestyle barely changed.
The greatest compliments I ever got were from friends who said: I knew you
when you were poor and I know you now that you're rich, and you're the
same person. That's all great until you wake up and realize you've become
poor overnight. I'm obviously not a Donald Trump fan, but something he
said during one of his bankruptcies has stayed with me: "I'm walking around

town, and people don't realize, I'm worse than broke, I'm several hundred million dollars in debt. That's a very strange feeling."

So, there I was, with almost all my assets in a company that was deeply in debt, and on the hook personally for the money I had borrowed to buy back some of my stock following the troubles with the Mariner bridge loan. The world had turned upside down. In other words, it was a situation best summed up by Tim Matheson and John Belushi at the end of Belushi's "Was it over when the Germans bombed Pearl Harbor" speech in *Animal House*—when Matheson declares, "I think this situation requires a really futile and stupid gesture to be done on somebody's part," and Belushi adds, "and we're just the guys to do it!"

Saving Emmis was crazy, and likely futile, but I had run into that before, and at least this time, I was fighting for what I cared about most. There's a saying, "you never want to fight a war on someone else's homeland," and Emmis clearly was my homeland.

When our company collapsed in 2009, I referred to Kipling's poem "If—" a number of times, just to muster the courage and wisdom I knew I would need. The most important thing is to gather your team, clearly explain the current situation, and communicate what you're attempting to achieve. I can guarantee that when the bottom falls out, you'll need all hands on deck, with absolutely everybody's input, to come up with a survival plan. I believe the best part of our Emmis culture is the remarkable amount of trust in our leadership team. Everyone understands that their opinion is critical, and everyone understands that they will do whatever it takes to figure out how to right the ship.

Kipling's first line—"If you can keep your head when all about you are losing theirs . . ."—is the single most important aspect of leadership in a crisis. We put together a plan to slash costs as much as possible: employee salaries, 401K contributions, furlough plans, charitable contributions. You name it, we cut it. As the leader, I knew the cuts had to start with me, so I dropped my annual salary to $1. Naturally, I had friends comment that at a dollar, I was still grossly overpaid. Since my salary cut was noted in an SEC filing, the local and industry newspapers quickly spread the news. It became common for people to come up to me in restaurants and at industry events and hand me a dollar while proudly proclaiming that they were doubling my pay.

Our people knew that the senior managers were in the trenches with them every day and were bearing their fair share of sacrifices. Our history of being open with our people engendered trust—you can't ask folks to buy into your goals without it. I'm proud that at Emmis we had a significant reservoir of good will with our people, and when we needed them to make sacrifices to help save the company, they were more than willing. No one accepts pay cuts, furloughs, or benefit cuts happily, but our people did what was needed and were critical to our survival.

We tore the company apart, looking for creative ways to cut costs and pay down debt. Pat Walsh, then our CFO (now our president); Scott Enright, our general counsel; and Ryan Hornaday, then our treasurer (now our CFO) rewrote the book on crisis financial management. Selling the corporate jet was the one thing that broke my heart—as I mentioned, a plane is heroin for a workaholic—but it was not essential for our survival. We also used cash outside our credit facility to exploit a loophole in our Bank of America agreements and ended up tendering for nearly $80 million of our debt at fifty-seven cents on the dollar. When Bank of America found out, they were furious but calmed down when we pointed out the loophole. Of course, immediately afterward, they forced us to amend our agreement to prevent further below-market repurchases.

We also got creative with how we handled the proceeds from deals that didn't formally close (i.e., the sale of WVUE-TV, New Orleans) until we were in this predicament. When we closed in 2008, we used part of the proceeds to pay our senior managers and thus reduce regular operating expenses. We used the rest, along with a few other sources of cash not constrained by our lenders, to buy back more of our debt at a discount. In addition, we renegotiated several loan covenants; all gave us more breathing room to survive.

Reasonable people would ask why a company trading at nine times cash flow would even attempt to avoid bankruptcy if it is carrying thirteen or more times debt. As you already know, part of the problem lies with my obsessive desire to save Emmis, but there was another, more rational reason to save the company. Most radio and TV stations are valued on the books as a strict multiple of cash flow. In addition, the value of a company on the stock exchange includes the costs of being public, with corporate overhead a rather sizable portion. In a sale, however, you offer the station without corporate overhead. If your stations are valued at nine times cash flow, when you sell them without the overhead baked in, you will likely get a higher multiple.

Moreover, every radio and TV company has a significant number of assets that don't produce any cash flow. For example, if I own a station in New York that isn't profitable, that station is deemed to have no value based on its earnings statement. Nevertheless, people will pay a significant amount to enter the New York market, even if the station has no profit. We started Emmis by almost exclusively buying stations like this—as I mentioned, they're known as "sticks." For example, in 1984 we bought KMGG, Los Angeles, for the grand total of $11 million. The station had no ratings and thus no cash flow. A few years later, when it became Power 106, the station became one of the highest billing stations in America. We had been willing to pay $11 million because we wanted to own one of the twenty best signals in the market. As the station grew, and the Los Angeles market peaked in 2001 at over $1 billion in annual market billings, KPWR was generating over $40 million in annual cash flow, so an $11 million purchase produced remarkable returns. As one investment analyst cruelly reminded me (after the industry had declined precipitously), Power 106, at its peak, was worth over twenty times cash flow, or nearly $900 million!

As radio exploded in the 1990s, the value of unprofitable licenses skyrocketed as well. The all-time-high watermark was the $250 million purchase of KFSG-FM in 2000 by Raúl Alarcón's Spanish Broadcasting System. Not only was the station not profitable, it didn't even have a signal capable of reaching all of Los Angeles, and Alarcón had to get approval to move it to a tower site that we leased to him.

Although by 2009 prices were coming down dramatically, broadcasters still had values that were not reflected on their income statements and could be unlocked by selling those stations. Since I had started my career by buying "sticks," I had as much expertise as anyone when it came to selling them.

We decided that selling our second Los Angeles FM, KMVN, would be one of the best ways to reduce our debt. We had purchased "Movin'" from Bonneville International in 2001 when it was KZLA. It was LA's only country station and was underperforming, just as country music had in New York in the previous decade. While we knew that it was going to be difficult to make KZLA more successful in Los Angeles with its significant Hispanic population and its trendy Hollywood/Westside corridor, we decided it was worth the effort. Much of our thinking was based on the old adage: After you get out of Hollywood, Los Angeles resembles Des Moines more than you might think. We did our usual massive research and marketed heavily, but we were never able to break into the market's upper echelon. With a superb sales effort, led by Sales Manager Janet Brainin and Market Manager Val Maki, we were able to double revenue and grow cash flow fairly quickly, but it was clear country music was never going to be a ticket to great success in Los Angeles.

A few years later, Rick Cummings came to me with an interesting proposition he had gotten from retired Emmis president, Doyle Rose. Rick Dees, who had been a dominant force in Los Angeles radio for years as the morning man at KIIS-FM, had been cast adrift by Clear Channel to make room for the company's newest star, Ryan Seacrest. Seacrest, who later became host of *American Idol*, *Live with Kelly and Ryan*, and just about everything else on TV, was quickly becoming LA's dominant morning man. Still, research indicated that Dees had an incredible following in the market.

We were intrigued, especially since Doyle, who had become business and golf partners with Dees, confirmed that Dees was anxious to reclaim his spot in Los Angeles radio. The parting with KIIS had been painful, and he was dying to go up against Seacrest and Clear Channel. Our idea was simple; we'd put Dees on in the mornings on the new station and play a more adult version of KIIS's Top 40 format. Lots of research indicated that the older audiences loved and missed Dees, and we would pair him with music that appealed to his core listeners.

We did exhaustive research that indicated that Dees was beloved in Los Angeles and there was a significant hole in the market. KMVN, Movin 93.1 (the former KZLA), was launched in 2005 to much fanfare. Unfortunately, the station never took off. Dees still had loyal listeners, but there weren't enough of them to become a major force in the market. Rick Cummings, who had meticulously planned the project, was crestfallen and beat himself up about it incessantly. While failure normally led to nonstop needling within the halls of Emmis, we refrained because this one was too painful for Rick, and all of us knew it.

Finally, I pulled him aside: "Everything about this project made sense, the research told us it would work, your sense of the market told us it would work, and it just didn't. All I've ever asked you to do is make rational business decisions. If you do that, I'll never complain, and this was clearly a rational decision. You've been more right about radio programming than anyone in this industry. Let this one go because you made the right call at the time; it just didn't work out." Rick did let it go, although in his inimitable way, he always placed conspicuously, on the back of his desk, billboard advertisements of stations he had programmed that laid eggs. When a friend asked him why he displayed only the losers, he replied, "They always keep me humble!"

With KMVN going nowhere, it was a perfect candidate for deleveraging in a crisis. Fortunately, Bonneville, which had jettisoned the station eight years earlier, had decided to reenter the market. Bruce Reese, who ran the company for many years, was one of my closest friends in radio. When he and I discussed Bonneville's interest in buying back into Los Angeles, I said I would seriously consider selling KMVN back to him. One thing to remember during an economic calamity: It's great to have a buyer that is immune from the vagaries of the market. Bonneville is the broadcasting arm of the Mormon church and has always been able to rely on the church to fund its activities. I used to tease Bruce that, "In my next life, I want to build a business model around tithing, like you guys do!" I've bought, sold, and traded stations with the company over the years, and invariably, the people at Bonneville are as honorable, kind, and trustworthy as I have ever known.

Bruce and I had discussed a purchase price of $150 million, and we were nearing a deal in that range. Unfortunately, Alfred Liggins of Radio One had decided to liquidate his Los Angeles station, KKBT, as well. Alfred, who had bought the station for over $425 million from Clear Channel in 1999, was as desperate to pay down debt as we were. Despite having a better radio signal and a close friendship with Bruce, I made a major miscalculation. As Bruce and I were closing in on a deal, Alfred offered Bruce his station for $137.5 million. I debated dropping the price to match Alfred, but I knew that our signal was better, and that Bruce was going to change the format of whatever station he bought to a form of progressive rock. I thought that if I chased Alfred down to $137.5 million, chances were he would lower the price further, because I knew his lenders were more aggressive than mine. Besides, I reasoned, there were other buyers, and I thought I could get my $150 million price. Big mistake. Alfred made his deal with Bruce at $137.5 million and my other buyers disappeared. Here's an important lesson in an economic crisis: Don't assume a lot of buyers will show up. What made my decision more inexcusable was that "Movin" was losing over $3 million a year, and getting some cash for the station *and* eliminating the losses was critical to us and should have been my only objective.

Six months later, in April 2009, we were able to construct a lease/sale with Mexico's largest broadcaster, Grupo Radio Centro, for a grand total of $115 million. Grupo Centro had seven years to purchase the station, but we were able to put their lease payments in a special financing vehicle that gave us more capability to retire debt than an outright purchase would have. In 2013, we agreed to accept $85 million from them to buy the station early. When they needed to sell it in 2019, it only brought $35 million. This gives you an idea of the incredible decline of American radio throughout this period.

Just as we were gaining some breathing room, we had another bit of horrific luck. In the final quarter of 2009, Sláger, our Hungarian radio network, was nationalized (as detailed back in chapter eight). This incident gave rise to our motto: "When you think nothing can get worse, it *definitely* will get worse!"

All we could do was continue cutting wherever we could and harvesting every bit of cash to bring down our debt. As I mentioned, when we used cash that was not from radio station sales, we took advantage of loopholes in our loan agreements to buy our debt at a steep discount in the market. Our discussions with our lead bank, Bank of America, were always comical. We would do something to improve our balance sheet and they would complain. We would point out that it was permissible under our agreements, and they would note that while permissible, it didn't comport with what they thought was the "spirit" of the agreement. One lesson from this experience: When you are drowning and you reach for a life raft, you really don't care if it's a standard regulation raft! The banking industry was as upside down as the broadcasting industry; norms were being broken every day. Our job was simple: to survive. If we adhered to the letter of our agreements, we didn't mind if we ruffled a few feathers, and we did so regularly.

To give you an idea of where we stood at the end of 2009, here's a quick snapshot of Emmis, adjusted for station sales.

Revenues in 2007	Revenues in 2008	Revenues in 2009
$339 Million	$308 Million	$242 Million

Cash Flow 2007	Cash Flow 2008	Cash Flow 2009
$99 Million	$75 Million	$31 Million

Fortunately, by 2010, the economy had begun to stabilize, although radio was still reeling from the precipitous declines in revenue and cash flow. Nevertheless, a few bright spots appeared. Radio listening was holding up, foreshadowing a return of advertising dollars. Also, capital providers, sensing the industry had hidden value, started to hover around us. Sensing that the worst was behind us despite our staggeringly high leverage, I became more optimistic that there was a lot of unrecognized value in the company.

At the annual NAB Convention in Las Vegas in April 2010, John Momtazee, now our lead investment banker, came to me: Heath Freeman, a senior banker at Alden Global Capital, wanted to meet to discuss Emmis's future. John had worked with Heath on several deals, and I was happy to comply. Alden had taken a position in our preferred stock, which had cratered at the end of 2008, sinking from $15 to $1 per share. Part of that decline came from our suspension of the 6.25 percent dividends as soon as our business collapsed. The preferred shareholders were about to get two seats on our board after eight quarters of nonpayment, but that was a small price to pay to conserve cash. Alden, a hedge fund that had enjoyed great success in media, recognized the underlying value of our assets and came to us with an idea to take control of the remaining preferred shares. Heath suggested a partnership on the takeout. I told him I wasn't interested in resolving only part of our capital structure, but if they wanted to resolve all of it by financing our purchase of our common stock, I would be interested. We had been consistently telling the investment community that our stock was undervalued because we had assets that weren't performing in the current depressed environment. No one appreciated that performance would eventually improve, so we decided the best way to create value was to buy back our common shares.

Heath quickly jumped at the prospect. Like me, Alden saw the recession ending, and they knew that the performance of radio assets in the biggest markets was likely to improve rapidly. And we owned many of the country's most desirable stations. Now, if you have an MBA, or, come to think of it, command of third-grade arithmetic, you're probably asking: Why put more debt on a company with nearly thirteen times leverage at the very earliest stage of an economic recovery? My answer: With cash flows dropping by two-thirds, a great many of our stations had become unprofitable, despite their good positions in their markets and good ratings. In addition, the recession had devastated stations with lesser market positions, making marginal stations wildly unprofitable. Because I knew that outside capital still valued our assets, I thought financing the buyout of all our stock (going private) at $2.40 per share made sense. As usual, my thinking was based on how I could conclude the deal with Alden and quickly sell enough stations to fix our balance sheet. It wasn't an irrational position, especially in a rapidly improving economy.

We announced our agreement on May 10. Because Alden had to get the other preferred stockholders on board with the transaction, the first negotiations were with the non-Alden preferred stockholders. They were somewhat contentious and it took several months to reach an agreement. We then went back to Alden; they informed us they were no longer willing to go ahead with the transaction. Stunned, we said, "You can't do that." They said, "Fine, sue us." And that's what we did, with the lawsuit ultimately leading to a purchase of their preferred stock and a settlement that salved our wounds quite a bit. Since then, Alden has cast a wide swath through the newspaper business, and their take-no-prisoners approach has left a long trail of bodies in their wake. In 2019, when the firm was a bidder for the Gannett newspapers, several friends from the chain's *Indianapolis Star* called to ask me about Alden. There was one other bidder at the time—GateHouse Media—and the question was: "Who would you pick?"

That question reminded me of an old joke about a rabbi at a funeral. He's supposed to give the eulogy, but, standing at the graveside, he admits: "I'm new to this congregation, and I didn't know the deceased. So, in his memory, would someone say something nice about him?" The rabbi is stunned at the long period of complete silence. The rabbi asks again: "Really, would someone say something nice about the deceased? I didn't know him." More silence. The rabbi is beside himself. In desperation, he says: "Somebody, please, I'm really begging you, say something nice about this man!" Finally, from the back of the gravesite, a little old man steps forward and says: "Well, his brother was even worse than he was!"

In a similar vein, I quickly responded, "The other guys, no matter how bad they are, I guarantee you, Alden is worse." Apparently concluding the same thing, the Gannett board chose GateHouse over Alden.

I violated one of my trusted maxims when dealing with Alden: You never do good business with bad people. I didn't know much about Alden at the time, but I'd heard from a few sources that they were difficult. Looking back, I'm sure I was emboldened in dealing with them by the prospects of a recovering economy, a surplus of buyers, and a stock price that didn't come anywhere near the value of our assets. Still, the maxim holds, and I should have heeded it.

Years later, I reconnected with Heath Freeman, and I found him to be as likable as when we had first dealt with each other. I was also aware, from our original agreement with Alden Capital, that the firm's senior partner Randy Smith had been the one to kill our deal. Not Heath. The enduring lesson is that good people can work at places where they are not in charge, and you have to get a measure of how the company generally does business before you commit. And I should have been more wary of Alden's approach and avoided dealing with them.

The Alden experience reminded me that there are three types of bad people you should avoid. First, people who are constantly difficult—and usually impossible—to work with. In these cases, rely on your scouting reports; they don't lie. Second, people whom you once had a relationship with that has gone sour; business partners and spouses are prime examples. In these cases, never go to war with someone who will blow up your house. Some people are vindictive, mean, angry, or have just become totally irrational. If you sense that the person you're dealing with has become unbalanced, your best course of action is to make your peace and move on. If discretion is the better part of valor, then it's the only part of valor in this type of situation. Third, people you don't know but might encounter randomly, who are what, in Indiana, we call "batshit crazy." Never interact with them! My estimate is that in a country with 350 million people, at least two million fit this description. These are folks you definitely don't want to antagonize; just get as far away from them as possible.

After our Alden debacle, we were left with a significantly overleveraged balance sheet that was unsustainable. Unfortunately, since we were technically in a go-private process, we were effectively halted from doing deals, because any transaction would have to be disclosed, thus slowing down the process. As a result, for six months in 2010, we couldn't improve our situation. And a deadline was coming: we had negotiated a two-year standstill with our banks in August of 2009, but that meant that if we didn't fix our balance sheet by May 2011, the company would most likely default on its loan agreements, and its lenders would be able to take over Emmis.

Why May instead of August? Because we knew that our auditors couldn't give us a clean opinion letter in our annual audit, due by the end of May. Auditors have to study debt maturities and determine whether current operations, projected forward, will prevent default when the loans come due. They can't assume you will amend your bank agreements, or that you will sell assets or refinance your loans or improve your performance. Therefore, we were certain that, by the end of May, we would receive a "Going Concern Letter," which would be an act of default under our bank covenants, even though we could still pay off our interest and principal.

In an earlier era, you had a long-term relationship with your banks based on trust, and they kept your loans in-house. If you were in trouble, you could call up your trusted banker and say: "I've tripped a covenant and I'm technically in default, but I'll still keep paying my interest and principal. Can we waive the leverage ratio covenant?" Banks invariably charged a small fee; the covenant was modified to reflect the new market realities, and everyone went on their way. However, in the years leading up to the financial crisis, most banks quickly sold your loans to other institutions: pension funds, hedge funds, private equity funds. It was a way of spreading the risk and giving everyone a piece of the action. Unfortunately, when the economy dips, the value of the loans declines precipitously, and traditional funds head for the hills, selling their loan portfolios at a discount to distress-funds, known pejoratively as "Loan to Own" lenders. Distress-debt owners aren't looking for a long-term relationship; instead, they seek to buy your debt at a deep discount (in a significant recession, as little as 30 percent of the loan's face value). They wait eagerly for you to violate even the most minor of bank covenants, and then they pounce, using your default status to take over your company. Their theory is that your assets are worth much more than your loan, and by taking over the assets, they can reap outsized rewards when they liquidate them. During this period, I had more than a few friends who were in default, had their loans called, and lost their companies. And that's where we were headed.

Much of our debt was held by two very large hedge funds, Angelo Gordon and Canyon Capital. The Angelo Gordon fund was overseen by Gavin Baiera, known as one of the toughest lenders on Wall Street. In early March, I flew to New York to meet with him and discuss our situation. It was a very cordial meeting, and I remarked to one of our bankers that it had gone much better than expected; I was hopeful we could work out some relief. After the meeting, I flew to the West Coast to meet with our lenders at Canyon.

It was Friday, and that meeting wasn't going as well. Two of the junior lenders seemed largely indifferent to our situation, but one finally admitted he didn't have the authority to do anything, and the founder, Josh Friedman, would have to weigh in. My investment banker John Momtazee and I walked into Josh's office with the two younger bankers. Before we even started the conversation, Josh asked me a series of questions about Emmis, my life, and Indianapolis. It turned out that we had several mutual friends and Josh was fascinated with the history of Emmis. One of his closest friends was Jeff Modisett, who had been attorney general of Indiana during my friend Evan Bayh's tenure as governor. Josh asked, "If I were to call Jeff Modisett for a reference on you, what do you think he would say?" I replied, "Josh, I have no idea, but I really hope you make that call." The conversation continued, and Josh asked about our request to have Canyon buy out all of our loan under new terms, which included a better interest rate for them.

John and I were at lunch when my friend Jill Greenthal called to ask, "How do you think your meeting with Gavin went yesterday?" I said that I thought it went reasonably well. She then confided, "Well, I just found out that he really likes you, but he likes your company more and he has decided he wants to take it over." My heart dropped. I was aware that this was the world we were living in, but for the first time, I thought I was in real danger of losing Emmis.

However, less than an hour after lunch, Josh Friedman and his team called John. They wanted to buy out control of the loan and become our majority lender. By Monday, the agreements were done, Angelo Gordon was gone, and Emmis was saved. It was the closest I've ever come to a near-death experience, and it was certainly close enough!

Our debt holders weren't the only ones who understood how undervalued our assets were. Life is full of surprises, and here's one I call "the curious case of Kevan Fight." A former banker, Kevan had been CFO of Malrite Communications, a leading radio company during the golden age. After Malrite was sold in 1998, Kevan bounced around the industry for a number of years, consulting for various clients. He called me a number of times for advice and visited me in Indianapolis when he wanted more in-depth counsel on a project. At one point, unbeknownst to me, he decided that a nice, profitable venture would be taking over Emmis by partnering with one of our distress lenders (Angelo Gordon or Canyon). Kevan compiled an extensive due diligence presentation, describing all our assets, and analyzing the company and me, including details of my personal obligations. The book then laid out in great detail how he could dismantle Emmis. Apparently, he even had appraisals of how much he could liquidate our headquarters building for, all designed to convince our lenders that if they gave him a piece of the deal, he would generate outsized returns for them when they pulled the plug on us.

Now, I've had numerous calls from lenders over the years, asking if I would be interested in partnering with them to take over companies whose loans they had called. There's really nothing wrong with the concept. However, when you know the people about to lose their business (and in a small industry, often I do!), I'm troubled about participating in a process that will take away their life's work. Of course, Kevan was going a number of steps further. He wasn't responding to distress lenders asking for advice; he was actively seeking out *our lenders*, although he supposedly considered me a friend, or at least someone whom he sought out for free advice. I didn't learn about the extent of Kevan's activities until after we had reached our agreement with Canyon and secured our future, but when someone sent me his pitch book, I was appalled.

When I saw Kevan after everything was over, I have to admit, I was gleeful watching him squirm when I mentioned I had read his proposal to take over Emmis. But that was the extent of it; I am fortunate that I was born without a revenge gene. Besides, I've learned that if someone behaves abhorrently with you, they've probably acted that way toward others. My sense is, they'll probably spend a lot of time dealing with people who do possess an abundance of revenge genes.

Fast-forward to the middle of 2011: We were squared away with Canyon and our revenue was growing again, but not nearly enough to bring our leverage down to manageable levels. Enter Randy Michaels, an old friend, who proposed an arrangement that intrigued me. Randy had joined forces with GTCR, a successful private equity firm based in Chicago, and now he approached me with the idea of buying three of our stations and creating a new company, Merlin Media. He wanted to buy our two Chicago stations as well as one of our New York stations and package them with an FM he was buying in Philadelphia. His plan was to leave one Chicago station as a preeminent album rock station and convert the other three to all news. I loved the idea. While almost all music formats had abandoned the AM dial, it remained the province of news, sports, and information. Randy's theory was that listeners would ultimately shift their information needs to the FM band.

We were ecstatic to enter into an agreement, partially because I liked his idea, but more importantly, because we would receive $110 million in cash, as well as a significant equity stake in the new venture. All three stations had been battered by the recession, generating only a few million dollars of cash flow when we did the deal. When you sell assets that have little profitability for $110 million in cash, you can fix your balance sheet very quickly, and that's what we did. The Merlin deal validated my belief that even in a downturn, credible buyers would want to invest in radio. Phil Canfield, the lead partner of GTCR, believed in the idea and expected his firm to be well rewarded if the stations built a niche in the profitable all-news business, especially since the industry was rebuilding from its nadir in 2009.

Unfortunately, the project failed. Because all-news radio listeners skew older, they, like TV news viewers, are the most resistant to change. In New

York, they had spent years listening to WINS and WCBS; in Philadelphia, to KYW; and in Chicago, to WBBM. All were owned by CBS, all had great traditions in each market, and all were massive profit centers for CBS. In Chicago, CBS decided to block Merlin's move by simulcasting WBBM on an FM station they converted from a money-losing rock format. In New York and Philadelphia, CBS relied on force of habit and significant marketing to prevent the new stations from gaining any traction. Randy's idea was to target younger listeners, especially females, but they never responded. GTCR, like all private equity firms, was not blessed with significant amounts of patience, and they pulled the plug a few years later. In the last throes of the stations' existence, a friend called me to ask if we still had a significant equity stake in Merlin, and if so, when did we think we would see a return? "With any luck," I answered, "we should see some return on our money sometime in the next thousand years."

Merlin was sold at a loss; our equity was gone, and Randy and GTCR parted company. However, I still believe that, of all of the people I have known in broadcasting, Randy is the most innovative and creative. Rick Cummings and I have teased him for years that the only difference between him and us is that he has crossed lines we won't cross. He vehemently disagrees, but I've always thought that if Randy and Rick and I had actually worked together, we could have kept him out of trouble, and he would have led us to great success.

Although we had rejected Sam Zell's offer to merge our respective companies, we did a purely financial deal with him later in 2011. Several of our larger preferred shareholders wanted to be bought out, and they were willing to take a significant discount. Of course, Emmis being Emmis, we still had no actual ability to pay for the transactions, but as you should have figured out by now, a lack of cash didn't usually stop us. After Merlin, we were certain we would sell more assets, so we entered into a very expensive loan agreement with Sam and Nils Larsen, who was running much of Sam's business. The rate was ridiculously high, but the savings on the preferred shares were even greater, so we took the financing and redeemed most of our preferred shares.

By the beginning of 2012, our balance sheet still needed lots of work, but it was dramatically better after using the Merlin $110 million to pay off a hunk of our debt. Then, a short time later, I struck an agreement that really should put me in the transaction hall of fame. On the other side was Traug Keller, the president of ESPN Audio and Talent, and one of my closest friends (and golf partner). At the time, ESPN was locked in a ferocious battle with WFAN (now owned by CBS) for ratings in New York City. Traug believed that ESPN needed an FM station to shore up its weak AM signal. He knew that I was looking to get rid of more debt, and that I would be interested in parting with WRKS. A well-entrenched urban station, WRKS had dominated New York City ratings for many years. As noted earlier, in its glory days, Isaac Hayes had been our morning man, and it always ranked in the top five in the city. However, in 2009, the world had turned upside down for urban radio stations.

Arbitron (before they sold the business to Nielsen) had been roundly criticized for its diary methodology and decided to replace it with Portable People Meters, or PPM. A PPM is a small meter that listeners usually clip on their belts or carry in their purses. At night, the PPM is connected to a docking station, which transmits the person's daily listening back to Arbitron. The advantage of the PPM system is that it picks up the signal of whatever station is being listened to, unlike the diary system, which requires the diary keeper to write down what they remember listening to. Having spent most of my life in a business ruled by diaries, I can tell you that, years earlier, we had determined that most people who got a diary and were supposed to fill it out from Thursday morning until the following Wednesday night invariably waited until the end of the week to actually do it. Why did almost every radio contest in America give away its biggest prizes on Thursday morning? Because listeners would realize their diaries had to be mailed back that day, but they hadn't filled in anything all week, so at the breakfast table on Thursday morning, they furiously tried to remember what they had heard for the previous seven days. If a station was giving away a new car that morning, there was a better chance that listeners were hearing that station when they tried to recall what they had listened to all week, and the station would likely get credit for listening it didn't actually get. For years, we joked that we weren't in the radio business, we were in the diary retrieval business.

For urban music listeners, most of whom were Black, the discrepancy was even more pronounced. Urban music listeners gravitated to their favorites because these stations were integrally involved in their communities.

They identified with *"their* station" and diary returns became even more of a popularity contest than for other listeners. It was not uncommon for urban music listeners to write down in their diaries that they had been listening for three hours nonstop, but when they carried a meter, actual listening was a lot less.

In truth, all radio listening dropped precipitously. Arbitron's argument was: "Yes, PPM will only show 70 percent of the listening of the diary system, but advertisers will make up the difference because the ratings will be much more reliable." This statement ranks up there with the French general's proclamation that the Germans would never be able to penetrate the Maginot Line (I know they actually went around it, but you get the idea). Of course, PPM hit right during the depths of the recession, so radio's losses were magnified.

To give you an idea of how much worse PPM was for urban stations, under the diary system, WRKS and its competitor, WBLS, were always ranked in the top five of the market, and both were immensely profitable. After PPM was instituted, both became marginal players in New York City. In fact, while our cash flow declined from $8 million a year to under $1 million, WBLS, the flagship of Inner City Broadcasting, slipped into bankruptcy. The aggregate decline for both stations was around $15 million a year. The Sutton family, which had made WBLS an iconic brand, lost the family business as PPM and the recession took hold.

So, when Traug called about buying WRKS, I was very interested. Unfortunately, he had one problem. His parent company, Disney, had exited the radio business in 2006 and had no interest in buying any other radio stations. Still, Traug desperately needed an FM in New York. He and I finally determined that while he couldn't buy the station, he could lease it. As our discussions were nearing a conclusion, I had another idea. I called Josh Pack, managing director of Fortress Investment Group, with a proposal. Fortress, Yucaipa Companies, and Magic Johnson had recently purchased the assets of Inner City out of bankruptcy from the Suttons. Obviously, both WRKS and WBLS were struggling in the PPM system, and the end of the recession hadn't been enough to help either station. My idea was simple. If the new WBLS owners would pay Emmis for WRKS's intellectual property (format, playlist, logo, design, Station IDs), I would seriously consider selling the station to someone who would take it out of the format. Without a competitor, WBLS would dominate urban radio and the cash flow would grow dramatically. They loved the idea. I think my first ask was for $20 million, and we settled for $15 million.

After that, I finalized my agreement with Traug. Emmis would lease him WRKS for twelve years with annual payments starting at $8 million and ramping up to $12 million by the last year of the lease. Traug joked that, "I've just paid you more in a lease than the station was worth!" That wasn't true, but it was close; however, it was the only way he could get the deal done. I then went back to Josh and cemented our agreement to sell the intellectual property of WRKS for $15 million.

Because we were anxious to pay off as much debt as quickly as possible, we monetized the stream of payments for a lump sum securitization payment of $81 million, which was the present value of the deal. Since the lease was guaranteed by the creditworthiness of the Walt Disney Company, it was a low-risk piece of paper. At the end of the day, we got nearly $100 million in cash for a station that was struggling to make $1 million a year *and* we kept ownership of the license! Now, it's clear I've screwed things up countless times, but this deal put me on the genius side of the ledger, and it became legendary in our industry.

I couldn't have done it without Traug. You can't underestimate the power of his likability. As I've preached to both my children and my Emmis family, try to be someone that others want to see walking into a room. If you're likable, it's amazing how much more enjoyable your life will be and how much more success you will find. I guarantee that whenever Traug enters a room, people are happy to see him.

After the ESPN/Fortress deal, most of the pressure was off. As I mentioned, in the summer of 2012, we reached an agreement with Grupo Radio Centro to sell them LA's KMVN-FM. By that fall, we had paid off Canyon's credit facility, as well as the expensive Zell notes. We refinanced the company at slightly under 3.4 times debt and that was it: Emmis was solvent and ready to go on. It was exhilarating; with a uniquely creative team, some good luck, and incredible amounts of perseverance, we had accomplished what almost no one else had. While our expected growth rates were not much to be excited about, by the fall of 2012 survival was more than enough for us.

Top: At times of your worst crises, you always think of family. Wife Heather and daughter Cari. *At left:* One of my favorite pictures from a Mariners game. My son, Brad; me; and my dad, Sam.

13

An Existential and Financial Crisis

I 've focused on all of the things that we did to save Emmis during the Great Recession, but I was enduring a parallel crisis at the same time. When our stock collapsed, not only was the company underwater, but I was also in extremely dire straits. I was carrying a lot of personal debt, secure in the knowledge that my net worth was significantly greater than my obligations—until it wasn't. Years earlier, when I borrowed $25 million to buy back some Emmis stock from Morgan Stanley that had carried over from our Mariners deal, I discussed the obligation with Paul Taubman. At the time, he observed, "You're worth many multiples of the debt, you believe in Emmis, so of course you should do it." Paul was correct; it's just that I didn't pay all of it off when I should have.

When the world collapsed, I still had debt of over $7 million, as well as obligations from our failed attempt to go private. My personal debt was split between two local banks, all collateralized by much of my Emmis stock. These are called "margin loans," and your obligation to the bank is calculated as a percentage of the value of the stock they hold. If the price of your stock drops below the percentage required, you have to give the banks more stock to make up for it. Over a few short months in 2008–2009, my problems exploded. When Emmis's stock collapsed to under thirty cents per share, my guarantees were worthless, because the stock was close to worthless. At that point, the banks called the loan. While I had other assets, I didn't have many that were liquid, and it was clear that I was on the verge of personal financial destruction.

Both of my local bankers, with whom I'd had long relationships, were sympathetic, but they answered to corporate officers back at headquarters who neither knew nor cared about me. They just wanted their money back. My loans went into "workout status," a polite term for the most unpleasant part of the banking business. When you borrow money, you meet with your bankers in elegant offices, with fine leather chairs and rich mahogany appointments. When your loan goes into default or "workout," you meet in stark rooms reminiscent of detention halls in an inner-city high school. Your traditional banker has vanished, replaced by workout specialists who have little interest in anything other than when you're going to pay back the loan. If you choose to discuss how you're going to fix your business and repay them, they usually don't care to listen. Again, they just want to know when they will get their money. It's a painful, very cold process, designed to put the fear of God into a borrower who has fallen on hard times.

One of my closest friends, who was the former CEO of my major lender, was completely removed from the workout process. When my margin loans were called, he was able to keep the wolves at bay for a little while. During this period, he told me something I never forgot: "The problem with banks is that the one thing they're not very good at judging is character. Some people will march through hell to repay their obligations, while others will stiff you in a heartbeat. Unfortunately, too many times we don't distinguish between the two when we lend money, and we certainly don't distinguish between the two when we try to collect."

While I was given some time to work out repayment, it was clear that I was in deep trouble. Compared to the many opportunities we had to fix Emmis's balance sheet, my options were practically nonexistent. Once your loans have been called, you have to find solutions very quickly, and I had to tend to Emmis first. I had friends who thought I should declare personal bankruptcy, but I never seriously considered it. That left me painfully caught between a rock and a hard place.

I've said that you learn the great lessons about life in adversity, and I learned more about the foundations of my character during this period than at any other time in my life.

One of my favorite maxims goes: "Givers never take and takers never give." I've seen this behavior in more instances than you can imagine. Some people are comfortable being givers; others are comfortable as takers. If you are used to giving, the notion of taking is unsettling and foreign to you, and the same holds true for those who are takers. By the way, I'm not being pejorative about either side; it's just what I've learned about human nature. And what I've learned about myself is that I am a giver, through and through. That doesn't make me a better person, it's just who I am.

Being a giver has been ingrained since childhood. I used to tease my mother that we were always the softest touches around. Before he passed away, my father said to me, "Please watch your mother, she'll just give away whatever I leave her if you don't stop her." My dad proved largely correct—he just picked the wrong person to guard the henhouse. Every out-of-luck relative or friend would visit my mom (or me) with a tale of woe, knowing that there was a decent chance we would come to the rescue. For me, it was a point of pride that I could step in and help others, but it's clear that sometimes the recipients were truly deserving, and other times they had just discovered a very soft touch. For years at Emmis, the joke was that we had to have a buffer for me, because if not, I'd accede to every request for charitable support. Fortunately, we brought in the remarkable Lindy Richman many years ago to handle those requests, and she is a lot better than me at figuring out where our resources should be allocated.

This tendency is why my accountant, Bruce Jacobson, told me that whatever I would make in life, I would give most of it away. It's also why my greatest regret about Emmis's problems is that I haven't been able to make a difference for the things that I believe in. Before Emmis's collapse, I was a very regular, and usually significant, donor to USC, my kids' schools, the Jewish community, and a number of other civic causes. When my world turned upside down, all of that went away, and it affected me deeply.

Being a giver also means you're generous with more than money. Many years ago, my assistant, Peggy Johnson, gave me a Christmas gift, which was simply NO in large block letters. She put it on my desk so, just possibly, when someone wanted something, whether it was money, a speaking request, or just my time, I would consider turning them down. The joke among my managers was, "Thank God he wasn't a woman or he would definitely have been a nymphomaniac—he can't turn anyone down."

Another quality of a giver is that you're generous with people's feelings. My wife, Heather, laughs when we're at an event and someone walks up and says, "Jeff, I'm Joe Smith. I don't know if you remember me, but we met in 1989 and we had a nice discussion about Indiana's economic policy." I invariably say, "Joe, of course I remember you and remember talking to you." Naturally, when Joe walks away, she will say, "Who are you kidding, you don't remember what you had for breakfast today, let alone somebody you talked to once, thirty years ago!" I just like the idea that I can make people feel good about something and it doesn't hurt me at all.

Finally, a giver doesn't judge people harshly—you give everyone the benefit of the doubt. My wife puts it succinctly: "Don't ever ask Jeff about his opinion of someone, he'll always say he likes them. Ask me, ask anyone, but don't ask Jeff." I'm definitely guilty as charged, but I usually find some good in everyone, and most of my friends would tell you that makes me singularly incapable of sizing up people. It's the reason I take someone else along to important meetings, so that I can get a dispassionate analysis, without my usual optimistic outlook.

My view of people and my willingness to help out has become legendary among my friends. One day at lunch, Charlie Morgan, our Indianapolis market manager, joined our group and asked what I'm certain he thought was an innocuous question: "Jeff, I had a call from a friend of yours who wanted me to talk to his son about a job, and I wanted to know if he's a good friend?" The other six people at the table simultaneously erupted with laughter. For the rest of the hour, they regaled Charlie with tales of people who were supposed friends that I barely knew, all of whom would call for various favors for themselves or close relatives. After lunch, Ian Arnold, one of our attorneys, came up with the "Jeff Smulyan Venn Diagram of Friendship."

Jeff Smulyan Venn Diagram of Friendship

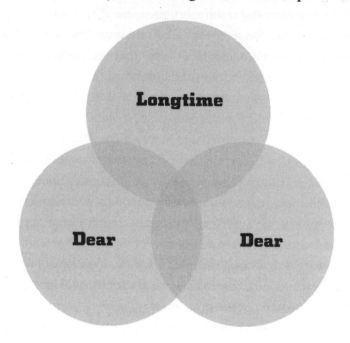

Longtime, dear, dear friend = highest level of friendship and loyalty (e.g., Gary Kaseff, Rick Cummings). Jeff would step in front of a bullet for one of his longtime, dear, dear friends—or tell stories about the time that they almost dated the Boston Celtics frontcourt together.

Dear, dear friend = second-highest level of friendship and loyalty (e.g., Steve Stitle). Jeff would, of his own volition, choose to eat a meal or see a movie with this person without the slightest feeling of guilt or obligation.

Longtime, dear friend = third-highest level of friendship and loyalty (e.g., Val Maki, John Beck). Jeff genuinely appreciates these people and would be a character witness for them in a homicide trial.

Dear friend = fourth-highest level of friendship and loyalty (e.g., the hostess at Champps, the person who got his order right at Subway or A&W). Jeff tips them when they give him the table he wants and would be willing to use his diet root beer float to put them out if they were on fire.

Friend = second-lowest level of friendship and loyalty (e.g., Kevan Fight). Jeff has actual, though potentially fleeting, disdain for them.

Distant relative, former employee = lowest level of friendship and loyalty. Jeff would recommend them to someone he knew for employment.

So, my identity was wrapped up in being a giver. But now that my stock had collapsed, I could no longer be the one that everyone asked for favors, nor the one who could solve everyone's problems. For the first time in my life, I was in a position where I needed the help of others, and it was a place I had never been before. It was excruciating. No doubt much of it was pride. I'd lived a charmed life for years, and it was incredibly humbling to admit that I could no longer be a giver—I would have to be a taker. Saving the company was a piece of cake compared to going to friends for money.

As I agonized over my financial crisis, I thought a lot about my core values. I had a law school professor, Frank Jones, who pronounced early in a first-year contracts class that everyone lives by their own "eight by eight." He then showed us a grid that included all of the values anyone might have. Some people value family, some value money, some value pride, some value power, some value fame, some value loyalty; in short everyone chooses the values that guide them. Long after I've forgotten every other thing about contracts, I've remembered that we're all guided by our own eight by eight.

In many ways, my values are aligned with my religion, and yet I'm still a bit of a cynic. I think that all religions basically espouse a few fundamental values: be good to your family; treat others with dignity; feed the poor; shelter the homeless; care about your community; uphold the faith; and don't kill anyone. Cynics like me note that religion has been a good way to keep people in line by promising a reward in the next life if they act civilly in this one, thus preventing them from killing each other. That idea may have been useful in ancient times, but it's not what's important now, at least for me. Still, I find it comforting to think that some higher power out there does, in some small way, look over everything that happens. Do I believe God is watching me and will answer my prayers when I ask him to help me sink a five-foot putt? No, for if I did, I'd surely be an atheist.

My commitment to Judaism doesn't stem from some mystical belief that we are God's chosen people, but rather that Judaism, which teaches the importance of family, education, and trying to heal the world, has done a better job than other religions of living up to its values over the centuries. Of course, it's not lost on me that Jews have always been a small minority, generally persecuted throughout the ages, which gives them more incentive to cling to those beliefs. Would Judaism have been as faithful to its values if the count were three billion Jews and only thirteen million Christians, or would we have had the same desire to impose our will on others as has been done to us? It's hard to say. I would hope not, but in my opinion, it is easier to uphold your ideals when much of the world scorns you.

Several years ago, I was called upon to roast my friend, Gordon Smith. Gordon is a past president of the NAB, as well as a former US senator from Oregon. More than anything, he is a devout Mormon and has been a lay leader of the church for decades. At his roast, I said, "Gordon, I just read a survey that said that the Mormon church was now the least liked religion in the United States. I have to admit, I'm stunned. As a Jew, I'm a member of a religion that has been the most despised for every day of the last six thousand years, and I'm wondering, what in the world did you guys do to displace us?"

All this introspection led me to another of my values: the responsibility to do what's right in a tough situation. Years before he died, my dad said to me, "You're in charge now." That meant he was counting on me to solve the family issues that he had shouldered for years. However, passing the mantle to me was the second-best thing he ever did. The first, which I'll cherish all of the days of my life, was what he told a family member years ago: "Jeff will always do the right thing. Whatever the right thing is, that's what he'll do. I won't always do the right thing, but Jeff will." I was incredibly proud of that, and it has guided me every day since he said it, and at times when I might be tempted to drift off course, it returns, firmly implanted in my brain. I've had a lot of nice things said about me over the years, far more than I deserve, but by far, this was the most meaningful compliment of my life. Second place isn't even close.

Finally, I swallowed my pride and did the right thing for me and my family. I reached out to my sister and a few close friends, who were incredibly kind and lent me money. I'm sure all of them will be embarrassed to see their names in print, but they all made a major difference in my life: my sister Dale, Greg Nathanson, Steve Crane, Jerry Reinsdorf, and longtime family friends Herb Simon, his brother Mel, and Mel's wife Bren. My attorney, Jim Dubin, also provided life-altering help. Nothing gave me greater joy than to pay all of them back, with interest, a few years later. When one of them received my repayment, he remarked, "Thanks, but of all the times that I've done this, no one has ever paid me back." Not paying them back would have been something I couldn't live with.

I had one other break during the crisis. Years earlier, my college and law school friend Mark Wapnick had come to me for help when he was starting a business. While practicing law, Mark had realized that courts waste tremendous man-hours by having numerous preliminary hearings on trial matters, and he determined that most of these hearings could be conducted over the phone. Mark and his partner, Bob Alvarado, started CourtCall, an audio-conferencing system for judges. CourtCall was designed to save the countless hours wasted in travel and in perfunctory appearances in court. Mark wanted $200,000 to help get the business off the ground. He still remembers a call we had with Bruce Jacobson, who summarily dismissed the investment, but added, "I don't think Jeff should do this, which means he will." Bruce was right, I invested the money, and Mark and Bob built a wonderful business over the next decade.

When the bottom fell out of Emmis, I realized my CourtCall stock was worth a significant amount of money, but there was almost no way to monetize it. The company didn't have the ability or the desire to buy it back, and as a private, closely held company, it would be difficult to sell. Enter Tom Quinlan, CEO of R.R. Donnelley & Co. Tom and I had become friends, because Donnelly published all of our magazines and we were a very good account of his. In addition, we shared the same banker, Julie Jalelian at Bank of America. Julie was discussing my plight and Tom explained that Donnelly had an investment basket that he could use to purchase my stock. CourtCall was a good investment for Tom, but he made it as a favor to me, not worrying about whether it would provide a good rate of return. It was an incredibly kind gesture, and it was a major reason I was able to stay solvent and have the time to solve all of our problems at Emmis.

Although both Emmis and I survived our parallel catastrophes, I was more convinced than ever that radio needed another source of revenue beyond advertising, or Emmis would soon be in trouble again. Unfortunately, the next craze the radio industry fixated on was not the panacea we hoped it would be.

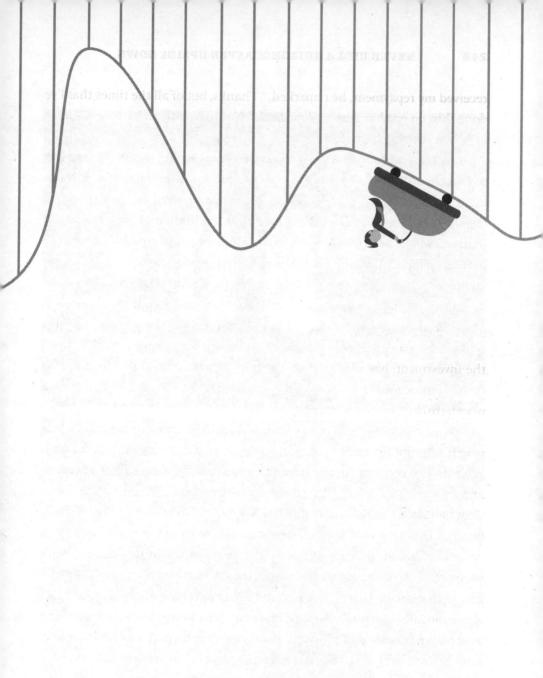

Top: With Radio Ink editor Ed Ryan, Donnie Osmond, me, and Pat Walsh at an industry conference. *Bottom:* Celebrating great ratings with Pat Walsh at Hot 97, New York.

14

The Search for Shiny
New Objects

When the dust settled after the 2008–2009 recession ended, we were still standing and our future was no longer in jeopardy. We retained a significant portfolio of radio stations— not nearly the size of our largest competitors, but strong ones in very good markets like Los Angeles and New York. Radio revenues had started coming back from their low watermark, but they only grew about 7 percent annually in the years that followed. Our digital advertising was picking up, but it was a very low-margin business; meanwhile, our core advertising revenues, always the heart of the industry, were stagnant. Consequently, radio was urgently on the lookout for a shiny new object to bring back growth, and that object was streaming audio.

One thing you can count on in a stagnant business is the impulse to find the shiny new toy, focus on it intently, and market it like crazy. I've seen this pattern a number of times, and the rise of streaming in radio was no different. It started in the mid-1990s—as the world wide web was gaining traction—and was a great way to reach a few of our listeners. Distributing radio over the internet was a novel idea that was gaining cachet.

Around this time, I got a call from Walt Kirkwood, one of my dad's bankers. Walt wanted me to talk to his nephew, Todd Wagner, who was building a streaming business with his partner, Mark Cuban. Todd came into my office late one afternoon and laid out his business proposition. Their streaming service, AudioNet (later to become Broadcast.com) needed radio stations for content; he proposed that AudioNet stream our stations, charge us a monthly fee of $10,000 per station, and insert their commercials in place of our commercials on the streaming version of our stations. They would then sell what had been our commercial time and reap the rewards. I laughed and said, "Todd that sounds like a great business for one of us." I then added, "It seems to me that I can hire two interns from any nearby university and pay them minimum wage to do the streaming and keep the advertising for myself. I'm not sure why anyone would pay you a fee *and* let you keep the advertising revenue!" Our conversation was pleasant, but their business model was clearly a nonstarter, and when he left, I thought to myself, who in his right mind would take their deal?

Of course, over the next six months, several hundred broadcasters did just that. Now, I'm sure that they didn't pay Wagner and Cuban anywhere near $10,000 a month, but it was still a ridiculously one-sided arrangement. My favorite story came from Randy Michaels, who was running Jacor at the time. By the time they met with Jacor, they had already signed up several hundred stations. Randy always joked that, if he had listened to their entire presentation, he would have thrown them out of his office, but in the first two minutes, they told him about the sizable inventory they were getting from all of their customers. Randy's first question was: "Who is selling all of your inventory?" They said they didn't yet have a sales staff, so he tossed out, "Give me ten percent of your company and I'll sell all of your inventory for you." Cuban and Wagner accepted on the spot, and Randy and Jacor became instant owners of Broadcast.com.

Broadcast.com went public in 1998, and its stock soared 250 percent on its first day of trading, reaching a market cap of over $1 billion at the end of the day. The company grew steadily and, less than nine months after the

IPO, Yahoo paid $5.7 billion for it. Within a year, Yahoo realized the hype for Broadcast.com was dramatically greater than the reality and it slowly shut down the business. Randy and Jacor sold their 10 percent share shortly after the IPO, and made over $150 million from their ownership stake. Of course, the best part of the story was that Randy and Jacor had sold all of the inventory for Broadcast.com's entire stable of stations for over eighteen months, and the grand total was a measly $930,000! When it came to Broadcast.com, there never was a *there* there.

I'm not a fan of Mark Cuban for a lot of reasons, but I give him credit; right after selling his business to Yahoo for $5.7 billion, he quickly sold his billion dollars of Yahoo stock—a brilliant move, considering that the Broadcast.com deal tanked Yahoo. The deal was called one of the worst internet acquisitions of all time, and the company effectively shut it down a year later. Even twenty-plus years later, Yahoo has never recovered. Broadcast.com was a skillfully marketed concept, and it made people believe in an idea that was an illusion.

My Broadcast.com experience partly explains why I have always been skeptical of streaming, but there is another overriding reason. It happens to be a bit of a historical anomaly: In the United States, broadcasters don't pay royalties to performers, but streaming companies do. This disparity dates back to when the copyright laws were written, during a time when broadcasting was the nascent industry the government was protecting. Performers have fought to change the law ever since, but broadcasters have foiled them at every turn. Howard Berman, the former congressman who led the charge against my industry, summed up the problem succinctly over lunch one day: "Jeff, my district includes all of the record labels, so I'm always going to fight for their rights, but the record industry is dominant in only one congressional district, mine. On the other hand, broadcasters have a strong presence in every congressional district in America, so when I want to get the law changed, who do you think wins every time?" Howard was right, and as a lifelong broadcaster, I can promise that we will keep sending in the NAB to wage the war against the recording industry every single year. Broadcasters pay publishers and composers through organizations such as ASCAP and BMI, but, from radio's standpoint, another significant royalty to performers would probably drive many radio companies into bankruptcy.

And, remember, from its nascent days on, radio was responsible for exposing listeners to music—those listeners would then go out and buy records.

Another problem with streaming audio is that it's an extremely inefficient delivery mechanism. I have given the following example in countless speeches to the industry, and it is illustrative: "I have a station in Los Angeles, KPWR. My only cost of distribution is the cost of my electricity to power my transmitter. My outlay runs about $65,000 a year, and for that, I can either reach one person in Southern California or all fifteen million. It's the same cost either way. My station actually reaches about three million people a week, and for those, my distribution cost is my $65,000 electric bill. Now let's imagine I took down my radio tower and could only reach my listeners through streaming. I would have to reach each person, and the data costs to reach three million of them would be about $1 million per year, and that's just my cost to *send* my signal; my listeners, in turn, would incur similar data charges to receive my signal. And I incur those costs before I have to pay sizable performers' royalties that I don't have to pay using my over-the-air signal. It is a staggering differential, essentially several million dollars versus $65,000." While in the intervening years since I started making these speeches, those data costs have come down, they still exist, and they mount up quickly.

The above is why Pat Walsh's favorite saying was: "Every time you take a listener from over-the-air to streaming, you take a customer who gives you a 35 percent profit margin and you make him a customer who costs you a minus 10 percent margin. Same customer, same content, totally opposite result." All of us at Emmis quickly realized that for all its cachet, streaming was a shiny object with almost no chance at profitability.

Streaming audio is filled with untenable economic models; those companies that keep going are taking in capital from outside sources. For example, we knew the founders of Pandora very well, and Rick even gave them some help in their early days. While we liked them a lot, we used to joke about their business model. Once, on an earnings call, after being asked about Pandora, I infamously said, "We made more money this morning before breakfast than Pandora has made in twelve years." Another example is TuneIn. Rick and Pat had become close friends with John Donham, TuneIn's CEO, and, as a favor, we took a small stake in the company—over my vigorous objection. TuneIn's business strategy was different from Spotify's and Pandora's. The company merely provided a platform for thousands of stations, with each station paying its own royalties and data charges. TuneIn's business model was to sell its own commercials that ran before listeners could tune in to their favorite stations. Time has proven me correct; that business model didn't work either. Our investment (fortunately only $500,000) became worthless. Finally, Spotify has been the world's leader in streaming audio, with a market cap of $45 billion, in spite of annual losses that have exceeded $1 billion. Spotify contends that it will become profitable in the next few years, but I have my doubts. Pat and I even joked that for our next business venture we should just take $20 million and short Spotify (that is, bet the stock would go down), but we concluded that with our luck, either Tencent or Alibaba (the two Chinese media giants) would decide to pay $100 billion for it and we would be wiped out.

The challenge that all streaming audio companies face is that they not only have distribution charges, but they also pay significant music royalties, usually over 60 percent of their gross revenues. As the music industry has shed CDs and other physical products, it has come to rely on streaming revenue for the majority of its income. Worse, Apple entered the space in 2015 and agreed to royalties of over 70 percent, which it could do, because it doesn't ever need to make money with its streaming business; it just wants customers in its ecosystem. Amazon, with the same goal of attracting customers to all its businesses, entered the space in 2016. Bottom line, whether you are paying 60 or 70 percent of your business for music rights, you will continue to be unprofitable for a long, long time. Apple (and probably Amazon) are happy to pay high royalties, which will consign their competitors to a business with no hope of ever becoming viable.

When Bob Pittman became chairman and CEO of iHeartMedia (formerly Clear Channel) in 2011, he immediately shifted the focus of the company to the iHeart app, attempting to drive his over-the-air listeners to the streaming app. I don't know how much money Bob has spent promoting iHeart music, but if you've ever listened to his stations, you know the app is touted every hour. In addition, he has spent hundreds of millions of dollars sponsoring concerts and making deals with automobile companies and portable device makers, trading advertising time for placement of his app. In essence, Bob views his commercial inventory as unlimited, so he gives lots of it away; the net result is that his radio stations, which have always provided almost all of his profits, have been filled with countless commercials that dramatically damage the listening experience. In a 2012 discussion about the challenged economics of streaming, Bob merely said, "Yes, we have to get the royalty system changed." That's as likely as getting the North Korean government to adopt democratic reforms, and in the ensuing years, neither has come close to happening.

For fun, I used to speak at radio conferences and ask for a show of hands when I asked: "How many of you are making money streaming audio?" I'm still waiting for the first person to put his hand up.

However, just because streaming audio isn't a viable business model doesn't mean it doesn't have great consumer appeal. For years, the business has attracted massive amounts of capital, lured to the notion that streaming is, "the next big thing." I will be curious to see what happens to that capital as the promise of profitability continues to stay on the horizon.

One of the things you learn in business is that your enterprise may not be replaced by another viable enterprise but by a hobby (i.e., something that loses money consistently). It doesn't matter that the hobby isn't viable; if it kills your business, you're still dead. Streaming may not be economically viable, but it has attracted millions of listeners who love the on-demand nature of the experience, and they will continue to prefer it as long as it is available.

We're now seeing the same transition to streaming in video, otherwise known as the "over the top" model (OTT, as noted earlier). Today, the cable industry is being battered by multiple alternatives, from the wildly successful Netflix, Disney+, Hulu, Amazon Prime, and a host of others. While the parallels are inexact, there are similarities to what I've observed with streaming audio that make me believe that OTT may lead a lot of people down a rabbit hole with the loss of countless billions of dollars. However, this model is wonderful for consumers, because, as we've discussed countless times in our offices, streaming is just a staggering transfer of value from distributors to consumers.

Google's YouTube is one of my favorite examples. It has achieved remarkable viewership by showing everything imaginable under the sun. By far the leader in streaming video, it has no peer; nothing else comes close.

Every year, I attend the Aspen Institute's communications forum. It's a great chance to spend a few days hanging with academics, regulators, public interest types, and representatives from some of the largest telecom companies— people that I wouldn't ordinarily get to know—and discussing subjects I don't usually think much about. The forum is a perfect "fish out of water" experience, and I love doing it every summer.

Every year, before we arrive in Aspen, we always receive a packet of reading materials, and in 2016 our packet included an analysis of YouTube. When reading through the report, my mouth dropped open: according to the latest financial statements, You Tube had $4 billion in annual revenue and $6.5 billion in annual expenses. It was hard to comprehend that the most successful video streaming service could be losing $2.5 billion a year. I could hardly wait to get into the session with a fellow attendee, a Google executive, to determine if the numbers were accurate. Absolutely, she confirmed, the report was accurate.

Another regular attendee at Aspen went one step further, noting, "I know for certain that Google has lost $20 billion on YouTube in the last decade." Of course, the staggeringly profitable Google could easily afford loss leaders, but the magnitude still stunned me. If Google, whose costs of data transmission were lower than anyone else's, and whose content was theoretically cheaper than anyone else's, couldn't come close to making a profit, the business model seemed as challenged as we had seen in streaming audio. However, since that conference, YouTube has added YouTube TV (which distributes major channels), and the combination plus continued growth appears to have pushed YouTube into profitability. Because it is enmeshed in Google, it's hard to get a completely accurate assessment. Nevertheless, it appears that—with You Tube's massive reach and user-generated content— Google has found a way to make streaming video profitable.

The advantage of streaming video over audio is that many of the new video platforms are subscriber based, and video consumers are definitely more willing to pay fees than audio consumers; however, achieving profitability is still a significant problem. To induce subscribers to pay, the content has to be compelling, which is why Netflix spent $17 billion in 2020 to create and buy content. Ironically, Netflix's content costs are almost as much as their total subscriber revenues. How can they keep going? Again, the capital markets believe that at some point, Netflix will become wildly profitable, so the cash spigot is turned on until they get there. With Netflix having a market cap of $270 billion, they can keep up their exorbitant content costs for a long time.

Of course, with more competitors, there is a question of whether Netflix, or any OTT service for that matter, can acquire and keep enough subscribers to create a profitable model. Right now, everyone is in a race to acquire subscribers, so the question of whether streaming can be profitable has been put off for another day. Most analysts expect Disney, with its massive library of compelling content, to have the best chance with its Disney+, but even Disney projects $5 billion of losses before they approach breakeven, and I think that number is overly optimistic. But it's going to be fascinating to see how the streaming video business shakes out, and whether any of these services will ever be profitable.

At Emmis, we knew the answer as far as streaming audio was concerned. It was merely a shiny object that took everyone's minds off the fact that our core advertising business was slowly eroding.

Just as in 1998, when I became a contrarian about the economics of unlimited radio consolidation, so I was an outlier again about the economics of streaming. Did we still stream all of our content? Of course. We always believed that wherever our customers were, we had to be there as well. However, we viewed the expense as another marketing cost. In 2016 we decided to put out a premium product, combining Power 106 and Hot 97 in an app called Where Hip Hop Lives or WHHL. The concept was to give consumers a behind-the-scenes look at the two biggest global hip-hop brands, with all sorts of premium content mixed in. The genesis of the idea was that we had lots of listeners all over the world, especially in Germany and Japan, who consumed countless hours listening to our stations. However, it was almost impossible to monetize these listeners. Since most of our advertising sales were local, we couldn't get an automobile dealer in Secaucus or Burbank to pay anything extra for foreign listeners. Obviously a Hot 97 aficionado in Düsseldorf wasn't going to hop on a plane to go to Secaucus to buy a Honda. We decided that if this international audience had such a great affinity for our two hip-hop stations, we could bundle their programming together, add in valuable extras, and with luck, entice those listeners into subscribing to the app. The hope was that we would also be able to sign up our listeners closer to home. We spent a lot of time and money preparing Where Hip Hop Lives, and when it was ready to launch, I went over the projections with Rick. If the app could really attract several hundred thousand subscribers per month, at five dollars each, it would be a very profitable business. However, Rick and I both feared that our projections were wildly optimistic. After a year, when it turned out we had absolutely no demand for a paid subscription model, we abandoned the project.

Perhaps music industry icon Jimmy Iovine said it best in his interview with *Billboard*: "The streaming services have a bad situation, there's no margins, they're not making any money. Amazon sells Prime; Apple sells telephones and iPads; Spotify, they're going to have to figure out a way to get that audience to buy something else."

We also invested a significant amount of money in various digital initiatives, under the capable leadership of Angie May Cook. Angie built a team of digital experts who created a number of innovative products that greatly enhanced our brands and were compelling to our advertisers. Digital did produce good revenue for us, but it was nearly impossible to generate great margins on the business. For radio in the last decade, digital has masked the decline of traditional spot advertising, but it has never been able to replace the majority of our lost advertising dollars or the accompanying operating margins. I've viewed digital as another shiny object that has allowed us to avoid confronting the reality of our business.

Today, we're faced with another shiny new object: podcasting. So far, its economics are looking a lot like the streaming model. Several large companies are in a race to create the most content and provide the most attractive packages for advertisers and consumers. Spotify has led the way, buying up hundreds of millions of dollars of programs and ancillary services, including their $100 million purchase of Joe Rogan's controversial podcast. Of course, giving Joe Rogan $100 million up front means that Spotify will have quite a challenge getting much of a return on their investment. Still, I can easily understand their strategy of becoming the dominant player in podcasting. Remember, most of Spotify's business is music, and they pay over sixty cents of every dollar to the music industry. Spotify has not had any success becoming profitable with that model. I'm certain they believe that if they can attract millions of listeners to their spoken word podcasts, they will be able to balance out the disastrous royalties they pay on music, since, currently, no royalties are paid on spoken word programs. Of course, podcasters are now trying to extract separate royalties for their programs, but until they do, Spotify's desire to transition to a new revenue stream makes sense. Except for one big problem.

The podcast business has practically no barriers to entry; there are now over two million podcasts, with thousands of new programs added each day. For a distributor to find a hit podcast *and* keep the profits is an almost insurmountable challenge. As usual, iHeart has jumped on the bandwagon with both feet, creating and buying as many podcasts as possible in an attempt to use their tonnage to make their "podcast network" attractive to large advertisers. In its zeal to create winners, iHeart has resorted to its usual high-cost system, promoting a few podcasts every week on their 850 radio stations. This massive advertising blitz certainly generates more awareness, but it also makes radio stations run more and more commercials; as we have seen, that makes their listeners much more likely to reject their core product, the radio programming. The jury is still out on this gambit, but I'm fairly certain it will have the same results as their iHeart music app: monumental promotion costs, a billion downloads, and nominal listening. Or as I would put it, throwing more shit up against the wall for a second time and hoping that this time it sticks.

Podcasting is certainly an attractive business proposition for consumers. Listeners have a myriad of choices (two million and counting), and over 40 percent of the public listens to podcasts every month. However, they predominantly listen to the most popular, which consist of maybe several hundred podcasts. Therefore, the chances of creating a hit are staggeringly low. The *New York Times* has a podcast, *The Daily*, which has been a great winner, with approximately four million listeners per month. However, the revenue is from advertising only, and the costs are significant; the *Times* has deployed nearly one hundred people to produce the segments. National Public Radio (NPR) has also deployed many of its people to produce long-form programming that it distributes as podcasts, and five of them are in the top twenty for listeners and probably average about ten million listeners per month, combined. Other examples include *Dateline NBC* and *ESPN Daily*.

Usually, these successful podcasts are created by companies with significant manpower that can be allocated to content creation, and it's possible they can turn a profit. However, these winners are few and far between, and for every one of them, thousands of other podcasts have a minimal number of listeners, making them barely attractive to advertisers. There have been a few attempts to convince consumers to pay for their subscriptions to podcasts, but so far, they have had no success.

As the land rush continues for podcasting, my sense is that the industry is another shiny new object that at the end of the day will create a few winners and many, many more losers. Emmis has entered the fray, but from a different angle. In 2019 we purchased a small business that produces podcasts for major brands. Because many brands believe a long-form podcast is better than emails or newsletters, a number of companies have decided to enter the field. We've been very successful in producing content for many retailers and others who rely on our skills to produce high-quality podcasts. We get paid a fee and our clients are thrilled to be able to communicate with their most loyal customers in an informative and entertaining way. It's a profitable, fun niche to be in, within the podcast space. If someone decides to bring us an idea for a hit series, we'll be delighted to produce that as well—for a fee—however we're not investing in acquiring content.

But let's put streaming video and podcasting aside, and go back to the 2000s, when streaming audio was all the rage. Although the exact numbers were hard to find, I was convinced that this "shiny new object" wasn't the answer to radio's stagnant growth and diminishing margins. Yet it wasn't until 2009 that I discovered an ingenious way to put the industry back on a growth trajectory, provided I could just get them on board. Everything I had learned about being an entrepreneur and using group dynamics to get everyone behind my vision was about to be put to the test.

Top: Paul Brenner conceived and ran the NextRadio project. *Bottom left:* The NextRadio phone app. *Bottom right:* The NextRadio logo.

15

No Good Deed Goes Unpunished

After the 2008–2009 recession, the radio industry was clearly stagnating. Its revenues only rose about 8 percent from the bottom in 2009 and then languished for several years. Digital provided some new revenues, but the industry entered a period in which annual growth was stuck at a measly 0–2 percent, and margins slowly declined. We were convinced that the industry needed a catalyst to spur growth, and it wasn't going to be streaming audio, which we considered fool's gold.

For years, a small group of industry CEOs had met every three months, and in 2008, David Rehr, then president of the NAB, told us about a novel idea. In Europe and Asia, phone companies were making FM tuners available in phones. The chip cost consumers five dollars per phone, and they were buying them in droves. The phone manufacturers were completely on board, because their cost per chip was nominal, and their customers loved the idea of getting a portable radio in their phones. He strongly suggested that we should lead the effort to get the chips sold in the United States. None of us had been aware of the FM chip, and we were very excited.

Someone in the room that day knew that Emmis had worked on a project with Nokia in Finland—back then Nokia was the global leader in cell phones—and suggested I take charge of the project. In retrospect, I should have turned it down, but I was intrigued.

The more I studied the idea, the more I fell in love with it. It was no secret that radio's portability was dying. Gone were the days when millions of Sony Walkman radios flew off store shelves. And when was the last time you saw someone walking down the street with a boom box? Radio was being relegated to in-car listening and not much else. Even in 2008, clock radio sales were starting to decline precipitously, and most in-home listening was on the wane, a problem that has grown exponentially since.

Meanwhile, as the dawn of the iPhone approached, cell phones were becoming ubiquitous; if we could become an integral part of that experience, we could revitalize our portability. I began to study every aspect of the project, talking to phone executives around the world and learning everything I could. The most important, and the most challenging, factor was who controlled the customer experience. In much of the world, the phone manufacturer did. In Europe, most people bought their phones from the manufacturer, and for them, adding a radio was another nice profit opportunity. When you went into the Nokia store in Amsterdam, or the Sony store in Tokyo, they were more than happy to sell you a phone with an FM tuner.

As one phone executive explained, "In the United States, your problem is different. The experience is almost completely controlled by the phone companies. You don't go into a Nokia store in the US, you go into an AT&T store, and they want to control the entire ecosystem. The US phone companies want to make sure that when you buy their phones, they control every part of your experience, and a radio that can reach their customers through their phones and sell advertising time is definitely not something they'll be willing to do."

I ran into this problem as soon as I started discussions with American phone companies. However, the landscape was changing. Apple had introduced the iPhone, and it was revolutionary. No longer was the phone just able to make calls and texts, it was becoming a mini-computer, capable of doing everything that is second nature to us more than a decade later. All of its competitors realized that Apple had completely disrupted the phone experience, and they rushed to compete. As they built their own mini-computer phones, they did something that, for our industry, could prove game changing. They had Qualcomm and other chipmakers include an FM tuner in their new integrated chipsets. It was a universal standard in almost every smartphone in the world.

My fervor for this project came down to one simple point: a streaming radio station goes through a data network, which racks up costs, and the broadcaster is subject to significant performers' royalties. In contrast, the FM chip keeps the listener in our own terrestrial system—the same system that has been the center of American radio since 1921. You send a signal over your tower, it is picked up by a receiver, and there is nothing standing in between you and your listener. You pay no data fees, you have no extra royalties, and there is no gatekeeper to prevent you from selling your time. As I mentioned, this business model had allowed us to earn 35–40 percent profit margins, as opposed to streaming, which always lost money. I was convinced that if we could succeed with the smartphone, the industry would receive a very badly needed shot in the arm.

Of course, while no gatekeeper could block our terrestrial signal from reaching a listener, the phone companies were in charge of turning on the FM chip, and they became the most problematic gatekeepers of all.

Several years into the project, while I was locking horns with the phone companies, Kevin Gage, then head of technology at the NAB, concluded it wasn't enough to turn on the chips. As Kevin said, "The consumer of the future is not going to be happy just looking at a radio dial, when we are competing with so many other things in a phone that are far more compelling." Kevin's vision was a radio ecosystem that would be fully interactive. When a song popped up, you got a picture of the album art on your phone, later supported by lyrics to the song and a myriad of other possibilities, including the ability to buy and download the song instantly. When an ad came on the air, you clicked a link to the advertiser's website to get more information. When a radio station ran a contest, you didn't have to be the tenth caller, you just clicked on another link and you were entered. Kevin's vision laid out a system that was clearly a game changer for our industry.

It turns out our chief technology officer, Paul Brenner, knew Kevin and had already been discussing his ideas. Paul proudly told me: "Jeff, we can build that system." As a result of early talks with Apple regarding their iTunes store, Paul and his team had been working on various forms of inter-activity. In fact, Paul was leading the industry effort with iTunes, and his work formed the genesis of the system he envisioned.

I assume that Kevin went to our larger competitors about building the system, but no one seemed to have much interest. All of them, especially Clear Channel, now renamed iHeart, had shifted their efforts almost solely to their streaming audio projects. When the NAB came to us in 2010 to build the system, we gladly accepted their offer, especially since it included $750,000 to help defray development costs.

By accepting the challenge of building out the new ecosystem, which we quickly dubbed NextRadio, we were now fully committed to the project. Because we believed that radio had to regain portability and do so profit-ably, we viewed the effort as critical to preserving the future of the industry. That's what kept me going through the years we fought to launch NextRadio.

It took Paul's team more than a year to build out the ecosystem, and I can still remember the reaction when we rolled out an early version to a number of industry CEOs at an NAB meeting. Watching the faces of my peers observe what NextRadio could do was simply exhilarating. Everyone marveled at it, everyone pondered all of the ways they could utilize it, and everyone thanked us for what we were doing for the industry. Well, almost everyone.

At a lunch with my friend Bob Laikin, I was explaining the challenges of dealing with the phone industry, forgetting that, before he sold his business, he had been one of the world's largest independent cell phone distributors. Bob said, "Jeff, why haven't you called me about this? I've been dealing with these people for thirty years!" Bob quickly put me in touch with Larry Paul-son, who was then a senior executive at Qualcomm but had worked with Bob, and before that had been a senior executive at Nokia.

Meeting Larry was a godsend. He understood all of the challenges we faced with the phone industry, and because he was at Qualcomm, knew everything about the technology that placed chips in phones.

From my earliest days on the project, my encounters with phone exec-utives were largely surreal. Gordon Smith, who had replaced David Rehr as president of the NAB, was a former US senator who was able to arrange a meeting with just about anyone on Capitol Hill. Ed Markey, then a congressman from Massachusetts, was an early advocate of our work. Markey believed, as did so many others on Capitol Hill, that the ability to turn on a radio during an emergency would be lifesaving when the cell system went down, as happened in tornados, hurricanes, and even earthquakes. In the direst emergencies, when the power grid goes down, the cellular system goes with it. So does television. The radio tuner, however, is independent from the cellular system, and even if many broadcast towers lose power or are wiped out in a massive storm, the odds of all of them being destroyed is quite remote. If just one broadcaster could survive, people could get lifesaving information.

In one of my first meetings on Capitol Hill, before the widespread adoption of the iPhone, Gordon, Kevin Gage, and I met in Ed Markey's office with a senior executive from AT&T as well as a lobbyist from CTIA, the wireless industry trade association. They listened politely to our discussion about the need for the FM chip to be activated in their flip phones and agreed with Markey's point about the value in an emergency. "However," the AT&T executive noted, "what you want is just technically impossible with our transmission system in the United States. We'd love to do it, but we just can't." Then, in one of my favorite career moments, I pulled out of my pocket an AT&T phone that Kevin had found, which included, of all things, an FM tuner. I quickly noted, "It's funny, but THIS is an AT&T phone and it has an FM tuner ready to go." For emphasis, I turned on the radio, which I made sure was tuned to WTOP, Washington's news station. The executive was totally speechless but mumbled, "Gee, I didn't realize we could do that."

Throughout the project, I met many phone executives and liked a lot of them, but my initial encounters always reminded me of Jerry Reinsdorf's line about George Steinbrenner: "How do you know if George is lying? When his lips are moving!" In my first few years of the FM chip experience, that was precisely my sentiment about American phone executives. I can still recall a congressional hearing with phone executives who were adamant that there were absolutely no FM chips in cell phones. Despite countless charts, graphs, and sworn statements about the universal availability of the chips, the phone industry lobbyist was unmoved. Finally, one of the state regulators, who was also testifying, rattled off about five other industry misstatements that had been made and noted, "I know you guys must tell the truth sometimes, but I'm at a loss to know when it has happened!"

The project had great momentum in lots of places. With the weight of the NAB firmly behind it, it was wildly popular with broadcasters. In Congress, almost everyone loved the idea of consumers having a lifeline in their hands in times of emergency. Craig Fugate, head of FEMA, was another godsend. Craig had been director of Florida's Division of Emergency Management, and during his long career had experienced many hurricanes; he knew that the cell system and the power grid quickly went down when the worst storms hit. Craig fervently endorsed our efforts.

While I had no illusions about the magnitude of the task, I knew that radio needed to do *something*, and streaming wasn't it. With the introduction of the PPM, Rick Cummings and Mark O'Neill, who had analyzed our data for years, noticed a slow, steady decline in radio listening, which the PPM was magnifying. Persons Using Measured Media or PUMM was their standard measurement statistic, and Rick constantly updated us about ever-falling PUMM levels. Once, after seeing months upon months of PUMM declines, I jokingly issued an edict to Rick and Pat Walsh: "From this day forward, the word PUMM is forever banned at Emmis. I never want to see it in an email, a memo, or in any discussion. It shall be known as the word that can no longer be uttered!" It became a running comedy bit among the three of us, as in, "The thing that I can't discuss declined a lot in New York this month, and Los Angeles isn't any better."

Interestingly, by 2015, several engineers had developed a device, called Voltair, that was able to transmit enhanced radio signals that Nielsen's PPM system could detect. Nielsen at first cried foul and claimed that the boxes were illegal, or at least against the spirit of the encoding system. That triggered a furious run on Voltair boxes, which no one would publicly admit they had. All of us bought as many as we could, knowing that Nielsen would have to recognize them eventually, which they did. Rick used to joke when a competitor's ratings spiked, that, "looks like they got their Voltair this month." It is quite likely that the signals that Voltair transmitted were background noise no one was listening to, but it had the desired effect. As Voltair, and Nielsen's version of it, became universally deployed in the industry, ratings went up by about 15 percent. Industry leaders and analysts hailed the rating increases as a "renaissance of radio." We had no such illusions. As Rick noted, "In two years, when this cycles through the industry, PUMM levels will start declining again, just as they always have." For those two years, however, Voltair did its job, and everyone in the industry was ecstatic about our sudden listening rebound. Of course, Rick was right, and once Voltair cycled through, listening levels declined steadily, as they have to this day.

Because I've had a lifelong passion for radio, and because we had become both emotionally and financially invested, I became obsessed with making NextRadio work. As I've stated before, I love trying to do something that everyone else says can't be done, and the fear of failure has never deterred me. With missionary zeal, I started a quest to sell the idea to broadcasters, and I accepted every speaking invitation that was offered—and there were many. At first, it was hard for people to comprehend the full economic value of their terrestrial signal, but as time passed, and people realized that streaming audio couldn't be monetized, they began to understand the concept. In addition, Paul and his team had built a compelling ecosystem for NextRadio, and broadcasters began to realize that if adopted, NextRadio could generate significant new revenues that had eluded them.

However, the most daunting challenge was getting NextRadio installed in cell phones, and we knew from early meetings that the phone industry would erect massive barriers. Ironically, we almost made a breakthrough with Apple shortly after NextRadio was introduced. Paul had previously spearheaded the team that had built interactivity into the iTunes system and he knew several key Apple executives. Also, my friend Ron Sugar, a fellow trustee at USC, was one of the seven Apple directors. During one of our golf outings at a trustee retreat, I mentioned our challenge with Apple, and Ron graciously offered to introduce us to senior leadership. We had promising discussions, but according to Paul, Apple's history with the radio industry on the iTunes project had convinced them that it was easier *not* to work with radio. Besides, Apple has never been willing to have anyone make much money in their ecosystem.

I went to Larry Paulson, who had been closely monitoring our situation, and he devised a plan for our industry. He concluded that we were going to have to buy our way into the phone companies and suggested that we start with a smaller carrier; if successful, we would be able to demonstrate that the system worked, and that would put pressure on everyone else. It was a brilliant idea. As luck would have it, my longtime friend Larry Glasscock was on the Sprint board. Glasscock introduced us to Sprint CEO Dan Hesse, and after several meetings we struck a deal: The radio industry would pay $15 million a year for three years, and in exchange, Sprint would activate the FM chip and place the NextRadio software in all their phones (about one hundred million) over the next three years. At our final meeting, I brought along several other radio CEOs, to make sure we had a consensus, because the industry was going to have to pass the hat to fund the deal. Everyone agreed that the contract with Sprint was essential if we were ever going to get a foothold in cell phones.

It was only after we started to raise the funds for the Sprint deal that I began to understand the nature of another, very significant problem: Bob Pittman.

When our project started, Mark Mays, CEO of Clear Channel, had been one of its most vigorous advocates. He helped in any way he could and provided counsel at various points. His company, however, was in the process of being sold. In 2006, Mark, his brother, Randall, and their father, Lowry, sold control of Clear Channel to a venture headed by Bain Capital Partners and Thomas H. Lee Partners, two prominent private equity firms, for $26.7 billion. The deal, with its regulatory hurdles, took almost two years to be approved; by the time it was ready to close, the lenders balked at the price and the terms, because the economy was getting very tenuous. Bain, Lee, and the Mays family sued the lenders, and finally, in May 2008, reached a deal for a slightly lower price, and it closed later that year.

The Mays family became billionaires and it was perfect timing for them. Although the company's stock had languished since its deal with SFX in 2000, the family made quite a haul. As I've noted, the SFX deal was the harbinger of decline for the entire industry because it finally caused Wall Street to question radio's bullish projections. By the time the Clear Channel deal finally closed, the credit markets were in disarray, and by the end of 2008, it was apparent that Bain and Lee were in a hole they could not climb out of. Mark continued to run the company for two years, but, with the economy in free fall, it was tough sledding going forward. By the end of 2010, Mark Mays announced he was stepping down, and shortly thereafter, Bob Pittman was named CEO.

I knew Bob vaguely; I'd had only one meeting with him, years before, but it was memorable. In the early 1990s, Bob had called to say he needed to meet with me. Meeting at the Hotel Bel-Air bar when we were both in Los Angeles, Bob asked, "Jeff, I have an opportunity to buy two AM stations and switch them to heavy metal. Should I do it?" In my usual skeptical fashion, I responded, "OK, Bob, I know that's not your real question, what is your question?" He said it was definitely his question; he could buy the stations cheaply and thought it was a great idea. I told him, "Bob, the people who listen to heavy metal have no interest in listening to AM radio. The fidelity is awful, and most of your target audience won't even know how to tune in to the AM band. This will never work." He then explained that the price was a bargain, and I gave him my standard response: "Sometimes free is too expensive!" I have no idea if he ever bought the stations, but I do know that no one in this or any other parallel universe has ever made heavy metal work on AM radio.

Bob was a known commodity when he took the job, and one friend said, "If he sells the industry, he'll help all of you. If he imposes his strategic thinking on your industry, he'll kill all of you." Make no mistake, Bob is one of the best salesmen I've ever seen. He's magnificent in front of a crowd and presents his case brilliantly. One of my close friends described watching Bob with a group of senior finance executives: "Bob had very smart people absolutely convinced that what he was saying was brilliant; when he spoke, they nodded in agreement, and paid rapt attention to his every word. It was remarkable, because he was sputtering complete nonsense, but he had intelligent people believing him!"

Perhaps Bob's greatest skill is building his own brand. Two of my Emmis board members knew Pittman from his early days in broadcasting and both marveled at his ability to craft his image. One noted, "Bob is now credited with being the genius behind MTV, and he's the only one who ever gets credit for its success, but I know of other people who had as much to do with building MTV as he did, but Bob took all of the credit and history now recognizes Bob and only Bob." The other told me, "Whenever a group of us got together, we knew that whatever idea Bob pitched was the exact opposite of what we should be doing. He had the uncanny ability to pick the wrong course of action every time."

There was also an industry legend about Pittman's role as the architect of the AOL/Time Warner merger. When the deal was done, Bob received kudos as a driving force behind it. By the time it was considered the single worst merger in American history, Bob had already jumped ship and escaped with his reputation intact. Of course, I learned Bob's secret a few years later. When Pittman joined Clear Channel, he brought in his own public relations team.

So, I had heard all the Pittman stories when he took the helm of Clear Channel, and when I saw him at his first industry event, I was impressed by his ability to articulate the case for radio. He may have been "Bob Pitchman," but he really was good at it. Years later, I marvel at his ability to tell a story convincingly, even when I know it is a lot closer to fiction than fact.

When Mark turned over the reins to Bob in 2011, I hoped we would have a good relationship. Since the company had been such a fervent supporter of NextRadio, I had some faith that he would remain aligned with a goal the industry firmly supported.

I got my first inkling that things might go badly before we even closed the Sprint deal. When I called to give him updates, he would ask the same question in slightly different ways, sometimes over and over again. The first time he did it, I thought he was just a slow learner, but after a few more calls I finally said, "Bob, you keep asking me the same questions over and over again, and every time I give you the same answers. It seems like you don't really want to hear what I'm saying." It was becoming clear that, while publicly supportive of the project, he was quietly trying to undermine it.

Paul Brenner, who was running the technical side of NextRadio, was also picking up signals that Clear Channel—now called iHeart through Pittman's massive rebranding campaign—was not going to be on board. After a trip to Germany to meet with automakers, Paul raced into my office and announced that two separate German automakers had disclosed that iHeart was pitching them on replacing the standard tuner with their own app; it would provide all the over-the-air signals, but *through* the iHeart app. I told Paul I should throw him out for reporting such a ridiculous notion. First, iHeart was basically attempting to become a gatekeeper, stepping in between broadcasters and their listeners: "Paul, that's like the radio industry letting iHeart become what cable is to TV. That would be insane. If iHeart decides to charge broadcasters for a place on their system, and we don't pay it, we're out of the automobile! Besides, if the iHeart app is the only tuner in cars, that would be an egregious antitrust violation. You're letting one company control the access of everyone else." I told Paul that he must have misunderstood, but later that summer, I learned that he hadn't.

After we closed the Sprint agreement, we had to garner industry support. We agreed on a fee schedule based on total company revenues, and as the largest company, iHeart had the largest bill. Shortly before meeting to take a final vote on whether to fund the deal, Paul was called into a meeting with Jeff Littlejohn, iHeart's head of technology. They had been friends for years, but Paul knew that Jeff was merely carrying Pittman's water and had no input into any decision. Littlejohn announced that iHeart wouldn't participate unless the entire system ran through their app, essentially confirming what the German automakers had told him earlier that summer.

It was clear that Pittman wasn't going to help anyone else in the industry unless he received all or at least most of the proceeds. After several people in the industry pushed back, the radio companies agreed that the fifteen largest would meet to vote on the deal. As we went through the presentation about the Sprint agreement, there were numerous questions, but it was clear that everyone but John Hogan, iHeart's COO, were firmly in favor of the deal. In the middle of the meeting, Pittman strode into the room, interrupted the meeting and said, "I don't know why we're voting on a deal with Sprint; we should go get a deal with AT&T or Verizon." I have no idea whether Bob knew or cared what our carefully crafted strategy had been, but I strongly sensed that his goal was merely to kill the deal so he could figure out how the capture the entire venture for himself. After listening to him for a few minutes, I stated, "Bob, before you joined us, we had already thoroughly discussed why the industry needs to start with Sprint, and why it makes no sense to start with another phone company." By now, it was clear that any burgeoning Pittman/Smulyan romance was dead, and I had no problem abruptly cutting him off, especially when I was certain I had the votes. We called for the vote, everyone supported it; even John Hogan reluctantly voted yes. John couldn't be seen trying to undermine the rest of the industry, and since Pittman had already left, he wouldn't have to incur Pittman's immediate wrath.

After the meeting, Lew Dickey, who ran Cumulus, discussed the project with me. Lew had always been a skeptic, and this day was no different, but he gave me a rare compliment: "Jeff, I have no idea if you can really pull this whole thing off, but I watched how you saved Emmis, and I marveled at it. You had absolutely no negotiating leverage in any deal that you did, and you figured out how to do it. I can't imagine you're going to have any leverage with the phone companies either, but I'm interested to see you try." I said, "Lew, we'll have more leverage with the phone guys than Emmis had with our banks. Let's see what we can get done."

When the Sprint deal was announced, I made certain Pittman was the first name in the press release, well ahead of mine. I knew that if he got top billing, it would make him at least a bit more supportive of our efforts.

Now we were off and running. Gordon Smith suggested that we meet with Bob and try to get everyone on the same page. When we got together with Bob and John Hogan, Bob opened the meeting by asking for our strong support for his push to get streaming rates down, and I told him that as long as he supported NextRadio, he would have my full support. Bob then went on about how the only thing that mattered to the industry was the streaming issue. By now, he had completely repositioned iHeart as a massive streaming audio service, and he had already spent hundreds of millions of dollars in on-air promotion, making certain that everyone who listened to the 850 iHeart stations was constantly reminded to find their favorite stations on the iHeart app. To this day, the greatest share of the company's revenue still comes from those 850 stations, but iHeart continues almost exclusively to promote its streaming app. I violated one of my cardinal rules by engaging Pittman on this: Never try to convince someone that his core values are invalid. This is true whether you're trying to persuade them that their politics, religion, or even wardrobe is inappropriate. It's a losing battle, but on this day, I couldn't resist. When Bob went into his standard "this is just like what I did at MTV," I started to smile, although it was probably more of a smirk than a smile: "Bob, this isn't anything like MTV, unless you think we can get AT&T and Verizon to pay for radio, like the cable companies did for cable channels." Bob dismissively replied that when MTV started, it didn't get paid. True, but the immense value of all cable channels was only created after receiving subscriber fees. Even when you're getting a scant twenty-five cents per month, across a cable universe of eighty-five million homes, that's a quarter of a billion dollars of annual revenue before you sell one commercial. It was crystal clear that no phone company was going to pay for radio signals the way cable had for MTV and so many other channels.

As our discussion continued, I told Bob that it would be great to get royalty relief, but that was a tall order (as it still is years later). Royalties, however, weren't the only costs that made streaming inefficient; the massive data charges were also an impediment. At this point Bob stunned me by retorting, "We don't pay any data fees." I said that they must have reinvented the laws of physics, because everyone incurred data charges. Bob was insistent and even asked John Hogan, "We don't pay for data, do we?" Now, I'd known Hogan for years, and his reputation as the ultimate company man was very well deserved, so his answer didn't surprise me: "Gee, Bob, I don't know, I'll have to look that up." John looked at me and the expression on his face was priceless; it practically screamed to me, "Jeff, if you think I'm going to tell this guy he's completely wrong, and what he just said is complete nonsense, you're crazy. I just ducked his question, which is as much as I'm going to do." Our conversation continued, and I explained that our listeners had expensive data charges, too—remember, this was years before data charges were bundled into plans that masked them effectively. Bob, now in rare form, responded, "People don't care about those charges, they'll pay anything, even one hundred dollars a month." By now, I was in disbelief and said, "Bob, I'll make you a bet, you go home to Mississippi and ask the first ten people you see if they would mind paying a hundred dollars a month for their data charges. I'll bet you nine of them would laugh at you."

When we left the meeting, I told Gordon, "I feel like the rest of the industry is stuck in the back seat of a car and Pittman and Hogan are Thelma and Louise and they're about to drive the rest of us over a cliff with them." It was an eerily prophetic statement.

I confided to Rick and Pat after the meeting that Bob was turning iHeart on its head, completely retooling the company around a strategy he didn't understand at all. In fairness to Pittman, I think he was just playing a different game. He was running a company that was completely underwater, and he saw the massive valuations of the streaming enterprises and most likely assumed that if he could get significant listening for the iHeart app, he could spin it off at a high enough value to solve the company's massive debt problems. Bob would have been the perfect person to hype the system and unload it, but after a few years, it would become clear that he would have no takers.

Still, begrudgingly, iHeart stayed on board, and as we passed the hat, they paid their fair share. I look back at the Sprint payment process with mixed emotions. When we did the deal, I thought the NAB, with its large administrative staff, would be in charge of managing the collection. I was stunned when the NAB told me that Emmis would have to be in charge. After thirty years in the business, I couldn't think of anything more frustrating than obtaining and collecting commitments from hundreds of broadcasters, but this gargantuan task landed in my lap. I should have realized that this was an early indication that the NAB was slowly drifting away from the partnership I thought we had.

I should also say, most broadcasters were terrific. Most understood the importance of the project and that they needed to do their fair share. However, others relished being free riders, content to let the rest of the industry do the work, while they would enjoy the benefits if the project were successful. Every year, we had a shortfall, and every year, Emmis, Ginny Morris of Hubbard, Bill Hendrich of Cox, and David Field of Entercom pitched in to make up the difference so we would meet our commitment to Sprint. I confided to friends that after thirty-five years in business, I had discovered that my job was "receivables clerk," and it was a very unenviable role.

Still, NextRadio made progress. The agreement with Sprint created a good amount of interest, and it gave leverage to members of Congress to pressure the other carriers. Paul knew that John Legere, the mercurial head of T-Mobile, was famous for his social media usage and his Twitter challenges, so Paul issued his own. He told John via Twitter that if he accepted NextRadio on T-Mobile phones, the radio industry would promote his latest initiatives. Legere instantly accepted, and we worked out an agreement and had our second carrier. Paul was also able to make deals with smaller carriers and was able to get NextRadio installed in phones that weren't controlled by the major phone companies. We saw usage grow, not as much as we had hoped, but we were definitely getting traction. Paul also had success placing NextRadio in Mexico, Peru, Argentina, Canada, and South Korea. While each deal was tedious and time consuming, we were convinced that we had a good chance of regaining radio's portability.

Of course, there were storm clouds. The two biggest carriers, AT&T and Verizon, as well as Apple, seemed largely indifferent to our efforts, and they used their significant lobbying ability to blunt our efforts on Capitol Hill.

One of the most exciting byproducts of the NextRadio launch was the response from the auto industry. Ford and other automakers were fascinated by the system. Along with Ibiquity Digital Corporation—the company responsible for digital radio installation in cars—we formed a coalition to explore how we could import the technology into the dashboard of the future. For Paul and me, it was a valuable hedge; even if we couldn't completely revive radio's portability, preserving our position in the car by providing a compelling ecosystem was going to also be critical for radio's future. After all, the car was the one place where we were dominant, and with interactivity coming to cars, it was critical that we stay relevant in that environment.

The fragile peace we had made with iHeart was suddenly shattered when, in 2014, I received a call from David Field, CEO of Entercom: "Bob Pittman is furious that you want to put NextRadio in cars, and he wants it stopped immediately." I was astounded, since we had been constantly updating the industry on automaker interest since the initial launch of NextRadio in 2012. Knowing that David was one of Bob's few close friends in the industry, I reminded him that all of us had been aware of the auto initiative for years, and he needed to refresh Bob's memory. David agreed to discuss it with Bob, which culminated in the most bizarre meeting of my career.

We gathered at Bob's office in New York. The founding group of nine leading companies had been reduced to five: iHeart, CBS Radio, Entercom, Cox, and Cumulus. Apparently, the previous year, Bob had decided he wouldn't meet with the larger group. Therefore, I had to wait outside the office. Irving Azoff, a close friend of iHeart COO Rich Bressler's, ran into me in the waiting room: "What are you doing outside when the rest of those guys are inside?" I laughed and said, "Long story, Irving, long story."

Bressler was in the room because the new rules granted iHeart two representatives, while the other companies could only send their CEOs. I was allowed into the room only for the discussion of NextRadio in cars, which

I was spearheading. Bob Struble, CEO of Ibiquity, was piped in by phone, since he was integrally involved in our effort to build interactivity into cars. Pittman started with his usual monologue: "Look, I know automobiles better than anyone in this room, and I know consumers better than anyone in this room, and I can state definitively, that there is absolutely no interest or need for interactivity in cars. They want the standard radio tuner, and that's all they want, and we will not support putting anything else into cars." When he was done, Struble responded: "Bob, we've spent years on this, we've conducted tons of research and we've spent the last decade with automakers, and I can tell you that interactivity is coming to cars, and we need to be a part of it." Pittman quickly dismissed Struble, noting, "Your business hasn't been much of a success, so why should anyone listen to you?" It was a despicable put-down. Ibiquity, like the rest of the radio industry, had labored for years to get digital tuners into cars, and while they had had some success, it was a slow process, for two reasons. First, unlike SiriusXM, they weren't paying automakers to be placed in cars, and second, despite our fervent desire to see digital or high-definition radio succeed, every one of us knew that consumers weren't exactly clamoring for it.

When Pittman finished dismissing Struble, I jumped in: "Bob, let me see if I understand you. You're saying that the tuner is the only thing that matters, correct? And by the tuner you mean the dial that goes from 88 to 108?" After Bob nodded, I moved in with the coup de grâce: "Bob, you realize that the tuner you are talking about was invented for the 1946 Studebaker. Don't you think we've come a bit further than that now?" I noticed the smiles on the others in the room, but clearly the put-down wasn't exactly resonating with Pittman. He continued to insist that I was wrong, and I responded, "You're still talking about 1946 technology. There's no other technology invented in 1946 that's still around today."

He continued with his argument, until I mentioned the '46 Studebaker again, when he snapped, "Goddammit Jeff, stop mentioning the 1946 Studebaker!" Unable to resist, I parried, "OK, Bob, let's call it a 1973 Dodge Dart; it's still ridiculously old technology." By this time, there was more smoke rising from his head than from the Vatican when a new pope is selected, but I no longer cared. Most people in the industry recognized that Bob only specialized in self-serving jargon, but unlike the others, I not only had no problem calling him on it, I sort of relished it. If he were going to lead us all over a cliff, I would at least suggest he take his hands off the wheel before we got to the precipice.

As the meeting went on, we told Bob that we were going to meet with the automakers at the upcoming Consumer Electronics Show, and we would report to all of them on our progress. Afterward, two of the other CEOs called to explain that they were baffled by Bob's position and that they loved the '46 Studebaker remark. I told them both: "You don't need to tell me how you feel, you need to tell Bob." I doubt they ever did.

The '46 Studebaker line became famous, although costly to me and Emmis. Rick, Pat, and I were sure that after the meeting, Pittman would strike back at us, and six months later, we had ample evidence. Emmis was finalizing negotiations with our star morning man, Big Boy, whom Rick had discovered years earlier, when Big Boy was a security guard. Rick was also his mentor and father confessor, and the station had made him nationally famous. In fact, when I presented Big Boy with his twenty-year Emmis employee watch, he broke down and cried in front of his wife, his kids, and all his fellow employees. When his contract was up for renewal, we thought it highly unlikely he would ever leave. We made a mistake in not renewing it before our exclusivity period ended, but as it turned out, it didn't matter. We were paying him slightly under $1.5 million per year and our proposal was for slight increases. Then, as the exclusivity period ended, iHeart stepped in and offered double his salary, numerous trips on Pittman's private jet, and a syndication plan that would significantly enrich him. After a long debate, we finally agreed to offer terms substantially similar to iHeart's offer; however, it was too late. We concluded that if Big Boy seriously thought about our new offer, Pittman would merely double his again. Unlike us, he had almost no balance sheet constraints, for iHeart was already hopelessly underwater and they had managed to stave off bankruptcy for years. When it was over, and Big Boy was gone, we forever referred to it as the "1946 Studebaker agreement."

On the NextRadio front, we continued to work with Ibiquity and the automakers, without any noise from iHeart. However, a few months later, Paul got a call from Littlejohn announcing that we were to turn off all of iHeart's 850 stations in the NextRadio system, immediately. As part of our original agreement, we had placed Emmis stations in iHeart Radio's app, and also gave them a number of free promotional commercials every week. In exchange, they went into the NextRadio system, with an unspecified number of promotions for us, which they conveniently never ran. When our programmers complained about running their spots when they weren't running ours, we told them we were doing it to "keep peace in the industry." Now, iHeart was escalating to all-out war, and it couldn't come at a worse time.

Unbeknownst to most, we were in the final stages of an agreement with AT&T. Gordon Smith was close friends with AT&T's head of government relations, Jim Ciccone, and Gordon had had some good initial discussions with Jim about joining NextRadio. Jim hosted Gordon and me in his office, and we explained that the radio industry was ecstatic about promoting a deal with AT&T and would use our massive reach to promote whatever he wanted to promote. Half-facetiously, he asked what we would do if he turned us down, and sensing a chance for some levity, I stated, "Well, then we will use our massive reach to say everything about AT&T that you don't want us to say!" Jim was very likable, and we reached a tentative agreement.

While the lawyers were working away, we got iHeart's call. I called Gordon and said, "We both know that if iHeart pulls out of this, it will kill the AT&T deal, the industry will appear to be dysfunctional, and all of this will go away." Gordon readily agreed and offered to step in. He called Bob and convinced him that he did not want to be blamed for killing NextRadio. By this time, several years into Pittman's tenure, any illusion that he was going to try to help the industry had long since vanished, and, with the exception of David Field, I knew of no other industry executive who believed Bob's motives were benign. In fact, several of David's most senior leaders marveled at David's inability to see that Bob had no intention of helping Entercom or anyone else.

Gordon reached a truce with Bob. In exchange for iHeart remaining part of the NextRadio platform and being publicly supportive, NextRadio would cease negotiations with automakers until an NAB-funded study could be done. Peter Smyth, CEO of Greater Media, was named chairman of the study, and Bill Hoffman, CEO of Cox, was named his co-chair. Three research firms were hired, including Marshall Cohen's, who had done all of Pittman's research for years. The process went very well, and although it took nine months, the three firms reached a unanimous conclusion. A call was set up between the NAB, Smyth, Hoffman, Pittman, me, and several other industry leaders to go over the findings. It was a rather straightforward presentation that concluded that, with the exception of a significant number of sixty-five-year-old or greater listeners who wanted the standard tuner to be left unchanged, everyone else had a strong preference for interactivity.

During the call, when one of the presenters noted that "interactivity is the key to your future," Pittman jumped in and said, matter-of-factly, "Of course, I knew that." After the call ended, another member of the committee called and said, "Can you believe that, we spent all this time and money on this, and he admitted that he knew the whole thing was ridiculous. Can you believe this guy?" I told him that Bob's goal all along was to negotiate with automakers without the rest of the industry at the table. He had bought himself nine months, and I was sure he had made the most of it. Bob didn't believe his own arguments any more than the rest of us did, but his bluster served his purposes.

Such were the waters we were treading in. We had one more glitch before the AT&T deal was done. While we were anticipating a final sign-off, we were told that a senior AT&T executive who had previously approved the deal had changed his mind and was now opposed. We knew it had to be someone in the highest ranks of AT&T. The two-week delay seemed interminable, but in the end, Jim Ciccone convinced Randall Stephenson, AT&T's CEO, to approve the agreement over strenuous objections, and we had our first major carrier in the fold.

The night before we were to announce the agreement, we decided that I should give Lew Dickey and David Field a heads-up. Lew, because he was convinced we would never get one of the two big carriers, and David, because in spite of his consistent support, he always had one foot planted in iHeart's camp. I called David late in the afternoon and discovered we were both in Nantucket, eating a few blocks away from each other. We agreed to meet for a drink after dinner. It was my anniversary, and Heather, my daughter Sam, and I were dining when the waiter brought us a bottle of champagne with a note that said, "Happy anniversary and congratulations on a remarkable achievement for the entire industry. All of us are in your debt." I was completely blown away by David's gesture. Later that night, over drinks with David and his dad, Joe—a friend of mine since my early days in the industry—David proposed a toast: "To Jeff and my dad, the only two people I have ever known who really could do the impossible!"

The AT&T deal changed a lot of perceptions, inside and outside the industry, and Verizon and Apple would clearly need to take notice. We even had some broadcasters who were finally willing to pay their NextRadio commitments, but collections remained a tedious challenge. Still, it was exciting to know that we were getting more traction as we rolled out the system.

Shortly after we reached an agreement with AT&T, the tenor of our discussions with Verizon changed. Previously, Verizon had been almost violent in their opposition to incorporating NextRadio, but with the other three major carriers on board, they knew they were going to incur the wrath of public safety officials if they didn't join us. We reached an agreement with Verizon, and we were certain we were on our way, with only Apple, the biggest challenge, to crack.

While we were getting NextRadio installed everywhere, we were disappointed at the usage rates. We noticed it and so did several critics. Affinity for the app was high, scoring very well in app store ratings, but people didn't seem to be listening as much as we had hoped. We spent a lot of time trying to improve the experience, but it was clear that the dogs weren't eating the dog food. One day, Paul walked into my office and explained the problem. We had launched NextRadio in Mexico, Canada, Peru, South Korea, and Argentina, and Paul noticed a disturbing trend. He discovered that in other countries, where the commercial load was less, there was much more affinity for the product, and being the ultimate data geek, he had done more analysis. He pointed out that after about seven minutes of interruptions an hour, listeners started tuning out, and it was hard to get them back. He showed that in other countries, where seven to eight minutes of commercials was the norm, listeners were loyal. However, when the spot advertising load was twelve to sixteen minutes an hour, listeners found it intolerable and went away.

This problem had started during the consolidation era, after the Telecom Act of 1996. As capital flowed into the system, debt came with it, and the industry entered a cycle of overleveraging from which it has never fully escaped. With debt comes the need to generate revenue, which makes commercial limits evaporate. In my early days in the industry, it was hard to find a radio station running more than eight minutes of commercials an hour on the FM band. By 2015, it was hard to find any running less than twelve minutes an hour. While not the only culprit, iHeart was the worst. Not only were they burdened with significant barter deals, but they were always scrambling to put ad inventory on the books to beat the industry revenue average, which they promised to do every quarter. In addition, their stations were loaded with at least two extra minutes of commercials every hour, one to promote the iHeart app, another to promote upcoming concerts and iHeart music festivals. Rick noted that the problem was staggering in smaller markets like St. Louis; he showed me a commercial log in which several iHeart stations were averaging twenty-two minutes of commercials an hour! Even in their largest markets, where it was critical to compete for higher-valued listeners, they amped up the advertising; their logs in Los Angeles revealed that, compared to us, CBS Radio, and Cumulus, they were averaging three to four minutes more an hour than everyone else.

Paul's conclusion was that our industry was oversaturated with commercials, and that was the reason listening had declined rapidly in the home and couldn't get a foothold in our portable devices. We were left with only the car, where our listeners were captive. We realized to our dismay that our problems were not going to be solved by giving the industry portability. I studied our listening numbers and realized that no matter how "cool" the NextRadio app was and how many features it provided, there was no way we were going to get people to consume radio in other environments with the impediment of the number of commercials we ran. The industry was clearly not creating a compelling value proposition for our listeners.

As I dug into the numbers, I also looked at the data behind the iHeart streaming app, because, unlike Spotify and Pandora, its primary focus was local radio stations. I knew iHeart brilliantly marketed the app, which had been downloaded over one billion times, but those actually listening were a small fraction of those listening to Pandora and Spotify. Worse, neither Pandora nor Spotify had spent any significant amounts marketing themselves. In contrast, I calculated the costs that iHeart had incurred, including: the value of the several million commercials they ran each year; the cost of the music events and festivals wrapped around marketing their app; and the value of the inventory they had given away over the preceding years to all the automakers, appliance makers, and others, to include the app in their cars and devices. The total was absolutely staggering. The unique listener proposition of the iHeart app centered around their radio stations; despite some other content, the core of the iHeart app was radio listening. And while iHeart had thrown billions of dollars at the concept, the app was an absolute laggard in the streaming competition. In a perverse way, Bob Pittman's experience with the iHeart music app helped me make a critical decision about Emmis. The year before, we had purchased WBLS and WLIB in New York. Armed with Paul's analysis of radio listening and my analysis of iHeart's costs and metrics, I could see that buying more radio stations made little sense. For someone who passionately loved the industry, the NextRadio results and our competitor's metrics made me realize that the challenges of owning radio stations were now almost insurmountable. We never bought another radio station.

Paul, as usual, was ahead of me. He had been studying the numbers for quite a while and came to a fascinating conclusion. While we were never going to have gigantic numbers of listeners on cell phones, we did have decent penetration; that, coupled with installing the NextRadio system in cars, meant we would be acquiring massive location-based data. The great secret of Google and Facebook has been their ability to accumulate and process staggering information about individual consumption. Now the radio industry had something unique: the ability to follow listeners as they constantly moved around their marketplaces. One of radio's great advantages has always been that people listen closer to their purchasing decision. You might see an ad for something while watching prime-time television, but that information is usually hours old before you are actually ready to make a purchase. With radio, you are in your car, many times headed to a retailer when you hear the commercial, and that is very valuable for advertisers. What we determined was that, for the first time, we could provide accurate, real-time data through our system. Instead of just the anecdotal information the industry had relied on for decades, we could demonstrate the effect of an ad campaign on visits to stores, because we knew exactly when people were in those stores, or at least in the parking lot. Initial tests provided great results for several advertisers; Paul and his team were certain this could be a winning pivot for the industry, and that the focus of NextRadio needed to shift dramatically. We still wanted to be in every cell phone and every automobile, but we now realized that the listening data had the ability to radically improve radio industry economics.

Here's why: While almost all advertising is sold on a cost-per-ratings-point basis, radio has always been a secondary or tertiary medium, meaning our pricing was significantly below television and even magazines and newspapers. When Google and Facebook demonstrated the value of their data, they were able to take pricing to an entirely different level, because they could provide advertisers with massive information about consumer behavior. The result was that their ad pricing was in most cases three to four times radio's average. If we could level the playing field with them on data aggregation, provide better location-based information, and use the proven value of broadcasting's ad retention, we could quite possibly pull off a monumental breakthrough for the industry.

Our hypothesis also offered an elegant solution to our industry's albatross, the overcommercialization that was slowly killing all of us. If we could provide quality, location-based data, the value of our advertisements would triple or quadruple. By doing so, broadcasters could sell a fraction of the commercials they had been selling and still receive more dollars. That could bring our crushing commercial load down to less than eight minutes an hour, finally making radio listening more attractive. Paul presented his ideas at an NAB convention, and everyone in the room seemed to realize this angle could have major consequences for all of us.

Although the value of data was foreign to most broadcasters, the impact of Facebook and Google was not. Everyone in radio had been severely affected by the inroads both had made in the local and national marketplaces. When we explained how we could now compete, with more compelling data in a more user-friendly environment, a light gradually went on in the minds of most of our peers. Within a year, every major company began to realize that this was going to be a critical element in its ability to compete, and most heartily endorsed the pivot. However, we were continuing to fund the operation, and the costs of building out a data-capturing enterprise were significant. All of us at Emmis, especially our board, noticed that our losses building out NextRadio were continuing to mount, because we were essentially funding American radio's entire research and development effort. We couldn't appeal to the NAB, since they had already helped cover the sizable shortfall for the last Sprint payment when iHeart refused to pay. Our only choice was to pass the hat. From the beginning of the NextRadio project, it's hard to imagine how many times people in the industry would stop me and thank me for "saving the industry." In addition, it was gratifying, but somewhat comical, that I received just about every award the industry could offer. After a few years of this, I finally told friends: "Stop thanking me, stop giving me awards, and just help us fund this thing."

Paul laid out a detailed budget of what it would take to fully fund the rollout of the industry's data plan, around twenty-five million more dollars before we could begin monetizing our efforts. Busy working on their own data program, iHeart was clearly not going to help, but their unwillingness to support the rest of the industry actually galvanized everyone else. After a number of years, all had finally realized that iHeart was going its own way, and if the rest of us didn't have a plan, it would build its own system and siphon off whatever revenues were available to the rest of us.

Paul was convinced that our location-based, over-the-air data was far superior to anything iHeart could build, and with the rest of the industry firmly on board with NextRadio, we would be accumulating far more information than even the industry's largest company could collect.

By the spring of 2018, after long deliberations with our board, we concluded that unless others provided meaningful support, we could not continue to go forward. We called a meeting in Indianapolis in April, and most of the largest broadcasters sat in our conference room as we laid out, in great detail, all the costs and benefits of the project. After a lengthy discussion, the decision was unanimous: we had to go forward. As several noted, the industry had no choice. If we didn't, radio would continue to decline, and we would also leave iHeart with its own system, which would further hasten our demise.

Everyone agreed that each company would fund a share that matched their proportional size, and they would be granted equity in NextRadio based on an approved formula. Our goal was to raise $25 million in new capital that would easily fund the project until it was able to be monetized. At the end of the meeting, we were heartened, not just by everyone's support, but by their fervor as well.

However, as with all things in radio, we were facing formidable challenges. Cumulus, the industry's third largest player, was just emerging from bankruptcy and was clearly unable to lend its economic support. Entercom was in the process of purchasing CBS Radio, and, while normally having a charter supporter get more heft would be a good thing, we knew that David Field's new clout was likely to yield demands that we feared would be unreasonable. Ironically, iHeart had also just filed for bankruptcy, but since Bob Pittman had managed to convince the bankruptcy court to pay him $10 million to steer the company through the process, we were certain he was still firmly in control.

As we were working on everyone's commitments, we received a message that proved to be a harbinger of doom. Bill Hendrich, who ran Cox Radio, called to let me know that the company had stopped all investments. Shortly after, I learned Cox was putting its broadcast stations up for sale, which it did the following year. Bill, one of my favorite people in the industry, had said at our meeting that all of us had to support the project, and that if we were unwilling, we were sealing our own fate. From day one, Cox had always stepped up and helped the effort, and their leadership was critical. Unlike publicly traded companies, the Cox family enterprise was privately held, with a long tradition of leadership in every industry they entered. Also, the Cox family was worth billions, and they lent significant credibility to every venture they backed. Without Cox's financial support, I knew that keeping everyone else engaged and committed would be challenging.

I also knew that replacing Cox's funds would be nearly impossible. After the ten largest groups, the rest of the industry just didn't have the resources. Most smaller companies, who had always supported our efforts, had balance sheets that would not allow them to make multimillion dollar commitments.

Throughout the summer, we scrambled to put the funding in place. Ginny Morris of Hubbard, Mike Dowdle of Bonneville, and David Field of Entercom were fully on board. Caroline Beasley, who ran her family's company, Beasley Broadcast Group, was supposedly supportive, but we could never pin her down. In addition, Mary Berner of Cumulus indicated that when they worked through terms of their bankruptcy, she would do everything possible to provide funds.

We agreed that we had to have a final plan in place to announce to the industry by the NAB radio convention in September. Numerous smaller broadcasters had been briefed about the data aggregation plan, and all were solidly on board. We hoped to announce the new funding along with a list of at least twenty other broadcasters, who, while not financially supporting the effort, were committed to every other part of the project. We finally reached an agreement that we could go forward with $16 million, short of our goal, but with the notion that others, like Cumulus and Beasley, would commit after the project was initially funded. We were excited for the project, until we got another jolt: David Field announced the week before the conference that he would not support the venture unless either Beasley or Cumulus also stepped up. Since we had agreed that we would go forward, I was disappointed, but not totally stunned. Cumulus had already told us they wouldn't be ready to commit by September, so that part of David's request made no sense. All of us also knew that Caroline would refuse to make a commitment until the last minute. I was certain that she would only join once she knew the train would leave the station without her. Others agreed with my assessment, and I began to see something else afoot.

We had set our deadline for the NAB convention, and David requested another week to see if he could get both Beasley and Cumulus to commit. I was frustrated, because we were losing all the momentum we could gain by announcing widespread support at the NAB event. However, by this time, Field was committing more money than anyone else, so I agreed to his request. While I was now fairly certain where this was going, I had no choice but to play out the hand. David and Caroline had been very close friends for years, and it was incomprehensible that he couldn't convince her to join an effort that she and her key people had vigorously endorsed a few months before.

Naturally, the next deadline passed without support from Caroline, and I told David that we were going to shut down the business. David then began a series of negotiations proposing that Entercom step in and take over NextRadio, which I had known was going to happen as soon as the first deadline was changed. David and his CFO had always said they either had to help fund this project or they were going to have to build their own data system. Paul was certain that either they were bluffing or completely misunderstood what it would take to build the system we had spent years putting together. After we told David that we were going to stop funding NextRadio, he started proposing various alternatives, all of which would have given him control of the venture for a nominal amount of money. My initial fears about David's increased hubris after he had gained control of CBS Radio were borne out. It appeared that David had realized that it would be a lot cheaper to wait for us to get ready to shut down NextRadio and then take it over rather than spend a fortune and start from scratch. We went back and forth for several weeks, and I finally concluded that rather than accept next to nothing for a project we had spent ten years and millions of dollars on, I would shut it down. The decision was painful, but I had realized from the start that solving the industry's problem was an immensely difficult challenge.

David was furious when we actually shut down NextRadio. I am certain that he, most likely along with Caroline, was convinced he could control our enterprise for almost nothing. Now, without everything we had built, he was going to have to start from scratch and replicate several years' worth of work and do it without widespread support from the industry.

For some reason, losing NextRadio wasn't as excruciating for me as it would have been for others. Because by then, I understood Greg Nathanson's admonition: "You come up with some terrific ideas, ideas that will create value for everyone, and that will help the industry tremendously, but they require collective action, and it's impossible to get the people in your industry to act that way. They have too much history trying to kill each other for that to ever happen."

As with other ventures that didn't succeed, I was remarkably proud of the team we had assembled and the work we had done. And, always suspecting the project was a long shot, I had started hedging my bets long before we abandoned NextRadio.

Top: At a Moelis Golf outing in Pebble Beach after several of our radio sales. From left to right: Anand Gowda, Founder, High Bluff Capital Partners; me; John Momtazee; Chris Ripley, CEO, Sinclair Broadcast Group; and Alfred Liggins, CEO, Urban One. *Bottom:* At another Managers' Meeting, Rick and I regularly presented awards, usually laced with bad comedy bits.

16

Escape from Dresden

y early 2016, I had begun to realize that staying in our current businesses was akin to pushing water uphill—forever. I knew our managers were terrific. In every business we entered, we always moved
the needle. Our regional magazines won every imaginable award for editorial excellence, and the publishing side produced the best profit results in the
magazine industry. Our editors and publishers were viewed as rock stars.
Texas Monthly had already been an iconic brand when we bought it from
Mike Levy in 1998, and our team enhanced it over the years we owned it.
However, like radio, the magazine industry was in spectacular decline. We
decided that we would sell all our magazines except for *Indianapolis Monthly*
and essentially exit the space.

It's hard to confront the reality that businesses you've spent your lifetime building don't make sense to continue to own. It's doubly hard when
the people you've hired have done remarkable, groundbreaking work, day
after day for many years. I've always said, people accept death slowly. None
of us wants to admit that our hopes and dreams have vanished. I also felt
like I was letting down people who had spent years with us, but, more

importantly, I realized that we couldn't make their lives better continuing to own our properties. I've had another favorite saying for decades: No one is happy in a failing business, neither the employees, the shareholders, nor even your communities, because you can't provide anyone with resources when the business isn't succeeding.

We came to the bitter conclusion that everything we owned was going to be worth less tomorrow than it was today, and pushing water uphill was becoming more painful all the time. With my usual gallows humor, I told our senior managers that our goal was "to get out of Dresden before the fire-bombing," and every time we sold something, we joked that we were getting a little further away from the center of Dresden.

There's no question that I had a lot of regrets about continuing to stay in businesses that were declining, but radio, and to a lesser extent, regional magazines were what I knew and loved. I'm not sure if I had the chance to do it over again that I would act any differently. As frustrating as it was watching our various entities decline, I still had fun coming to work every day. Doing what I loved with the kind of team I had surrounded myself with buoyed me at every juncture.

The corollary to accepting death slowly is that you hang on to hope, even in the face of impending doom. Even on our worst days, I knew that our assets had value and that we could rebuild the company. After we extricated ourselves from the financial straits the 2008–2009 recession had put us in, we were confident that we would survive. However, as the years went on and we continued in the radio and magazine businesses, we realized that for us to create meaningful value, we would have to do something completely different.

As much as I loved NextRadio, I knew the odds of resurrecting the radio industry were slim. Looking at Paul's listening data was a watershed moment, and Rick's declining PUMM statistics were further evidence that it was time to make a change. The hardest part for me, and for those who are still in the business, is that radio has always been a special medium. It has a unique ability to make a difference in the lives of its listeners, advertisers, and communities, and in spite of its current challenges, it will be able to continue to do that for many years to come. However, we had an insatiable desire to find businesses that were growing. Nothing to me was more rewarding than watching Emmis grow spectacularly over our first twenty years. While it was painful to make the transition out of radio, I was determined to rebuild the company once again.

We reached an agreement at the beginning of 2017 to sell Power 106, Los Angeles, to the Meruelo Group for $85 million, a far cry from the station's peak value, but a reasonable figure in 2017. Alex Meruelo was a new type of buyer. A successful serial entrepreneur, he had grown up listening to Power 106. Owning the station was an opportunity for him to be in show business, which appealed to his desire to become more than a very successful businessman. Our negotiations were fun and challenging, but at the end of the day, I knew that his management style would be radically different from ours. Once he was bitten by the entertainment bug, he went on to buy several, much cheaper FM stations in Los Angeles, including our former KMVN, then KXOS, which Grupo Centro, in their haste to exit the market, sold to him for $35 million, a significant haircut from the $85 million they had paid us a few years before. Enjoying media, Alex's next stop was sports, where he purchased the NHL's lowly Arizona Coyotes. It always reminded me of the line: If you wanted to be in major league sports in the worst way, buying the Coyotes was definitely the worst way.

As we decided to divest our stations, we fully recognized that we were in a new era. Because capital had fled the industry, prices had declined precipitously. Not only did Wall Street view radio as toxic, but the commercial banks followed suit. While I was confident our radio assets still had much more value than we were given credit for, for the most part, I was going to need to find some nontraditional buyers: people who loved radio and weren't going to be guided by industry declines, or competitors in our same markets, who could reap the benefits of combining operations. Alex Meruelo was definitely the first type of buyer. It wasn't like the days when you could put your stations up for bid and find a number of suitors. When lots of people are bidding, you have incredible negotiating leverage. One day in the office I complained, "I haven't had negotiating leverage in a deal since Lincoln was shot!"

Selling Power 106 was a watershed moment for us. It was the station that, thirty years earlier, had catapulted us into radio's big time. Despite the loss of Big Boy, Power 106 remained a significant factor in Los Angeles, far removed from its greatest glory—as was all of Los Angeles radio—but still very profitable. As I mentioned before, when I first decided to buy it, the owner, Howard Grafman's company, was only interested in selling us their St. Louis and San Francisco stations. As I studied the Los Angeles market, I fell totally in love with it. With only twenty-two big FM signals in a metropolitan area of fifteen million people, the market would give us ample opportunity to grow spectacularly. Unlike New York, which had a larger population, LA's residents were captive in their automobiles, with a sprawling metropolitan area and little public transportation. When I was at USC law school, one of my favorite moments was when a professor who had been asked to consult on a rapid-transit proposal, asked our class: "What do you think the average Angelino would pay daily to ride a subway?" All of us knew that Southern Californians were wedded to their cars, so we all guessed it would be a nominal amount. We were way off: "People say you'd have to PAY THEM two dollars a day to ride a subway." It was a lesson I never forgot, and when Los Angeles finally built its rapid transit system, I was curious whether the economics were as bad as predicted. In short, yes. After billions of dollars to build a very user-friendly system, ridership has been anemic.

I convinced Howard Grafman to put his LA station into our deal in place of their less attractive station in San Francisco. Within two years after we had purchased what was then KMGG for $11 million, we switched the station to KPWR, Power 106. It was a forerunner of modern hip-hop, and the station was a spectacular success. Within a few months, everyone in American radio knew Power 106, and I marveled at how many imitators it had. Stations even stole our logo and our station identifiers. I had to laugh, driving through a small midwestern town one day and seeing a Power billboard. I was laughing as I listened to the station, thinking how hard it was going to be for that station's management to find the unique mix of Hispanics, young Blacks, and trendy Southern California suburbanites in a small, rural, all-white town in Middle America!

Rick Cummings was the architect of Power 106, the mentor to program directors for all of the thirty years we owned it, and the person who had a remarkable knack for identifying and cultivating talent. No one was more responsible for Power's enduring legacy than Rick, so it was not surprising when my daughter Cari called me when the sale was announced. "Dad," she asked, "I know you're at peace with selling Power, but how is Rick doing?" It was a sensitive and caring question, and I explained that Rick had come to the same painful conclusion that I had, that as much as we loved the station and its people, we both knew it was time to leave.

When the sale closed, we had a farewell party for the staff; it was a bittersweet event, but some of the stories bandied about made the evening more hilarious than melancholy. At the end of the night, we handed out envelopes to our people. We wanted to say thank you with very generous farewell checks. I was proud to have done it, and I didn't mind that the story leaked to the press in the following days. Numerous people mentioned that, "Only Emmis treats people this way, even when they're headed out the door."

Giving our people a farewell gift was a way to assuage our guilt, but it was also the right thing to do. Even though we were feverishly trying to make NextRadio work at the time, we realized that the rational thing to do was to prepare for a time after radio. In spite of our ties to the industry, our senior leadership was relieved that we were finally headed in a direction that might prove productive. Rick summed it up concisely one afternoon: "I love the radio industry, but I just want to win again, and I know we're not going to win in radio anymore."

I realized that for the first twenty years of our existence, Emmis was a group that looked at a proverbial hill, put a plan in place to take the hill, and then went out and took the hill. It was exhilarating. There isn't anything in life like building something from nothing, and we did it time and time again. Between 2002 and 2008, and especially after, we weren't winning; we were barely standing in place. Moreover, that same team who fearlessly took hills before, had, after years of stagnant performance, became a team that would look at the same hill and instead of being poised to take it, would worry about which rock on the hill would roll down, start an avalanche, and kill them. My mission, which I articulated many times, was to break that mindset and to create an environment in which we could win again. I used to joke to friends that "I've spent an entire decade not creating any economic value for anyone." We also used to joke that "Emmis is the home of absolutely no economic or intellectual capital." I was certain, however, that our group had plenty of intellectual capital, we just desperately needed to create economic capital.

I knew that as painful as it was to sell assets that we had owned for years, we needed to move on if we wanted to rebuild Emmis. Author Jim Collins says that to build an organization, some things need to die, and for us, it was the assets that comprised the bulk of our company that needed to die.

By my age, I've become acutely aware of my strengths and weaknesses, and throughout my story, you've seen many examples of each. One thing I'm really adept at is selling assets. I used to joke: "No one gets involved in my sales process," and our group was more than willing to leave me alone. Numerous times, I knew that Pat, Ryan, Scott, or Greg would have taken far less for an asset than I was willing to. Sometimes, of course, that led to epic mistakes, but more often than not, it worked in our favor.

My motto in these negotiations was that you had to employ the "Nixon madman theory." For years, I vaguely remembered a discussion about Nixon's negotiating strategy with the Chinese. According to the story, Nixon believed that the best way to bring the Chinese government to the table was for them to believe he was insane; he wanted them to believe that he was ready, at a moment's notice, to launch nuclear weapons at Beijing. The Chinese, fearing the worst, became very calm and focused on reaching a deal. By convincing the Chinese he was crazy, Nixon converted their intransigent stance to a willingness to engage in good-faith, rational negotiations.

For years, whenever we were in an intense negotiation, I was likely to use the Nixon madman theory, which usually led to a successful outcome. One day, years ago, Scott Enright walked into my office with a Nixon mask and said, "The difference between you and Nixon is that he just acted like he was insane; we want to present you with this mask, because unlike Nixon, we're pretty certain you ARE insane!" It was one of my favorite moments. I told him that the Smulyan corollary to the Nixon theory was that it was just as important to convince my own people that I was crazy, because if they believed I was nuts, they would communicate that fear to the other side.

While I was laughing about it, I was serious underneath. If your people think you're bluffing, they will radiate that to the other side. Therefore, you have to convince your own folks you are totally irrational, so they will communicate that fear to their counterparts. Trust me, it works!

Also in 2017, we sold our remaining magazines in Los Angeles, Orange County, Austin, and Cincinnati, as well as the Terre Haute stations we had acquired as part of the purchase of the Hulman group. By the end of the year, we were in negotiations with Ginny Morris of Hubbard and David Field of Entercom to sell our assets in St. Louis, which concluded early in 2018. By then, we had whittled our debt down to almost nothing, and we were able to start thinking about what lay ahead.

It was clear that Emmis was going to have significant value from the cash from the sales, and a number of friends assumed that I would merely sell the remaining assets and liquidate the company. However, seeing the possibilities led me to the exact opposite conclusion. For years, I had been an entrepreneur in industries that had been steadily declining. Because I had a remarkable team, we had survived when others hadn't, and while our holdings were worth a fraction of what they would have been if I had sold everything a decade earlier, I felt we had earned the right to do something else. I, like Rick and our entire team, was dying to compete again. I told them all that being able to look at an actual hill, build a plan, and take it would be even more exciting than it had been years earlier, because this time, we had known the pain of being unable to do so. Even though I was over seventy, the idea of being able to rebuild Emmis was positively exhilarating for me.

In 2019, after we disposed of our Austin stations and wiped out our last remnants of debt, Ryan Hornaday walked into my office and proudly proclaimed, "Congratulations, Jeffrey, we have officially retired the last of $1.6 billion of debt." It had been a long ordeal, but it was an incredibly rewarding moment.

At the time, we were also in final negotiations to sell a controlling stake in our two largest remaining stations, Hot 97 and WBLS in New York. By 2019, we had shut down NextRadio, and the industry's anemic growth made finding buyers even harder than ever. Unlike St. Louis and Austin, where our buyers had already been in the market and our stations provided a significant additional presence, New York had no one with the ability to buy our stations. While WBLS and Hot 97 were very profitable, FCC limits prevented our two largest competitors, iHeart and Entercom/CBS, from buying. Even without FCC constraints, neither could raise the capital anyway. David Field was in the throes of a challenging purchase of CBS Radio, which tied his company in knots, and iHeart was just emerging from bankruptcy. No one else in New York radio had access to capital, and by 2019, there was almost no one who wanted to enter the radio space.

Soo Kim and I had gotten to know each other a number of years earlier at a Moelis retreat and we discussed working together. Soo is a brilliant financier, who purchased Young Broadcasting out of bankruptcy and then parlayed it into buying Media General and then LIN Broadcasting, to become one of America's largest TV companies. After the LIN deal, he set his sights on Meredith Corporation, which was considering liquidating its television holdings. Soo lobbed in a bid, but Perry Sook, owner of Nexstar, decided that he would launch a competing bid to take over Soo's company, Media General. It was a fascinating three-way battle, and ultimately, Soo's shareholders decided to take Nexstar's cash and the company was sold. Soo was deeply disappointed, but television had been a very profitable venture for him. I realized that he envied my company's two voting classes of stock, for if he had had that structure at Media General, he would have been able to control his shareholder vote and fend off Perry Sook.

As we discussed various opportunities to work together, I would often kid him that he always courted me by telling me that he loved my strategic thinking, my great corporate culture, and my vision for the industry, but that, at heart, he really loved my two classes of stock. It reminded me of Gary Kaseff's commentary on me when I was single: "Jeff, women are attracted to you because: (1) You're good-looking, (2) You're funny, (3) You're charismatic, (4) You're smart, or (5) You're rich. Pick one and only one! (Clearly, the only possible answer was 5.) I told Soo that clearly the only answer was that we had two classes of stock.

With our investment banker John Momtazee's help, Soo and I spent several months constructing a convoluted agreement in which Emmis would split into two publicly traded companies: Old Emmis and Mediaco. Old Emmis would retain its real estate, its Indianapolis radio stations, its magazine, Digonex (its dynamic pricing company), WLIB-AM in New York City and the residual ownership of WEPN-FM (formerly WRKS) in New York which, as I noted, we were leasing to ESPN. Mediaco would buy control of Hot97 and WBLS. Emmis would receive just a bit over $100 million in cash and a 24 percent stake in Mediaco. By the time we closed the purchase in November 2019, Soo had also placed two small billboard companies into Mediaco. Both Old Emmis and Mediaco had two classes of stock. I retained my controlling shares in Old Emmis, and Soo had controlling shares in Mediaco.

With the close of that transaction, we were officially out of Dresden. Emmis had some good assets and well over $100 million of cash. Goes to show that it's never too late to reinvent yourself. Now it was time for us to prove to the world that we could create value, and I was as excited as I had been in years.

Top: My mother always said, "In life, you just have to laugh." Here are my son, Brad; my mother, Natalie; daughter Cari; and daughter Sam, laughing with her at a family dinner. *Bottom:* Son Bradley's family: Brad, Quinn on Brad's shoulders, Leslie, Liam, and Peri, their dog.

Epilogue

At seventy-four, I'm at an age when most sane people are either retired or very close to it. Yet for me, quitting is the furthest thing from my mind. As I've mentioned, I live by the adage that if you love what you do, you'll never work a day in your life. I've loved almost every minute of my career, even the near-death experiences. The ability to reinvent Emmis is one of the most exhilarating experiences I can imagine.

And yet, leaving the media industry behind has been painful. Unfortunately, media, and especially radio, is in a rut, and I've learned that once you're in a rut, it's almost impossible to climb out of it. You keep searching for magical answers, and they almost never come. In radio, I watched the fervor for streaming music disrupt many of my peers, when the ultimate answer was that it was an attractive proposition for listeners but an awful proposition for broadcasters. It was a perfect example of one of my favorite sayings, "All of life is a math question." The math for streaming audio was always challenging and the results were predictable. Now, radio is in the midst of the podcasting frenzy. It's a wonderful way for people to consume new information and it has attracted lots of listeners, but the problem is, with no barriers to entry, it's impossible to find a viable economic model, and only a few podcasts have generated significant profits. Moreover, a podcast's profits usually go to the content creator, with hardly anything left over for the distributor. So, while many peers are again spending a fortune in this space, I believe the results will be dismal. When you're in a rut, the easiest thing is to throw a lot of stuff against a wall and hope something sticks. I'm afraid podcasting won't stick, certainly not to the degree that it will solve the multibillion-dollar debt challenges of the industry. In short, it's just bad math.

For us, now is the time to try different things. We're embarking on new ventures, but of course, in true Emmis fashion, we purchased our first business, Lencore, a world leader in sound masking, just before the pandemic hit in 2020. There's nothing quite like buying a business that controls sound environments in offices and hospitals, just before all of the offices are closed and the hospitals are overloaded with COVID-19 patients! Still, we love the venture and we're excited that, as the world returns to some semblance of normal, it will provide the excellent growth that we've been missing for so many years. Our dynamic pricing business, Digonex, has also demonstrated that there is a great market for providing sophisticated price guidance for just about any business. Our goal for the next iteration of Emmis is to acquire businesses in the $100 million range. In addition, we've entered the special-purpose acquisition company (SPAC) market with a goal of acquiring businesses in the $1–3 billion range. Of course, I've joked that there are 350 million Americans, and there will probably be 300 million SPACS in the coming year. In the meantime, however, we've found a receptive market for the suite of services that we currently provide: corporate finance, legal, HR, IT, and general strategic analysis. Time will tell if we're successful, but the early returns are encouraging.

I have no idea if either of our strategies for acquiring businesses will work, but my job is to view them from the 100,000-foot level. Over the decades, I've come to realize that my value in any analysis is the ability to distill the essence of the problem. I have great associates who are incredibly adept at drilling down on the details of a project. My task, however, is to zoom out from the details and assess the overall picture. It's a skill I've honed from experience, and this perspective is the most valuable asset I can contribute to Emmis.

Going forward, I anticipate that Emmis will have some significant successes and probably a few screwups, too. I'm an incurable optimist, and that's allowed me to survive in the most harrowing situations. I've also chosen to look at the bright side of everything that's happened to me. I have a saying that sums up that attitude: "If any one of ten things had happened, my company would be a thousand times bigger, but if any one of ten other things had happened, I'd be sweeping streets somewhere, so how bad could my life have been? Find joy in anything you undertake and you'll find success and happiness."

I have so much to be grateful for, including the many incredible events I've gone through in my life. In this book, you've seen me reach so many highs and endure so many lows, but what is hard to understand, especially when you're young, is that your life really is a journey. There are no ultimate successes and no ultimate failures. Along the way, you'll have plenty of both. From an economic standpoint, we've rescued Emmis from certain extinction and have been left with an interesting company full of potential. If you look back at what I could have earned, had I sold Emmis fifteen years ago, my economics are an absolute failure. However, if you look back at what we endured to get where we are today, it's a staggering success. Life is like that—it's all in how you look at it. If you focus on everything that has gone wrong, you can be consumed by your setbacks. If you can focus on what's good, you can delight in your victories.

I am continuing this journey of life, and it will be what I make of it. I know that, no matter what happens, the experiences will be invigorating and the friendships will be what matter most. Ultimately, I'll be guided by my father's admonition to be someone who "always does the right thing," and my mother's adage, "In life, you just have to laugh."

Acknowledgments

There are so many people to thank for their help on this book, it's difficult to know where to start. First off, I have to thank my younger daughter Samantha, or Sammie as we call her. For years, on our drives to school, I told her the stories of my life and she convinced me to write them down, and this book is the result. When I finished my first draft, I sent a copy to my friend and former investment banker, Jill Greenthal. Jill read much of what I had done and felt there was definitely a real book in there. She strongly suggested I get a great editor, and mentioned that Phyllis Strong had just edited her husband Tom's book *Why Startups Fail*. After some consternation about really wanting to finish the entire project, I hired Phyllis and it was a wise decision. Phyllis has been a wonderful partner, guiding me through every step of the way. Letting me know when my stories or jokes weren't particularly funny, tightening up my sometimes wordy descriptions and convincing me to cut pontifications about subjects that weren't germane to moving the story forward. Phyllis helped me put a presentation together that led to David Vigliano deciding to become my agent (I'm sure with some gentle prodding by my friend Nick Khan). David found the perfect home for *Never Ride a Rollercoaster Upside Down,* in Matt Holt. When I first met with Matt, I was certain I wanted to work with him. He understood that my book wasn't the typical business book, with the usual twenty immutable lessons, and it wasn't strictly a memoir, but rather a merger of both concepts. Matt and his small, but mighty, BenBella team were great to work with every step of the way. Editor Katie Dickman always provided valuable insights and was great at moving the process along. Copyeditor Scott Calamar was a terrific resource and his encouragement about the quality of the book certainly buoyed my spirits when he submitted his edits. Brigid Pearson, who provided the excellent cover art, Jessika Rieck who oversaw the layout, Ross Burlingame who advised on the audio book and Mallory Hyde who oversaw marketing—all contributed immensely. Every person on Matt's BenBella team was as helpful as every other and while I don't know if I'll be writing any more books, if I did, Matt Holt would be the first person I would call.

So many people in my Emmis Family provided insights into various parts of the book. Scott Enright and Beth Ellis, our crack in-house attorneys, read over the entire manuscript with the goal of avoiding libel suits and keeping me out of jail. As in everything they do, they were thorough and thoughtful. Ryan Hornaday and Pat Walsh provided invaluable insights into my analysis of the economics of our company and industries we have been involved in. Paul Brenner was a tremendous resource on all of the twists and turns of the NextRadio experience. Rick Cummings was able to remember so many of the crazy stories throughout the long history of Emmis, and even back to our first venture at WNTS, nearly fifty years ago. Kate Snedeker, who has tried to manage my press relations for several decades, did her usual stellar job of commenting on my various observations. Deb Smulyan and Paul Fiddick provided me with some excellent insights into our experiences in international radio, especially the debacle in Hungary. Steve Crane helped me set the stage for so many of our earliest experiences from the start of Emmis. Gary Kaseff, who lived every crazy minute in Seattle with me, was another valuable resource as were Stuart and Tracy Layne who not only lived through Seattle, but radio in New York, St. Louis, and Minneapolis as well. John Beck, who ran St. Louis for us for over thirty years, also had fantastic insights. Randy Bongarten and Greg Nathanson helped me relive our adventures in television. Peter Lund was a great resource on the history of the television industry.

It was fun to have so many people check facts for me. Steve Goldsmith was able to remember several memorable events, as were Bob Struble and

Lisa Dollinger. Tony Vinciquerra was incredibly helpful in recalling the details of our Dodgers venture and Tom Ostertag provided valuable insights into our various experiences in Major League Baseball. Jerry Reinsdorf was expert at reminiscing about some of our most memorable experiences in baseball, as well as in other ventures. In my office, Lori Stadick provided lots of help, and Wendy Jackson, my remarkable assistant, helped me in just about every possible way, getting this project to the finish line. Greg Loewen was also a goldmine when it came to remembering numerous areas of Emmis's history.

There are also so many friends who reviewed parts or all of this book and gave great advice: My nephew, Todd Hoffman, who has spent a lifetime in the entertainment industry, read an early draft and provided wonderful encouragement. Jeff Warshaw, Andrew Luck, Tom Buono, Jill Greenthal, John Momtazee, Jim Dubin, Stuart and Tracy Layne, Chase Rupe, my daughters Cari and Sammie, my son Brad, and, of course, my wife Heather, Mason Goodman, Dick Leventhal, Norm Gurwitz, Bruce Ramer, Paul Taubman, Scott Bridgford, Mark Wapnick, Lenny Levine, John Dille, Jon Horton, Peter Smyth, Ron Elberger, David Letterman, Randy Michaels, Bud Walters, Bob Padgett, my sister Dale, Jeff Haley, Peter Smyth, Brian McNeill, David Suess, and my accountant, Rosanne Ammirati, who not only provided great advice but has kept my financial ship afloat for decades. All of them, as well as everyone at Emmis, and I'm certain a few I've left out, have given me great guidance and support—exactly what your friends always do.

A special thanks to David Faber, who understands more about the economics of broadcasting and sports (and just about everything else) than anyone. He not only read and commented on the book, but graciously agreed to write the foreword.

To those who have generously offered to write cover endorsements: Jerry Reinsdorf, Andrew Luck, Ken Griffey, Jr. and Ken Griffey, Sr. (with a special thanks to Brian Goldberg), David Letterman, and Evan Bayh.

A special thanks to my golf partner Traug Keller and to Norby Williamson, who were kind enough to be my pro bono sports promotion team.

Thanks also to Sandi Mendelson and David Kass, who organized all the promotion for the book.

To Mallory Hyde, who oversaw the promotion efforts for BenBella, and Jordyn Kirtley, who tried to teach me social media.

To all of the friends and family who helped me throughout my career and thus made this book and this wonderful journey possible.

Thanks to all of you!

Index